GW01375651

ORMEN LANGE
PIPELINES AND SHIPWRECKS

ORMEN LANGE
PIPELINES AND SHIPWRECKS

PETTER BRYN, MAREK E. JASINSKI AND FREDRIK SØREIDE

© Universitetsforlaget 2007

ISBN 978-82-15-01131-8

All rights reserved. No part of this publication may be reproduced, stored in
a retrieval system, or transmitted in any form or by any means, electronic,
mechanical or photocopying, recording, or otherwise, without the prior permission
of Universitetsforlaget. Enquiries should be sent to the Rights Department,
Universitetsforlaget, Oslo, at the address below.

www.universitetsforlaget.no

Universitetsforlaget AS
P.O. Box 508 Sentrum
NO-0105 Oslo
Norway

Cover: Laboremus Prepress AS
Design: Laboremus Prepress AS
Binding: Bokbinder Johnsen AS
Printed: PDC Tangen AS
Typeset: Minion 10,5/14
Paper: G-print 130 g

INTRODUCTION

The Ormen Lange project is the largest industrial project ever run in Norway. But not only is this gas field development an enormous project, it is also a truly spectacular one.

In the late 1980s, Norsk Hydro came across a giant gas structure, deep below the seabed. The development of the field was initiated after several years of exploration and the gas discovery in 1997. The gas is extracted through subsea manifolds and then transported by two pipelines to a processing facility onshore. The processed gas is then exported to the UK where it will supply as much as 20 per cent of the market.

Modern seafloor mapping technology and 3D visualisation techniques were essential tools for the engineers planning and preparing the offshore installation work. But the technology also provides a unique insight into the impressive underwater world in this area.

Hidden beneath the waves, the underwater terrain close to the shore has dramatic narrow valleys and underwater mountains, and further out there is an enormous slide scar caused by the world's largest known submarine slide.

Through this terrain the project had to do extensive seafloor preparations – building rock supports for pipelines, and excavating and ploughing trenches. This could only be achieved by using many kinds of underwater technology, some developed specially for the Ormen Lange project.

The consequence analysis carried out prior to developing Ormen Lange included archaeological investigations onshore, as well as offshore in the pipeline route corridors. More than 60 archaeologists were involved in land excavation at Nyhamna in Aukra from 2002 until mid-2004 prior to the start of the development.

Marine archaeological investigations were also required, but it was not expected that any archaeological sites would be found that could not be avoided by re-routing the proposed pipelines. So it came as quite a surprise to the Ormen Lange team when archaeologists from the Norwegian University of Science and Technology (NTNU) discovered a historical wreck in the pipeline route close to Bud, in one of the very few areas where the underwater terrain made it impossible to re-route the pipeline.

A large collection of bottles and porcelain, along with a large ship's bell and cannons, were observed on the seafloor at a depth of some 170 metres. According to the marine archaeologists, underwater pictures from the site indicated the ship probably went down in the second half of the 17th century.

Although it is an important part of Norwegian and international cultural heritage, the wreck site could not be completely avoided by the Ormen Lange project. A challenging and detailed investigation of the historical site was commenced, including excavation of parts of the wreck site. The water depth created significant technological challenges for the archaeologists. The Ormen Lange project therefore also marks an important milestone for marine archaeology since archaeological excavation had never been done before at such depths. Through this project marine archaeology entered the deep ocean with proper methodology and proper tools.

The idea of writing a book about the project grew gradually as the project developed. The history behind the discovered wreck and the new technology developed to make deep water archaeology possible is presented in this book, together with the history of the Ormen Lange gas field development project. The result is two exciting stories that traverse the past, the present and the future, presented together in this book.

CONTENTS

5 Introduction
9 Engineers and archaeologists break new ground
11 Preface

13 PART ONE
PIPELINES

15 Ormen Lange: the background
23 Selecting the Ormen Lange development concept
33 The Storegga slide
43 Mapping the seafloor
49 Building underwater "roads" for the Ormen Lange pipelines
61 Marine biology in the pipeline routes
67 From the Ormen Lange field to Nyhamna – installing the Ormen Lange production pipeline system
81 From Nyhamna to Easington – installing the Langeled gas export line system
87 Constructing the Ormen Lange processing plant at Aukra

93 PART TWO
SHIPWRECKS

95 Maritime Fræna – a ship's graveyard
105 Shipwreck!
109 Why did we do it? – the Norwegian Cultural Heritage Act
113 Achieving a win-win solution
121 The deepest dig
131 The site below
137 Once on board, now in our collection
157 The historical puzzle and the Russian link

163 Afterword
166 Ormen Lange-prosjektet
171 Facts about Ormen Lange
172 Bibliography
174 Illustrations

ENGINEERS AND ARCHAEOLOGISTS BREAK NEW GROUND
BY EIVIND REITEN, PRESIDENT AND CEO OF HYDRO

The historical excavations in what is now the pipe trench between the Ormen Lange gas field and Nyhamna, is believed to be the most technologically-advanced marine archaeology project ever executed in such deep waters.

This is rather appropriate considering the excavations took place as a part of one of the world's largest and most technologically-advanced gas field developments ever.

120 kilometres off the north-western coast of Norway, a thousand metres below sea level and a further several thousand metres below the seabed, Hydro discovered in 1997 the gigantic gas field it named Ormen Lange.

In 2007, only ten years later, the largest industrial development in Norwegian history is completed – comprising technological solutions that certainly break new ground:

– A special excavator was invented to plane the bumpy seabed – operated by a PlayStation-like joystick 800 metres above
– The gas is produced from seabed templates rather than from a conventional platform
– The gas pipe climbs the 30 degree steep Storegga subsea landslide headwall
– The 1,200 kilometre long Langeled pipeline is now the world's longest subsea gas pipeline – made possible by special flow assurance technology and custom-made compressors, and a unique design to avoid formation of ice.

Ormen Lange is about to make history. Just as the archaeological excavations associated with the development have unveiled history – with a mysterious shipwreck containing thousands of artefacts from the late 18th century among the highlights.

The Norwegian coast is known for its rough nature and harsh climate. This has challenged seafarers over the centuries, and is the reason why the north-western shore, and Hustadvika in particular, is rich in marine archaeology.

The same demanding natural conditions have challenged petroleum activity and cultural historic excavations. Challenges that Hydro and partners, and the Museum of Natural History and Archaeology and partners, have overcome by breaking new technological ground.

Ormen Lange was a giant serpent in Norse mythology – and the name given by the Vikings to one of the biggest, toughest and most powerful Viking ships ever built, with the intention of challenging new frontiers.

In the Ormen Lange project, Norsk Hydro and the Museum of Natural History and Archaeology have certainly opened new frontiers in their respective projects, making the impossible possible.

Ormen Lange demonstrates that we can reach sea depths that were previously almost unimaginable, deal with subzero temperatures, cope with unpredictable conditions on the seabed, and meet the challenge of currents, winds and waves on a massive scale.

By mastering these challenges – which we've now done – these technologies and skills will enable us to master other, perhaps even greater, challenges in the future.

This goes for those who explore and extract petroleum resources as well as for those who search for traces from ancient times that help document and explain how we have become who we are today.

Hydro and our Ormen Lange partners are proud to have contributed to such a groundbreaking marine archaeology project, the scope and significance of which is well illustrated in this book.

PREFACE
BY NILS MARSTEIN, DIRECTOR GENERAL OF THE NORWEGIAN DIRECTORATE FOR CULTURAL HERITAGE

Norway has a very long coastline, with thousands of islets and skerries. The coast and the ocean are resources that played an important role in the movement of people to this part of the world and their settlement thousands of years ago. From time immemorial the ocean has given us wealth. People have lived, travelled, and made their living on the coast, and the remnants of these activities are also concealed below the surface. Although these traces are difficult to perceive and to interpret, they are at the same time a key source of knowledge. Until recently, shipping channels have constituted the most important transport artery for people and goods in Norway. However, the Norwegian coast is exposed and unpredictable as is evidenced by thousands of shipwrecks. The wreck that was discovered during the marine archaeological survey for Hydro's Ormen Lange pipeline is one example of an unknown tragedy. This is a relic of people who sailed along the coast and who probably found their final resting place there, telling their story as well as providing evidence of extensive contact with the outside world.

Over the last 40 years Norwegian marine technology has experienced a rapid development in the field of both science and technology. Hydro's Ormen Lange project has demonstrated that using the appropriate technology, underwater cultural heritage can be investigated and protected in a manner not previously possible. Archaeological investigations in deep water open up new opportunities but also present new challenges for developers and archaeologists alike. During the laying of the pipeline Hydro has attempted as far as possible to avoid conflict with cultural heritage. In cases where this was not possible, the conduct of the Ormen Lange project shows that the use of modern offshore technology allows scientifically acceptable investigations of wreck sites to be carried out in very deep water.

The oil and gas sector has been responsible for the development of the basic technology that archaeologists have employed in fieldwork in the project. Remote-controlled vehicles as well as sonar, seismic and extremely accurate positioning equipment enable the detection, registration and subsequent investigation of underwater cultural heritage with the accuracy that modern archaeology requires. The investigations have shown that with innovative modifications and tailored new solutions, equipment that has been developed to construct and maintain oil and gas installations at great depths can also be utilized in archaeology. The knowledge that the tools used to build enormous installations in the North Sea can also be used to investigate fragile archaeological discovery sites provides exciting opportunities for future management and research in marine archaeology.

Hydro's gas project will deliver North Sea gas to the continent. The experience acquired through cultural heritage management during this project will be of key importance in the planning and conduct of similar projects in the future. Close co-operation between the oil and gas sector and cultural heritage authorities in future years will provide invaluable knowledge of the people of the past and their use of the ocean and coast. Through the conduct of archaeological surveys as part of the Ormen Lange project, Norsk Hydro and the Museum of Natural History and Archaeology at NTNU (the Norwegian University of Science and Technology) have secured fresh knowledge of the international communication that seafaring represents.

PART ONE
PIPELINES

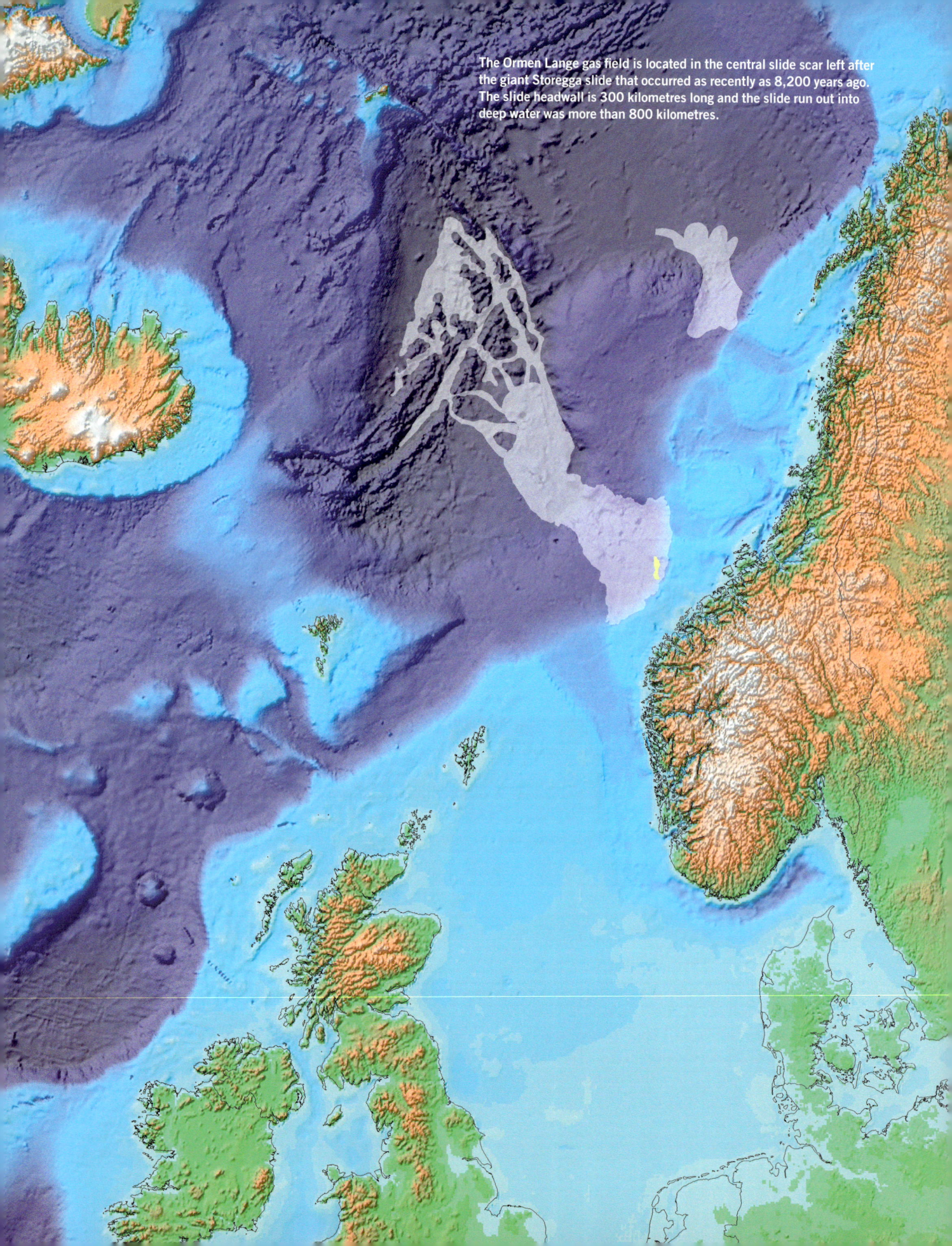

The Ormen Lange gas field is located in the central slide scar left after the giant Storegga slide that occurred as recently as 8,200 years ago. The slide headwall is 300 kilometres long and the slide run out into deep water was more than 800 kilometres.

CHAPTER 1

ORMEN LANGE: THE BACKGROUND

The modern history of the Ormen Lange gas field dates back to the late 1980s, when geophysicists at the Norsk Hydro research centre in Bergen came across what appeared to be a giant underground structure with a potential for gas accumulations. Seismic data showed the structure to be some 1,900 metres below the seafloor in water depths between 600 and 1,200 metres. However, a structure like this does not in itself normally provide sufficient criteria for investing in exploration activities and drilling for gas or oil.

There needs to be a source rock for hydrocarbons, normally carbon rich shale, as well as a porous sand reservoir that can store gas. The sand in the reservoir structure needs to be covered by a gastight "roof" to trap the gas. All these conditions appeared to exist in the structure named Ormen Lange.

The name of the reservoir derives from the Viking ship *Ormen Lange*. The ship was the proud property of Viking king Olav Trygvason; with a little imagination, the reservoir seen upside down resembles a Viking ship. The fact that the reservoir is over 40 kilometres long may also have inspired it to be called Ormen Lange, 'long snake' in Norwegian.

Geologists from Norsk Hydro reconstructed the geological history of the area and found that sand from mountain erosion along the Norwegian west coast was transported across the shelf area out to the Ormen Lange area following the rivers and valleys present in the early Paleocene period, 65 million years ago [1]. The sand was later covered by clay to form the tight roof of the reservoir. Gas migrated into the sand from carbon-rich, 85 million-year old shale below the sand as the pressure gradually increased from over 1000 metres of sediment that were deposited on top of the sand layer. The high temperature due to the deep burial combined with the high pressure "boils" the gas out of the hydrocarbon-rich shale.

The carbon-rich shale was formed in a warm period on earth with high production of organic material both on land and in the sea. Organic material was deposited in a shallow water basin and preserved due to the lack of oxygen, with about one per cent of the gas formed from this type of shale becoming trapped and preserved in reservoirs. At that time Scandinavia was also in a more southerly position due to continental drift.

The lightness of gas means it is found above water or oil in a reservoir. The boundary can sometimes be seen as a strong horizontal reflec-

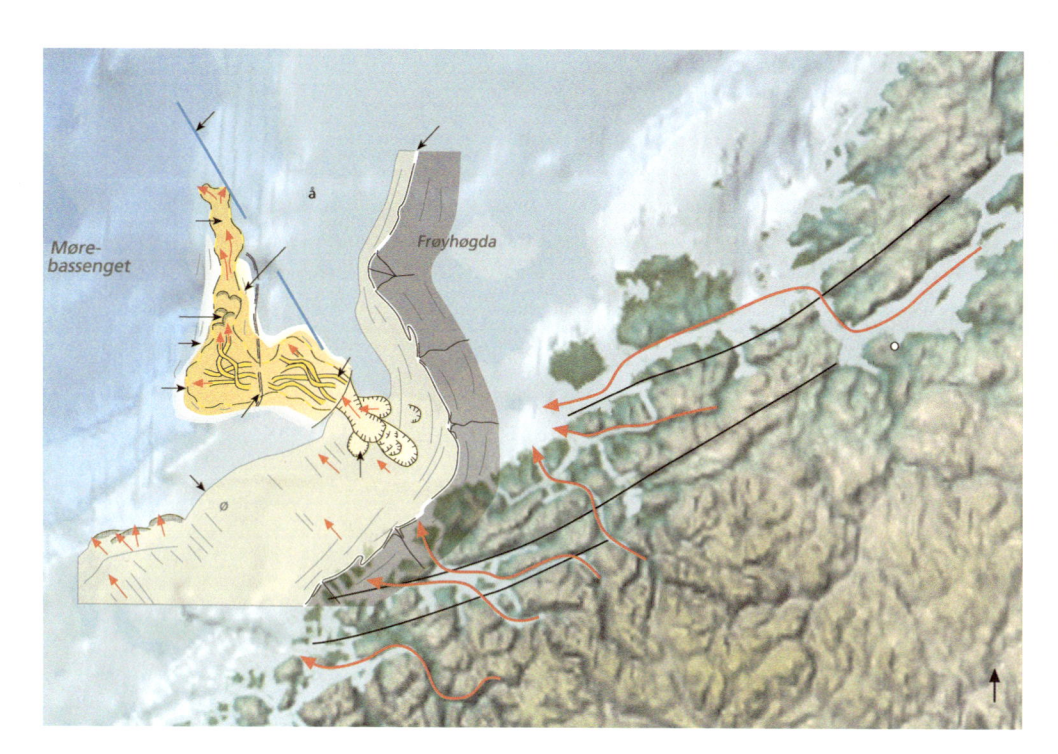

The figure illustrates how sand was transported from the valley system in Norway out to the Ormen Lange area some 65 million years ago. Norway's topography at this time had the same main elements as today, but ice has since eroded a deeper relief and created the deep fjords of western Norway.

tor, called a "flat spot". The geological sand layers undulate but the gas water contact is always horizontal, as it is in a glass of water when the glass is tilted. The Ormen Lange reservoir has a clear flat spot, which was a strong indicator for geophysicists of a gas reservoir above water. The amount of gas was uncertain, as was the quality of the sand in the reservoir. The only way to verify the presence of commercial hydrocarbons was to drill a well.

The findings indicating a large gas field remained confidential for several years, even within Hydro, while additional seismic data was gathered and new geophysical interpretations made. Competition is of course intense between the oil companies and Hydro clearly had an advantage in understanding the area's potential. Enthusiasm was high and Hydro nominated the area as an exploration priority area prior to the first deepwater concession round in Norway. This involves the oil industry advising the Norwegian Oil Directorate which areas it considers to have exploration potential before the Directorate decides which licence blocks are to be allocated to different companies.

In 1996 the deepwater area outside Mid Norway was opened up for exploration and the 17th concession round was announced with Hydro as operator for the structure known as Ormen Lange.

Extensive preparations began for the exploration, which in 1996 included a new 3D seismic survey to map the sand reservoir in detail. Based on the new seismic data Hydro started to prepare for the first well, scheduled to be drilled in summer 1997.

Hydro became the operator for Ormen Lange. The other partners in the Ormen Lange licence were BP, Shell, Statoil, Exxon and at that time also SDØE which represented the State's direct ownership of licences on the Norwegian continental shelf. SDØE was later renamed Petoro, the State-owned oil company in Norway.

Drilling in depths close to 850 metres was a real challenge. Never before had drilling been attempted at such depths in Norway. Particularly in such extreme conditions: minus 1°C on the seafloor, extreme current, and a rough seafloor terrain. Hydro had prepared thoroughly for the challenge by collecting all available knowledge about seafloor conditions, sea temperature, current, wind and waves in the deepwater area.

The Ormen Lange structure is located quite close to the steep headwall of the largest known underwater slide in the world, the Storegga slide, and during the preparation for drilling, the Hydro

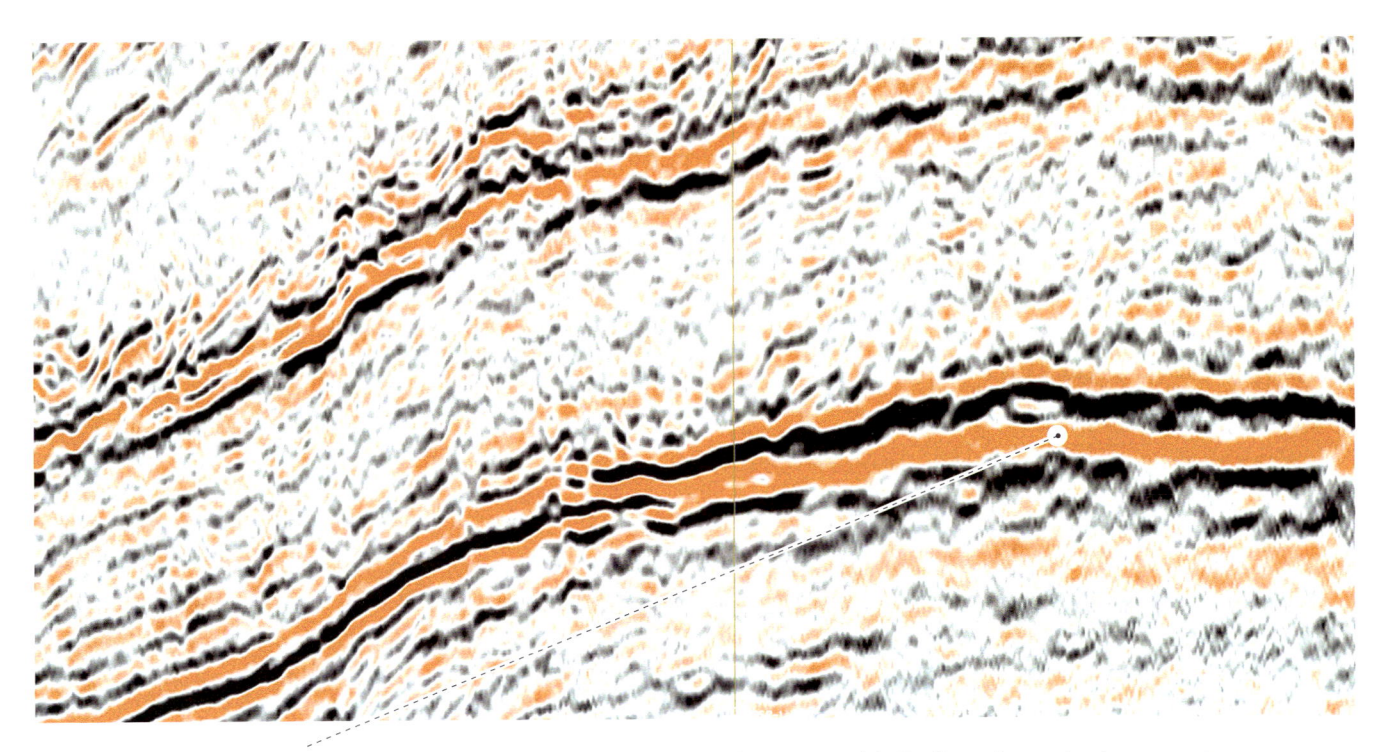

The seismic "flat spot" seen in the seismic sections through the sandstone reservoir in the Ormen Lange structure was a strong indicator of gas presence. The "flat spot" indicates contact between water and gas, with water below the gas.

team realised that the slide represented a huge challenge for hydrocarbon activity in the area. Scientists in Norway and other countries had identified the slide as a highly interesting feature, but as limited surveys and mapping had been performed very little was known about it.

The Storegga slide was thought to be very young in geological terms. There were indications that the slide was only about 8,000 years old, and that the slide event corresponded to traces of a major tsunami wave that inundated the cost of Norway and the shorelines of the other areas around the North Sea in the Stone Age. This could hardly be a coincidence: the age of the tsunami sediment was approximately 8,000 years. Wave heights of 10–15 metres had occurred in many places, with waves as high as 40–50 metres in certain spots. Geological cores from the slide area also indicated later slide events in the area.

During preparations for the first well, an unmanned mini-submarine known as an ROV (Remotely Operated Vehicle) was used to investigate the local area around the planned well location. The terrain was spectacular with slides blocks as high as 60 metres around the planned well position. The well location had to be moved to a relatively flat area where it would be possible to drill. The seafloor map and the survey video indicated some of the challenges to be faced if gas was discovered: large slide blocks with side slopes up to 75 degrees and numerous boulders of different sizes carried out by glaciers from mainland Norway over the repeated glaciations of the past 500,000 years.

There was a 25 per cent likelihood of finding commercial gas in the reservoir, which is quite high in statistical terms. Hopes were high, and amongst the drilling preparation team the expectations were closer to 75 per cent. Drilling started in summer 1997 and as the anticipated reservoir level came closer the Hydro team was extremely tense and excited. When the top of the reservoir was penetrated the 25 per cent hopes suddenly became 100 per cent.

The discovery was dramatic. It was potentially the largest gas field discovered in Norway since the Troll field. The potential was recognised by the stock market, which responded immediately when the discovery was announced.

Hydro's project leader for the Ormen Lange exploration project, Per Kjærnes, invited his team to a well-deserved celebration, knowing that years of challenging work were about to start.

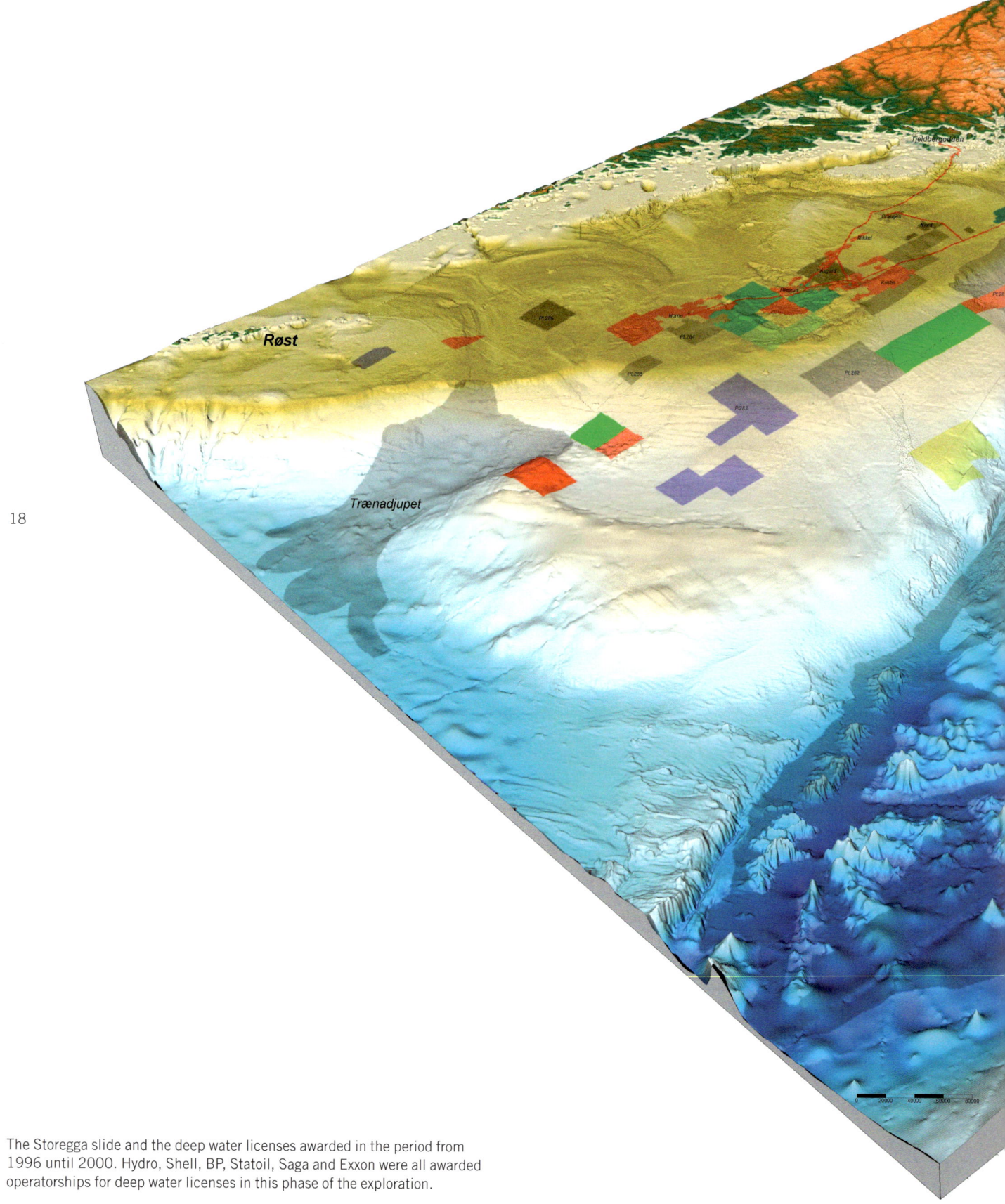

The Storegga slide and the deep water licenses awarded in the period from 1996 until 2000. Hydro, Shell, BP, Statoil, Saga and Exxon were all awarded operatorships for deep water licenses in this phase of the exploration.

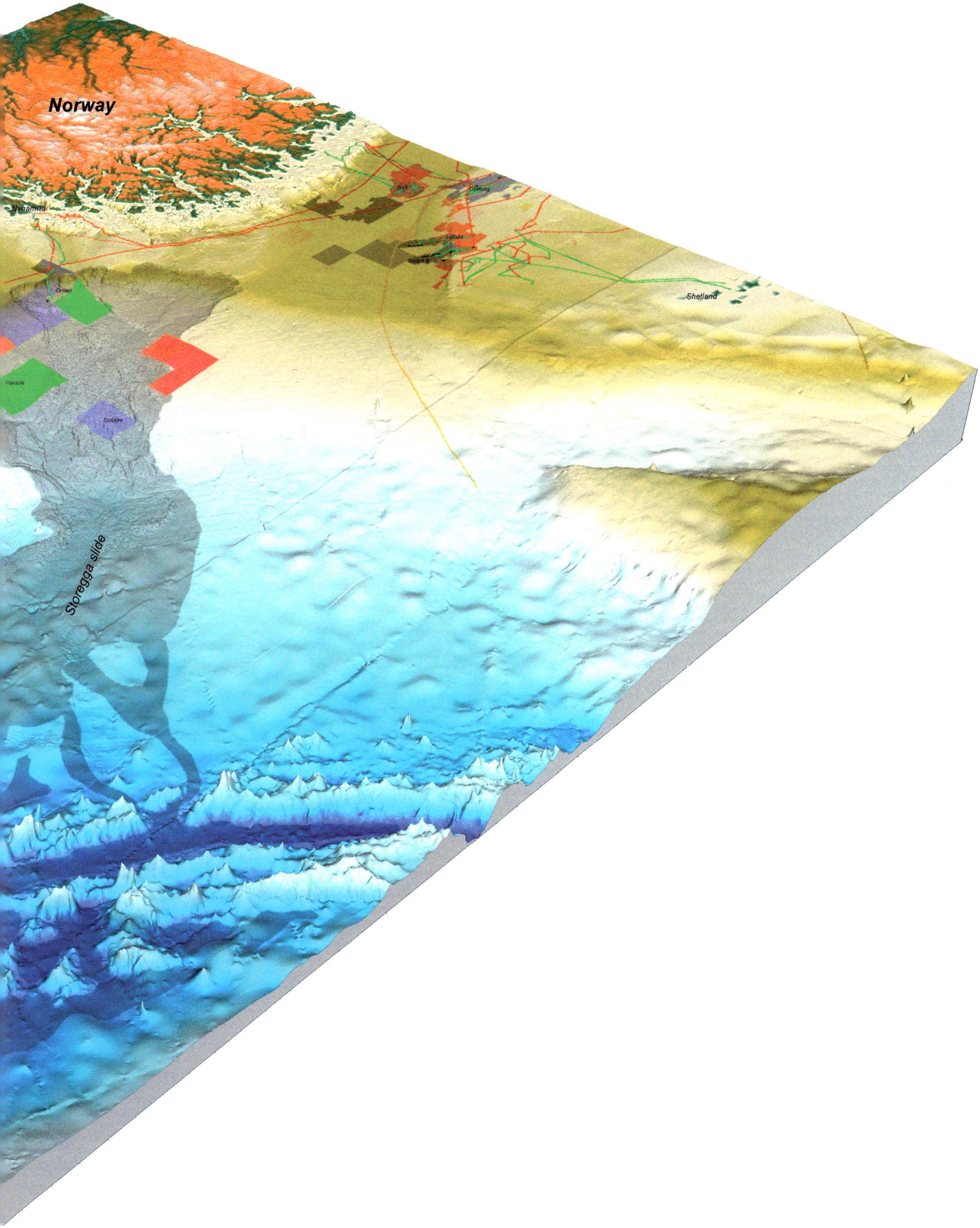
Norway
Nyhamna
Troll
Oseberg
Gullfaks
Snorre B
Ormen
Havsule
Solsikke
Shetland
Storegga slide

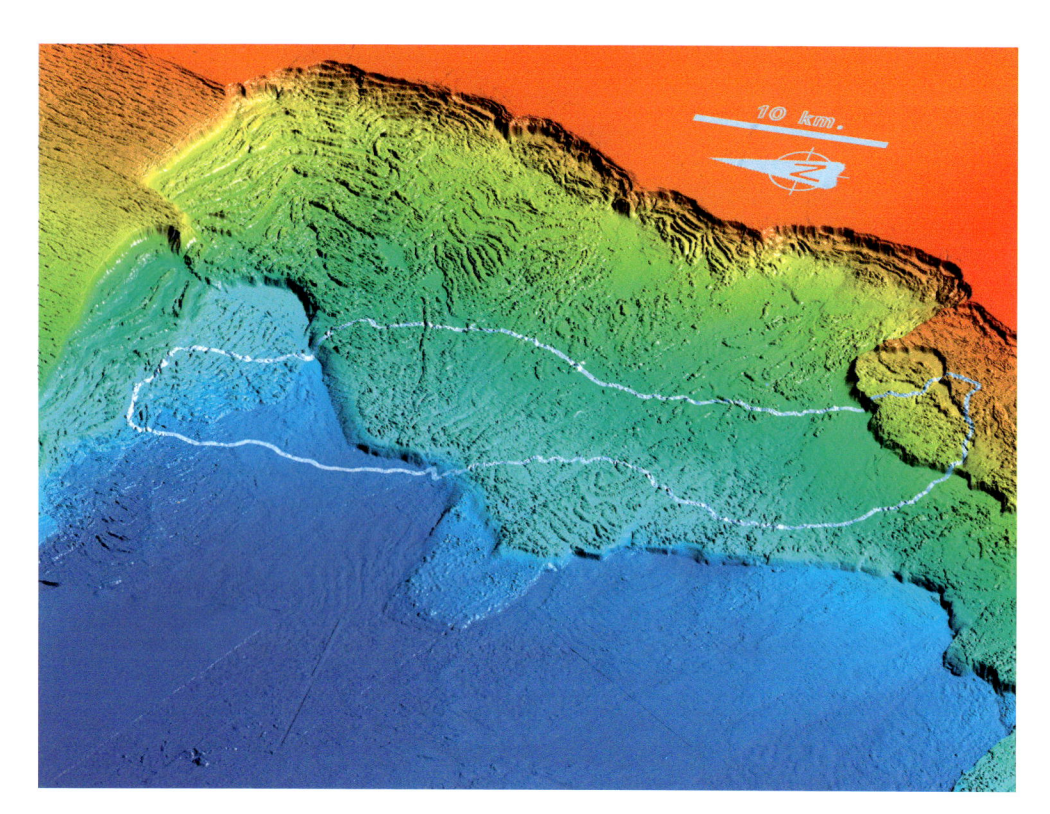

The Ormen Lange gas field is in the central slide scar created by the Storegga slide. When it was discovered in 1997 little was known about its architecture or morphology. Extensive seafloor mapping revealed the dramatic underwater terrain caused by the slide. Water depth of 300 metres at the shelf edge gives way to depths from 600 metres to greater than 1,100 metres (shown in blue) in the seafloor area above the reservoir.

The sand in the reservoir was of good quality, indicating that production wells could produce at high rates. It was, however, necessary to drill more wells to confirm the thickness, quality and extent of the reservoir. These properties along with the type of fluid (gas and gas condensate) determine the technical solutions needed to develop the field.

The gas had been discovered. The next step was to start the planning how to develop the gas field.

There were many questions to answer before the team could decide on a development concept and a schedule for the development:

- Can the reservoir be drained from the highest point? Will gas flow easily to the top of the structure? Where should production facilities be located in the field?
- Are the sand layers containing the gas continuous or cut by seismic faults? Do production wells have to be drilled in multiple locations? How many wells are needed? Can production be done with seafloor wells without a platform, or is a platform needed to support production?
- Should a large platform be constructed with gas processing facilities in the Ormen Lange field and gas exported directly to the European market? Or should it be sent to shore for processing before export through a pipeline?
- Can some of the gas be used in Norwegian industry and gas power plants? When would the gas be needed by the European market and where should it be exported?

The gas market was a key parameter when setting the development schedule. There were more questions:

- Would it be technically possible to develop a gas field in the slide area?
- Would it be possible to install pipelines in the rough seafloor terrain, unlike any previous area where oil and gas installation had taken place?
- Which location should be selected for the onshore gas processing plant in Norway if this alternative was selected?
- What were the costs for the various development alternatives?

Another major issue was the Storegga slide:

- Would it be safe to develop the field close to

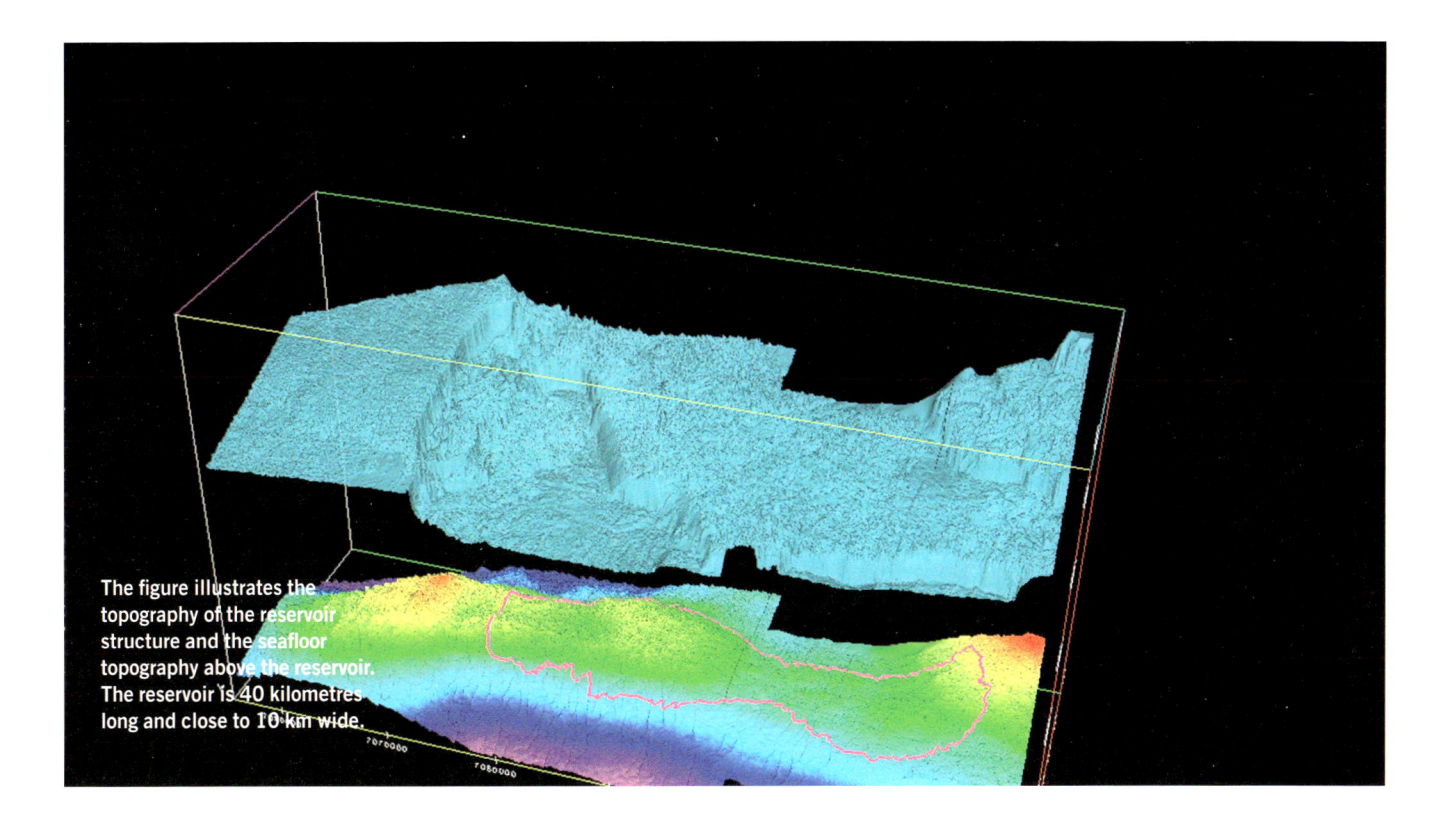

The figure illustrates the topography of the reservoir structure and the seafloor topography above the reservoir. The reservoir is 40 kilometres long and close to 10 km wide.

- the steep headwall of the world's largest known submarine slide?
- What about the stability of the steep headwall close to the reservoir position?
- Would seafloor stability be affected when gas was drained from the reservoir?

Many questions! To find the answers, an extensive technical study and drilling programme was required. The Storegga slide issue also required a lot of seismic data, seafloor data and geotechnical data to be collected, not only to clarify the slide risk but to help evaluate and select pipeline routes out of the slide scar. During the five years from discovery in 1997 to 2002, the Hydro project team answered one question after another and gradually narrowed down the options towards the final concept selection.

The technical director in this phase of the project, Tor Tangen, guided his team through all the complex decisions well within the required schedule. This work was performed in close collaboration with the Ormen Lange partners who contributed with technical expertise and performed some of the assignments. The size of the project and the many challenges it represented called for extensive collaboration to create the best value for the owners of the field. The project director for the Ormen Lange Project in this phase, Bengt Lie Hansen, diplomatically ensured the partners backed the recommended decisions and promoted an enthusiastic collaboration.

In 2002 the main concept was selected from the two main alternatives that reached final concept selection. One alternative was to build a gas-processing platform and export the gas through a pipeline via the Sleipner platform to Easington in the UK. The other alternative was to produce the gas from a subsea system with no field platform and send the gas to shore in Norway for processing. From the processing plant the gas would be exported through a pipeline via the Sleipner platform to the UK.

Pipeline route from Ormen Lange to Sleipner and Easington in the UK.

CHAPTER 2

SELECTING THE ORMEN LANGE DEVELOPMENT CONCEPT

Following the field's discovery in 1997 Hydro began studying different alternative development solutions and also the European gas market. Russia and Algeria were the main potential suppliers of additional gas to Europe but despite its distance to the market, it appeared supply from Ormen Lange would be competitive.

Distance was not the only criteria, however, regardless of the high cost of an export pipeline from Ormen Lange to central Europe. Potential customers such as Poland, for example, were also motivated by political pressure to decrease gas dependency on Russia as well as decreasing coal dependency for environmental reasons. Sweden was another potential buyer – the country required limited volumes to decrease its dependency on nuclear power plants.

Gas demand in the UK was also growing, but early indications were that Ormen Lange gas might not be needed until 2013–2015. However, the market situation changed between 1997 and 2001, indicating gas would be required much earlier in the UK. In addition to gas export pipelines to Continental Europe it made sense to consider export to UK.

One of the factors complicating the decision was a new EU regulation intended to open up the gas market. This meant it was no longer possible to sell gas on long-term contracts prior to field development. In practical terms this meant that Hydro and the other Ormen Lange partners could only assume customers would buy gas from the field at a reasonable price when production started.

However, the sudden introduction of large gas volumes on the market carries the risk of price erosion. The question was whether this potential price weakening could threaten the profitability of the new gas field. Uncertainty could not be completely ruled out, but the conclusion was that it would most likely be a temporary effect. A gradual build up of gas production was considered the best way to handle the risk. Flexibility would be important, and having a gas pipeline to both the European and UK markets would help spread planned production volumes over a broader market.

A final decision was taken: to export gas to the UK through a new pipeline and in addition connect to the existing gas pipeline infrastructure in the North Sea. A number of potential landing points in the UK were evaluated and Easington was ultimately selected as the landing point for the pipeline and the gas terminal.

The Sleipner Platform was selected as the con-

01 Subsea system to onshore plant

02 Deepwater platform to onshore plant

03 Shallow water platform

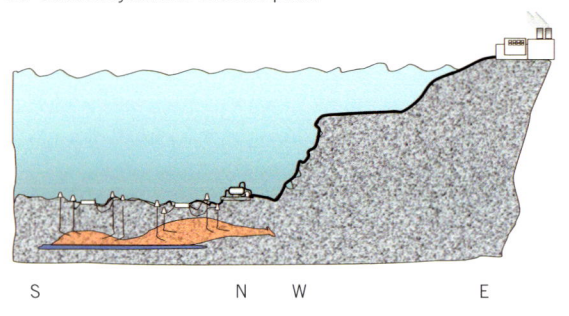

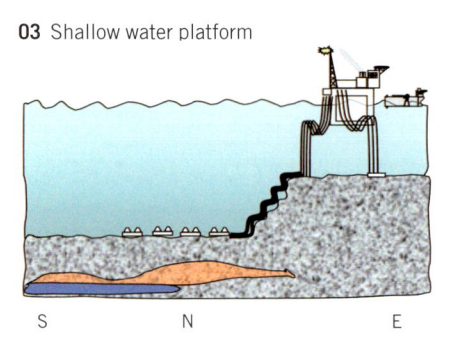

04 Deepwater platform

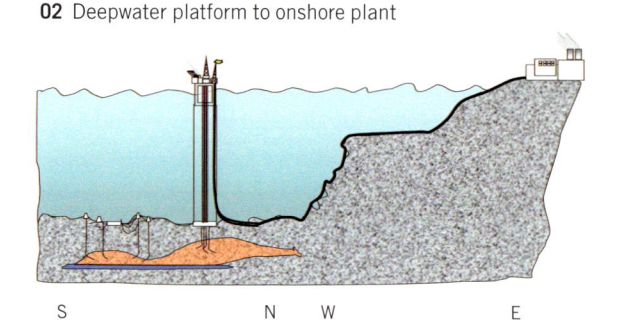

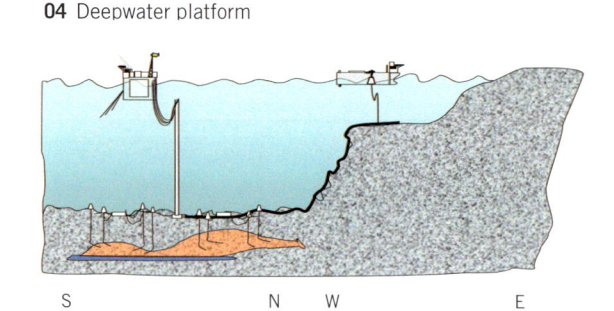

The four main concepts evaluated for production of the Ormen Lange gas field. Concept alternative 3 and 4 included full gas processing offshore and direct gas export to the European market.

nection point to other infrastructure in the Norwegian sector of the North Sea, which meant that gas from the Sleipner and other fields connected to it could be exported to the UK via the southern leg of the Ormen Lange pipeline.

The gas export pipeline from Ormen Lange to Sleipner was close to 800 kilometres, with a southern leg from Sleipner to Easington of 400 kilometres. The northern leg would have a diameter of 42 inches and the southern leg 44 inches since more gas would be exported from the Sleipner area. The 1,200 kilometer long gas export line would be the longest offshore pipeline in the world.

It was planned that the reservoir of 400 billion cubic metres of recoverable gas would produce around 20 billion cubic metres of gas annually in the first years. This corresponds to daily gas production of around 60 million cubic metres. To provide flexibility it was decided to base the facilities on a maximum daily production volume of 70 million cubic metres.

These sort of volumes are hard to imagine. To put it in context, production on this scale is equivalent to 20 per cent of the energy requirements of the UK, a country with over 60 million people and energy-consuming industry.

The market situation was now clarified and daily production volumes set. It was time to determine the size and capacity of production facilities, along with key parametres such as the number of pipelines, and the number and size of the production wells.

As mentioned above, four alternative concepts were selected for further evaluation, two of which were discussed extensively before the final decision was taken.

Should Hydro build a platform with production facilities in the field and treat the raw gas on the platform before exporting gas directly to the European market? Or would a subsea production system with gas transport and a gas processing plant in Norway be preferable before export to the European market?

In 1998–99, the subsea development concept was not an option the Hydro project team or the Ormen Lange partners thought would be economically viable. Controlling the production of such a large gas field in deep water 120 kilometres from shore was simply considered too high risk. Gas had never before been produced from a subsea field so far from shore anywhere in the world.

In terms of experience, however, the Hydro

Roy Backstrøm from Shell and Per Kjærnes from Hydro during a visit to one of the islands in the Kristiansund and Molde region during the site selection process.

team in Norway was a world leader in the field of subsea development. Its experience from the Troll field, one of the world's largest subsea developments, along with many other subsea developments created confidence that not only could such a long tieback to shore be done, but it could be done within acceptable risk margins. In parallel with the Ormen Lange development, the Snøhvit field was developed by Statoil in the Barents Sea. A similar subsea tieback to shore was planned for this field, which led Statoil to support the technical solution proposed by Hydro.

A strong reason in favour of bringing the gas to shore in Norway was the positive effect it would have on industry and employment, particularly in the local region of Møre and Romsdal. Development of the Ormen Lange facilities would generate many jobs and substantially increase activity. Long term, the gas processing plant would also add jobs to the area and taxes from the plant and pipeline system would contribute significantly to the area's economy. There would be great potential for additional future activity and gas-supply related industry would undoubtedly create opportunities in the area.

The points in favour of developing a cost-effective solution for the onshore alternative were adding up. Supporting the local community was a motivating factor, but the main issue for the owners was naturally to select the best development solution from a financial perspective.

A key part of the process of comparing cost, technical solutions and environmental and community effects of the development solutions was to find the best potential site for shore gas processing, along with the most cost-effective and technically-feasible pipeline route to shore.

Politicians from the Møre and Romsdal County were in favour of the shore solution as a way of boosting employment and income in the region. Local authorities initiated a project called "Ormen to Møre" supporting Hydro's goal to find the best solution for an onshore plant to compete with the platform concept. The high profile campaign generated a lot of excitement and enthusiasm throughout the region, and involved a lot of work keeping local residents, politicians and the press informed about the project's progress, decision processes, and the effect of alternative decisions.

Hydro's public relations strategy involved local communities in the process, including fishery and other local interest groups that would be affected

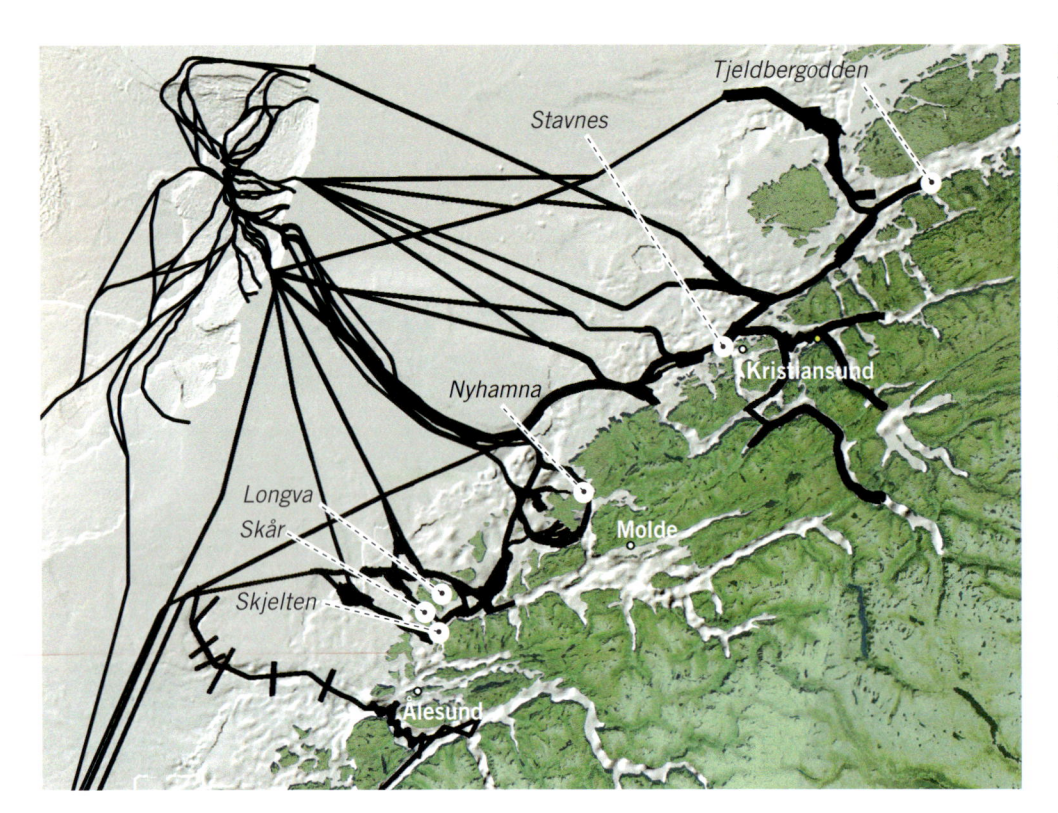

Many alternative pipeline routes were evaluated from the field to potential sites for the gas processing plant. Export routes from the alternative shore plant sites were also mapped. A pipeline across Aukra was also considered as an alternative gas export route due to the complex seafloor in the nearshore area outside Nyhamna. The many alternative routes out of the slide scar illustrate the challenge to find a feasible route for the pipelines through the slide terrain up to the shelf.

SITE SELECTION FOR THE ORMEN LANGE GAS PROCESSING PLANT

The "Ormen to Møre" project formed by the Møre and Romsdal County set about identifying potential sites for a gas processing plant along the coast. They came up with 14 alternative locations for the Ormen Lange project. Similar studies conducted by Hydro to see whether there were any other alternatives and to verify the sites proposed confirmed that the "Ormen to Møre" proposals were very well prepared and all 14 proposed sites were ratified.

The list included locations from Sand Municipality in the south to Tjeldbergodden in the north, with all the communities involved having put a lot of energy and enthusiasm into providing the information needed for further screening.

The list of alternatives was narrowed down using specific criteria including size of the area, other industrial opportunities, topography, existing infrastructure, environmental issues, effect on the local community, distance to the field and market, and cost of plant site preparations.

By December 2000, seven potential sites remained on the list:

- Tjeldbergodden in Aure Municipality
- Stavnes on Averøy
- Årsbogmyrene in Eide Municipality
- Nyhamna in Aukra Municipality
- Longva in Haram Municipality
- Skjelten in Haram Municipality
- Skår/Baraldsnes in Haram Municipality

More detailed studies were needed at the potential sites. Potential pipeline routes were mapped from the field across the shelf to each of these locations as well as a southwards route out for the gas export pipeline.

Particularly on a rough day, the many small islands and skerries along the coast can be clearly seen from the shore as waves hit them. The view above the water largely reflects the underwater topography – the terrain along the Norwegian bedrock coast is very irregular with many valleys and mountains under the waterline. Finding good pipeline routes in this kind of terrain was a

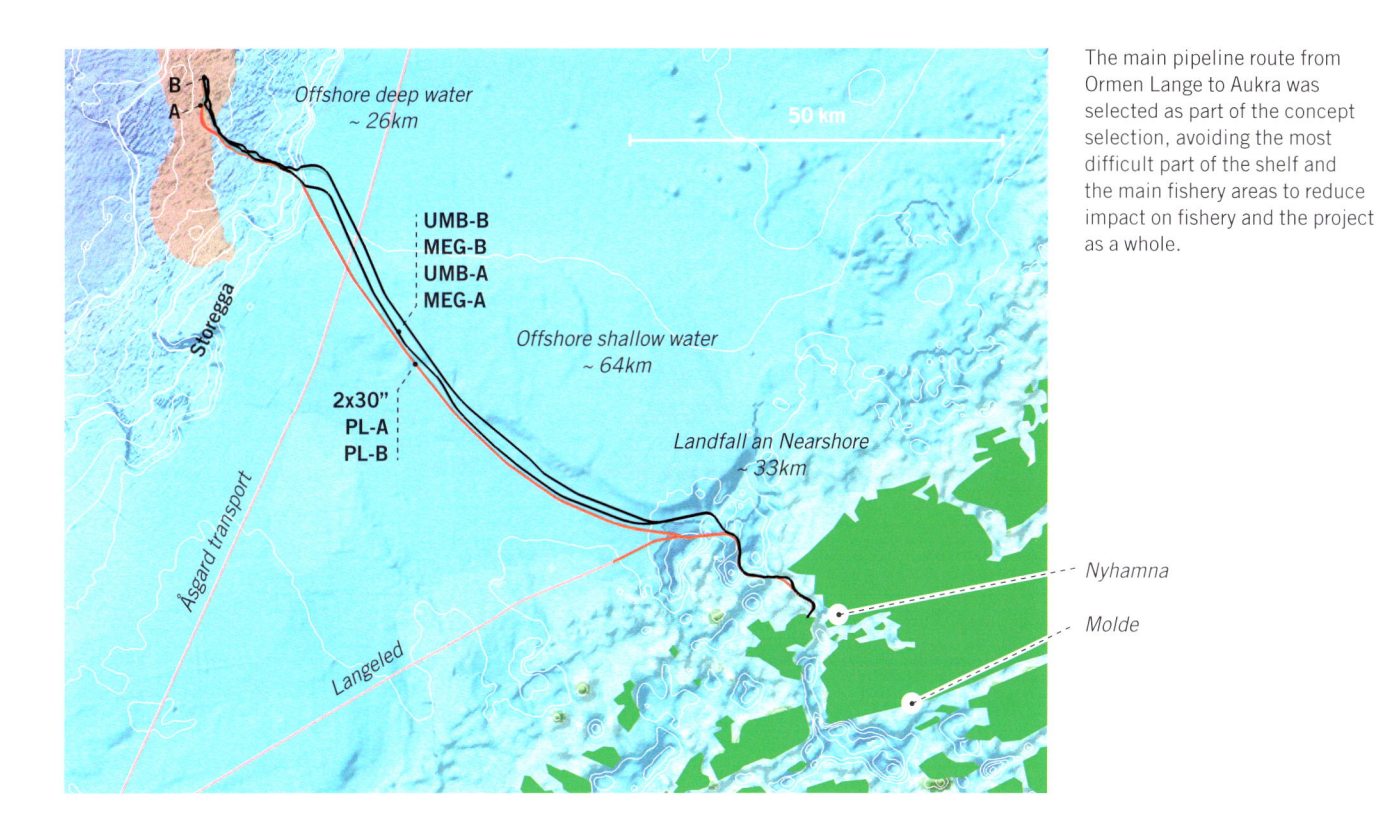

The main pipeline route from Ormen Lange to Aukra was selected as part of the concept selection, avoiding the most difficult part of the shelf and the main fishery areas to reduce impact on fishery and the project as a whole.

challenge, with mapping of potential routes made possible by modern seafloor mapping tools such as multibeam echo sounders.

The top four sites were to be selected between December 2000 and June 2001. Local communities promoted their locations enthusiastically and Hydro met a very positive response when gathering information for further evaluation. More detailed engineering was performed to calculate site preparation cost in terms of blasting, excavation and mass transport, cost of updating infrastructure, cost of power supply and other key factors.

As well as evaluating the requirements for the Ormen Lange project, possible future needs were also considered. Should the plant be expanded as a hub for gas from other potential fields in the area a larger site would be needed. Since oil companies were then at an early stage in exploring the deepwater area outside Mid Norway, it wasn't unlikely that other fields would be found and developed, and could be connected to the Ormen Lange processing plant.

In summer 2001 the four leading sites were announced: Tjeldbergodden, Stavnes, Nyhamna and Skår/Baraldsnes. Other municipalities were disappointed, but reassured by the openness and fairness of the process in terms of selection criteria and outcome.

The big question still remained however: would a full processing platform be built onshore? Should the decision fall in favour of an offshore solution, none of these sites would be selected anyway. As the site selection process went on, the local communities continued to invest in planning and technical work in preparation for the final decision.

The discussions on site selection were not only objective technical debates: political issues were also on the agenda. Statoil wanted to utilise the existing industrial site at Tjeldbergodden in order to increase its involvement in the Ormen Lange development and potential control in the production phase.

Existence of an established industrial site worked in Tjeldbergodden's favour as it would eliminate the environmental impact caused by new industrial development in another location.

Statoil's preference for Tjeldbergodden was also backed by local politicians and the labour organisation (LO). Its location in Trøndelag made Tjeldbergodden the only site outside Møre and Romsdal County – and hence made a political fight hard to avoid.

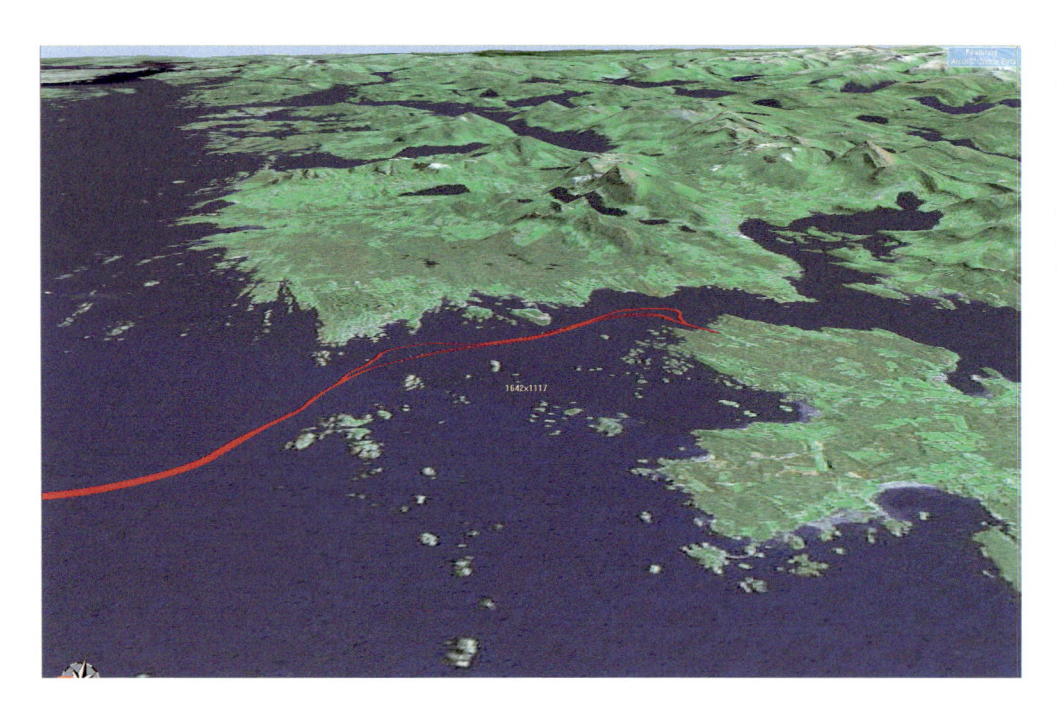

The planned pipeline route to the shore ran through the challenging near shore area to the landfall at Nyhamna on Gossen island in Aukra. The underwater topography is rugged, particularly in the area west of Bud. The skerries seen above the water level indicates similar conditions below the water level. The 3D image created by Hydro is based on Google Earth and a local terrain database.

Of the remaining four sites, Nyhamna at Aukra seemed best suited. There was plenty of space, and the pipeline route from the field to the plant was the shortest, and thus the least expensive, option. The site's relatively flat topography also meant the investment level was lower than for the other locations.

To avoid later conflict with archaeological sites that might stop development, studies were made at the four remaining sites to expose any potential issues. All four sites had acceptably low conflict levels despite many remnants from Stone Age and Bronze Age settlements being anticipated. The investigations clearly indicated archaeological excavation of the selected location would be needed prior to any development work and this had to be incorporated into the development plan.

The archaeological surveys were among the many detailed studies needed before the final site and concept could be selected. An assessment of total community impact was an inherent part of the preparation before selecting the final concept.

The final selection criteria involved investment cost for the plant and the pipelines, production cost in the production phase, production volume from the field as a function of distance (lower production volume with increased distance to shore), synergies with the existing facilities at Tjeldbergodden, environmental issues and local community impact. The potential for future development was also evaluated.

In the end Tjeldbergodden was ranked last after Nyhamna in Aukra, Stavnes and Baraldsnes. The final selection was made by the Ormen Lange partners in May 2002 following a further evaluation of the potential synergies with the existing facilities at Tjeldbergodden initiated by Statoil. This was a challenging period for the Hydro team as the intense involvement from project partners, politicians and the local community attracted a lot of media attention. Hydro ran an active public relations strategy to meet the expectations for openness and involvement in the process.

The Major of Aukra municipality, Aud Mork, had worked hard on the Aukra bid from early in the selection process and it was a great day when Hydro's project director Tor Tangen called to announce Aukra was the selected location. But a major potential obstacle remained: the offshore platform concept had still not been ruled out.

The final concept was to be selected in December 2002.

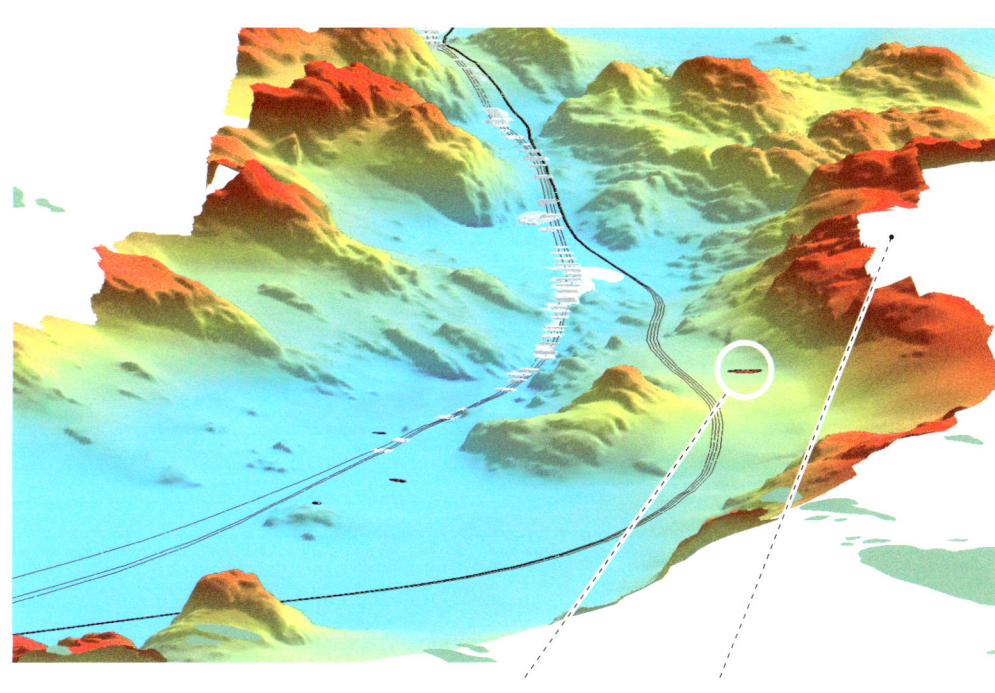

The historical wreck site was discovered close to Bud in a narrow part of the Ormen Lange pipeline route. Due to the narrow underwater valley, the gas pipelines were planned in a separate corridor to the small diameter service lines which initially passed through the wreck site. The routes are seen from shore towards offshore.

Historical shipwreck   *Bud*

Detailed evaluation of the area started as soon as the onshore location for the processing plant was selected, including marine archaeological surveys along the planned pipeline routes in the near shore area.

The routes mapped by the Hydro team had not shown any marine archaeological sites along the routes, but when the archaeologist from the Museum of Natural History and Archaeology (Vitenskapsmuseet) at the Norwegian University of Science and Technology analysed Hydro's survey data he concluded a more detailed survey was needed.

Then the day arrived that would change the course of the Ormen Lange project.

In August 2003 Hydro received a phone call from the vessel performing the marine archaeological survey that would have a major impact on the Ormen Lange development project: wine bottles, porcelain, and a ship bell had been discovered on the seafloor where the pipeline was planned for the MEG and umbilical lines. The large number of artefacts sighted on the seafloor were soon evaluated; the site was a historic shipwreck protected by the Norwegian Cultural Heritage Act (Kulturminneloven).

Onshore, plans for a major archaeological excavation were already well under way at the processing plant site which meant the Ormen Lange team was already familiar with land-based archaeology. For Hydro, however, it was a new experience to deal with cultural heritage on the seafloor; no previous Hydro projects had involved marine archaeology.

The initial plan was to carry out additional surveys and solve the problem by rerouting the pipeline. The narrow underwater valley and rough terrain meant that only one potential alternative route could be identified, and when this route was investigated another smaller historical wreck was discovered. The route also had other disadvantages which discouraged Hydro from selecting it.

The pipeline route was slightly rerouted from the first wreck, but the narrow valley made it impossible to avoid the defined wreck discovery area. The wreck discovery and the requirements for the Ormen Lange pipelines to pass through the area led to an extensive marine archaeological project financed by the Ormen Lange project.

The final concept was approved by all partners in 2003 following extensive negotiations. Exxon and BP were in favour of an offshore platform and Shell initially supported it too. However in spring 2003, Hydro finally convinced the project partners

The subsea-to-shore alternative was selected as the development concept for Ormen Lange. This figure illustrates the subsea templates and pipelines to the planned onshore processing plant at Aukra in Møre and Romsdal.

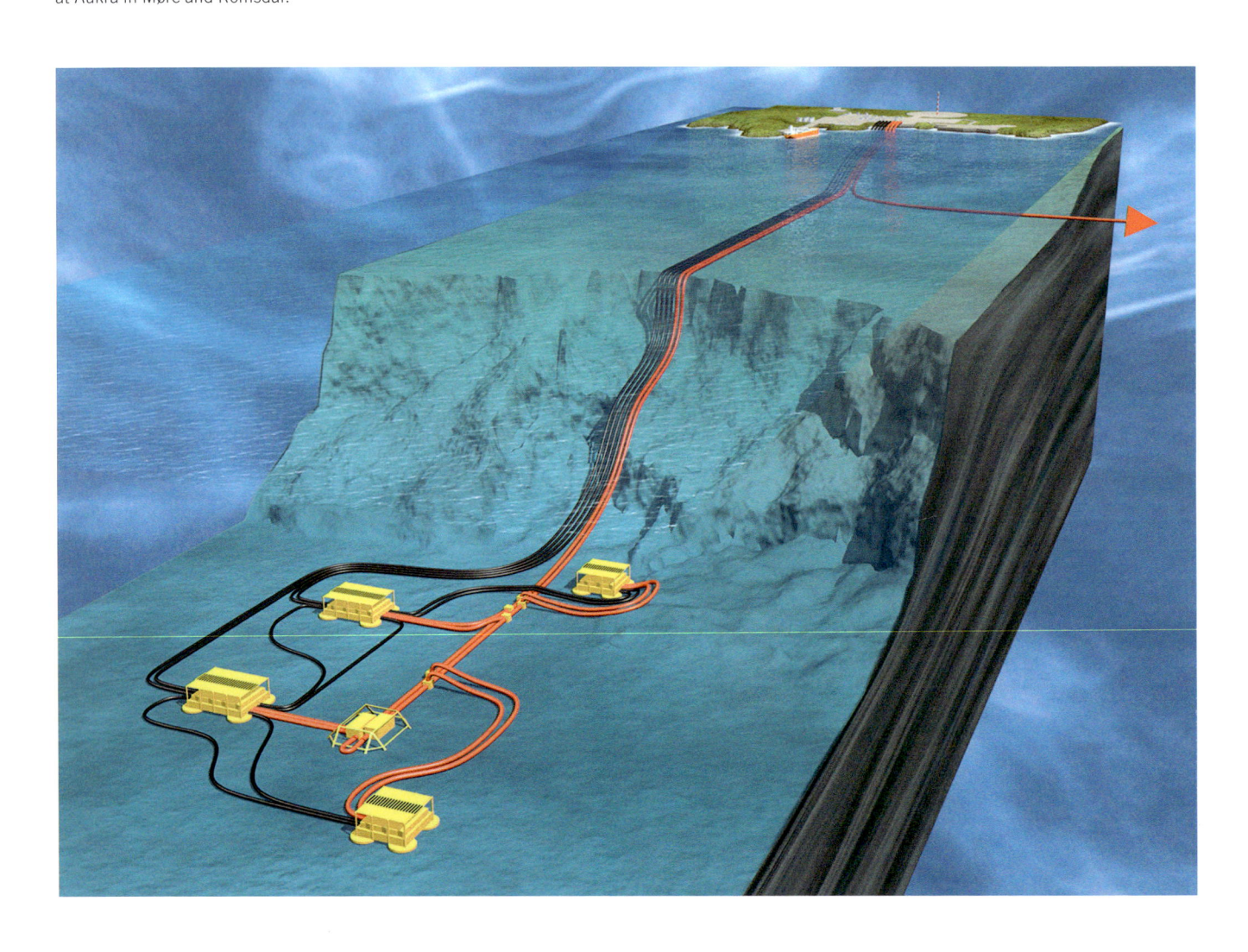

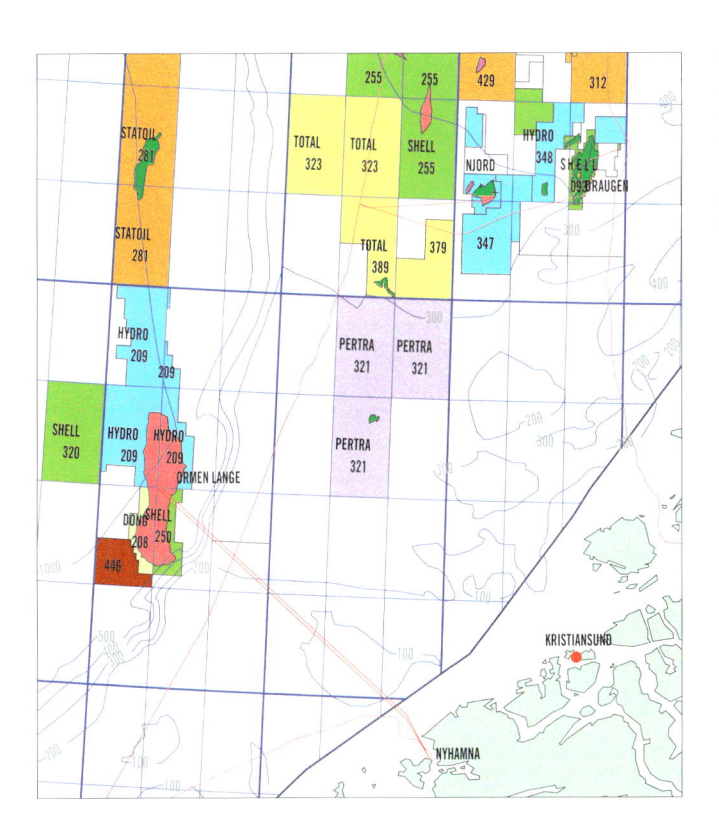

The Ormen Lange licence blocks and the reservoir boundary. Operatorship of the south-eastern block was awarded to Shell in 1999 with Hydro, Exxon, Statoil and Petoro as partners, although not BP.

that a subsea-to-shore alternative would work as well as the platform solution and they agreed to support the Hydro proposal.

This was cause for celebration amongst Aukra locals. 'Ormen to Møre' was no longer a goal or a dream, it had become reality.

OPERATORSHIP OF ORMEN LANGE

Hydro was awarded the operatorship of Ormen Lange in 1996. As the Ormen Lange field was so large in size physically, the structure was covering parts of three normal concession blocks. Two of these blocks were awarded in 1996 and the third in 1999, possibly delayed due to the high intensity of fishery in this area. Storegga is a very rich fishing area due to the upwelling of water in the Gulf Stream as it meets the sharp Storegga escarpment. The fishing industry was less than enthusiastic towards exploration activity in the area.

Operatorship of the third Ormen Lange block was awarded to Shell in October 1999. This came as a major shock to the Hydro team, which had assumed they would receive it.

The reason was most likely that the Norwegian authorities wanted to ensure Shell's global experience in deep water field development would be utilised in the Ormen Lange project. That Hydro did not have this experience was considered a risk.

Hydro and Shell each held an ownership share close to 18 per cent of Ormen Lange after the final licence block was awarded. Operatorship of Ormen Lange could be decided three ways: awarded to Shell, or awarded to Hydro, or split between the two. The Norwegian Petroleum Directorate (NPD) and the Ministry of Oil and Energy were to propose a solution with the final decision being taken on political level.

This was an uncertain and frustrating time for the Hydro team which had expected total operatorship of the field based on the initial licences. Hydro lobbied hard to convince the authorities it had the technical capabilities needed to develop the field, and in the end the Norwegian Parliament decided on a split operatorship: Hydro would be responsible for the challenging project development and Shell for the operation of the field after its planned start in 2007.

The announcement was cause for celebration amongst Hydro engineers. Major challenges in a spectacular project – for engineers there is nothing better. It was the Norwegian equivalent of sending a man to the moon.

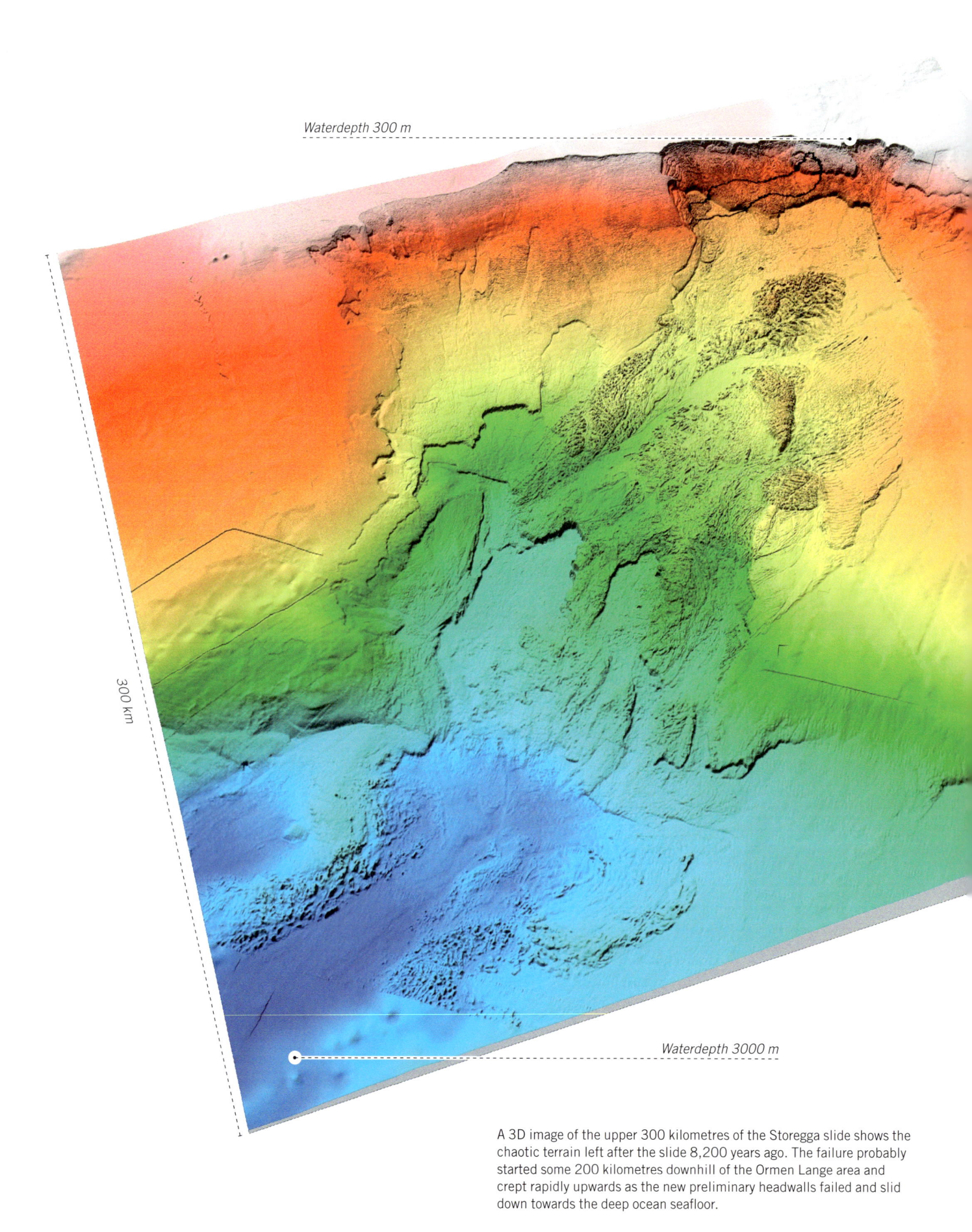

Waterdepth 300 m

300 km

Waterdepth 3000 m

A 3D image of the upper 300 kilometres of the Storegga slide shows the chaotic terrain left after the slide 8,200 years ago. The failure probably started some 200 kilometres downhill of the Ormen Lange area and crept rapidly upwards as the new preliminary headwalls failed and slid down towards the deep ocean seafloor.

CHAPTER 3

THE STOREGGA SLIDE

The Storegga slide is the largest known submarine slide on earth. The headwall of the slide scar is 300 kilometres long and forms the transition from the continental shelf to the deepwater margin outside Mid-Norway. Storegga is the name given it by fishermen who have long known of the dramatic change in water depth along the edge of the continental shelf, well before it was known to be a slide.

The slide occurred 8,200 years ago. Close to 3,500 cubic kilometres of sediment failed from the shelf edge, sliding out as far as 800 kilometres. The first 300 kilometres of run out is on the deep water margin from a depth of 300 metres down to approximately 3,000 metres. The slide sediments continued to run out on relatively flat seafloor for another 500 kilometres before stopping near the mountain range known as the Mid Atlantic Ridge.

Almost 90,000 square kilometres of seafloor was affected by the slide, an area one-third the size of Norway. The slide is a phenomenal feature that is extraordinarily interesting for all scientists involved in deepwater margins around the world.

THE STOREGGA TSUNAMI

Most Stone Age settlements in Norway at the time of the slide were situated along the coastline as fishing and hunting were the main sources of food. When a great noise erupted from the sea one day, and the water mysteriously disappeared from the beach, it is unlikely the coast-dwellers would have ever have seen anything like it before.

You could imagine them rushing down to the beach in astonishment, urgently collecting fish stranded on the shore when the water withdrew. Several minutes, perhaps even an hour, later the tsunami wave would have arrived, hitting the coastal areas along the west coast of Norway.

Tremendous waves of between two to three

The mapped run-up heights (blue dots) and the run-up heights from tsunami wave modelling (red dots) correlate well.

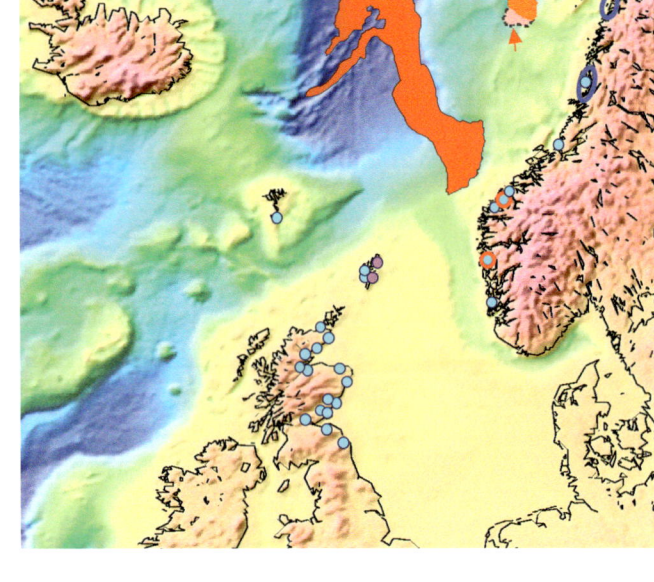

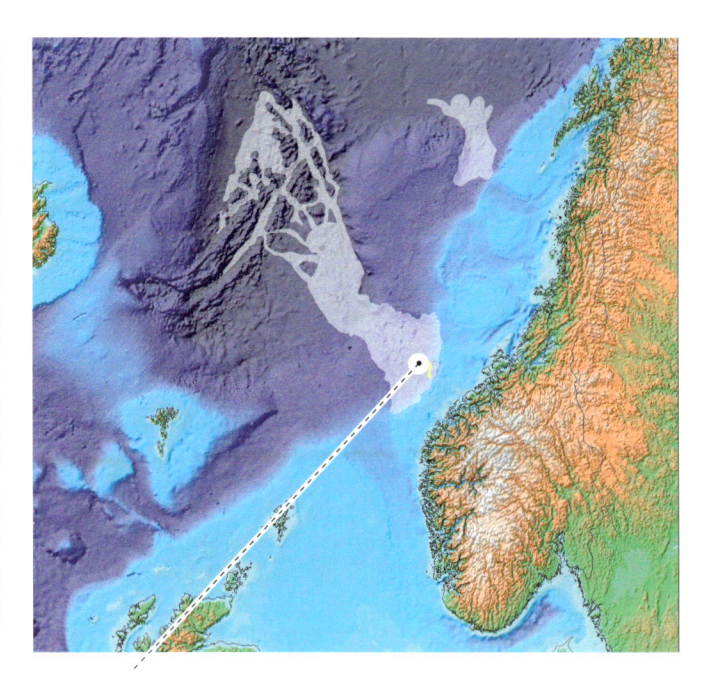

The Storegga slide.

metres and 12 to 15 metres high inundated the coast with devastating power. Tsunami modelling indicates that waves 30 to 50 metres high may have surged into narrow fjords or between offshore islands. The huge waves would have oscillated in the fjords for some time as their energy dissipated. Areas with long shallow beaches were most heavily affected by the waves, as they were in the South East Asian tsunami in 2004. Hardest hit with the most fatalities were the lower, flatter beaches where waves can have a long run up before being stopped by the landscape.

Flat areas like this along the Norwegian coastline would have been home to most settlements in the Stone Age. Many of these settlements would have been devastated and the coastal population undoubtedly suffered huge fatalities.

More recently, the tsunami that hit Indonesia, Thailand, India, Burma, Sri Lanka and east Africa on 26 December 2004 changed the way we think about tsunamis, our knowledge about how they happen and their devastating effect. The many casualities and our exposure through media to the waves and the affected areas was an effective lesson on tsunamis for most people around the world. It is easier to imagine the effect of the Storegga tsunami along the Norwegian coast having seen the coverage of the 2004 tsunami.

Since it is not known how the slide developed and at what speed, minor tsunami waves may have hit the coast prior to the major wave. However, even a relatively small wave would have had a dramatic impact along the coast, as no-one is prepared for events like this. When the maximum wave hit the coastline it would have had a devastating effect. The tsunami wave caused by the Storegga slide was two to five times higher than the wave that hit Thailand in 2004.

As well as hitting the Norwegian coast, the wave also hit all the islands and mainland around the North Sea. Waves of up to 25 metres have been "recorded" on the Shetland Islands in the catastrophic sediments left after the wave [1]. Such layers of chaotic sediment are typically found in lakes and peat bogs close to the coast but would here have been trapped as the wave inundated the coast and retreated as an enormous river. Remnants of trees and plants and even salt water fish in chaotic layers can be dated using the C14 method and tsunami sediments found around all North Sea coastlines have been dated and found to be around 8,200 years old.

Reconstruction of the sea level at the time of the tsunami indicates a local run-up of more than 20 metres on Shetland. The wave eroded and cut clasts of peat during run-up that were mixed with sand as the water returned to the sea. Carbon dating indicated an age of 8,200 years for the layer of tsunami deposits on Shetland. The tsunami mapping project, carried out as part of the Ormen Lange project, was led by assistant professor Stein Bondevik.

The expanding database gradually supported the idea that a single major tsunami event had affected this large area. Fish found in the tsunami sediments indicate the tsunami occurred in late autumn; the cycles of fish eggs can be seen in fish buried in sediments and preserved.

One of the steps in the process of identifying potential risks involved in developing the Ormen Lange field was to find out whether the Storegga slide had been a single major event or whether additional slides had taken place in the same area since the initial slide 8,200 years ago. If additional slides had occurred after the initial slide, had they been accompanied by additional tsunami events?

Extensive fieldwork by tsunami expert Stein Bondevik at the University of Tromsø concluded however that only a single tsunami wave of any significance had hit Norway from an offshore source after the ice age, namely the Storegga wave. The same conclusion could be drawn from studies of seismic data and sediment cores in the fjords. No more than a single Storegga tsunami had entered the fjords along the Norwegian west coast.

The reason the Ormen Lange team needed to understand the cause of the Storegga slide 8,200 years ago was simple: to establish whether there is a similar risk today. Was the risk of new natural slides too high to develop the field? Are the steep slopes close to the reservoir area unstable? Could draining of the reservoir lead to new instability in the area?

Scottish newspapers and other magazines such as *Illustrert Vitenskap* and *Scientific American* had run articles on the slide, emphasising the importance of getting well documented answers to these questions prior to any decision on field development. It was easy to ask questions and come up with frightening scenarios of new killer waves.

HOW WAS THE SLIDE RISK QUESTION SOLVED?

Hydro did not have the appropriate knowledge and experience to evaluate whether it was safe to develop the Ormen Lange gas field close to the steep headwall of the Storegga Slide. Therefore, a joint programme to map and study the slides and other seafloor phenomena in the area was started as early as 1996 to provide more information about the area.

Knowledge and experience were also sought from the academic world, both internationally and in Norway. An EU research project called European North Atlantic Margin (ENAM) was

Sensational articles in Scottish and Norwegian newspapers and scientific magazines raised frightening scenarios of new killer waves. Prior to field development it was necessary to reassure the community that the Ormen Lange project did not represent any risk of new tsunami generation slides.

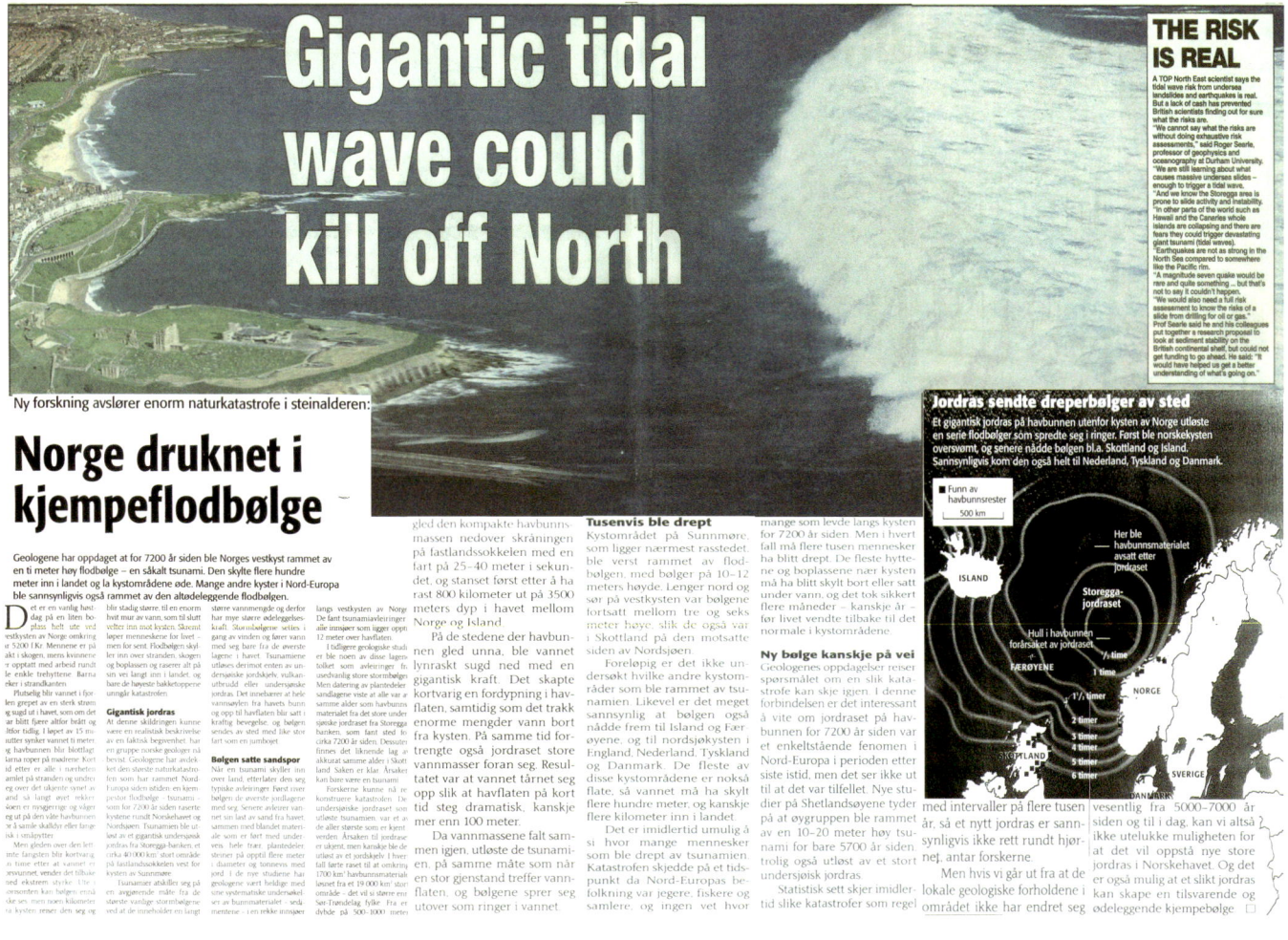

Petter Bryn during the Storegga slide risk evaluation.

already studying the European deepwater margin. The Universities of Tromsø, Bergen and Oslo were partners in this project with studies focussed on the Norwegian deepwater margin.

Over time, Hydro developed an active collaboration with the ENAM project, including joint fieldwork activities and complete exchange of data gathered by industry and academia. This co-operation ran until the slide issue was resolved in 2003 and included ENAM Phase 2 as well as a later slope stability project called COSTA.

In addition to practical co-operation on the mid-Norwegian deepwater margin, the teamwork gave Hydro access to the results of all deepwater margin mapping and research from all major academic programmes in Europe and Canada during the period. It was a win-win situation that helped update geohazard knowledge on a multidisciplinary basis, an outcome that since benefitted both academia and industry.

The major Norwegian contributors to the project were the Norwegian Geotechnical Institute, Norsar for earthquake expertise, the Norwegian Geological Survey, Sintef, and Scan Power for risk analysis, along with the universities. The British Geological Survey and Oceanographic Institute in Southampton also contributed to the final analysis of the slide risk. The survey contractors and the geotechnical drilling contractor were also important contributors, as drilling geotechnical boreholes at great depth in difficult soil conditions with many boulders was in itself a major challenge.

Hydro and the Ormen Lange partners clearly had a single objective for the research: to develop the Ormen Lange gas field. This naturally raised questions regarding independence. Would the conclusions from Hydro's slide risk evaluation be independent and objective? Would a positive outcome be acknowledged by the NGOs and the community as a whole?

To guarantee an evaluation of slide risk that would be as sound and objective as possible, Hydro involved academia in an integrated project team and ran an open process with exchange of data and results. A team was also set up including experts who were world leaders in the various topics being studied to verify the work programme, methods and results. The verification team involved tsunami experts, experts in geology and geophysics, earthquake experts, slide experts as well as experts in risk analysis.

Sintef led the verification process, with the team

0 25 50 100 150 200
Kilometers

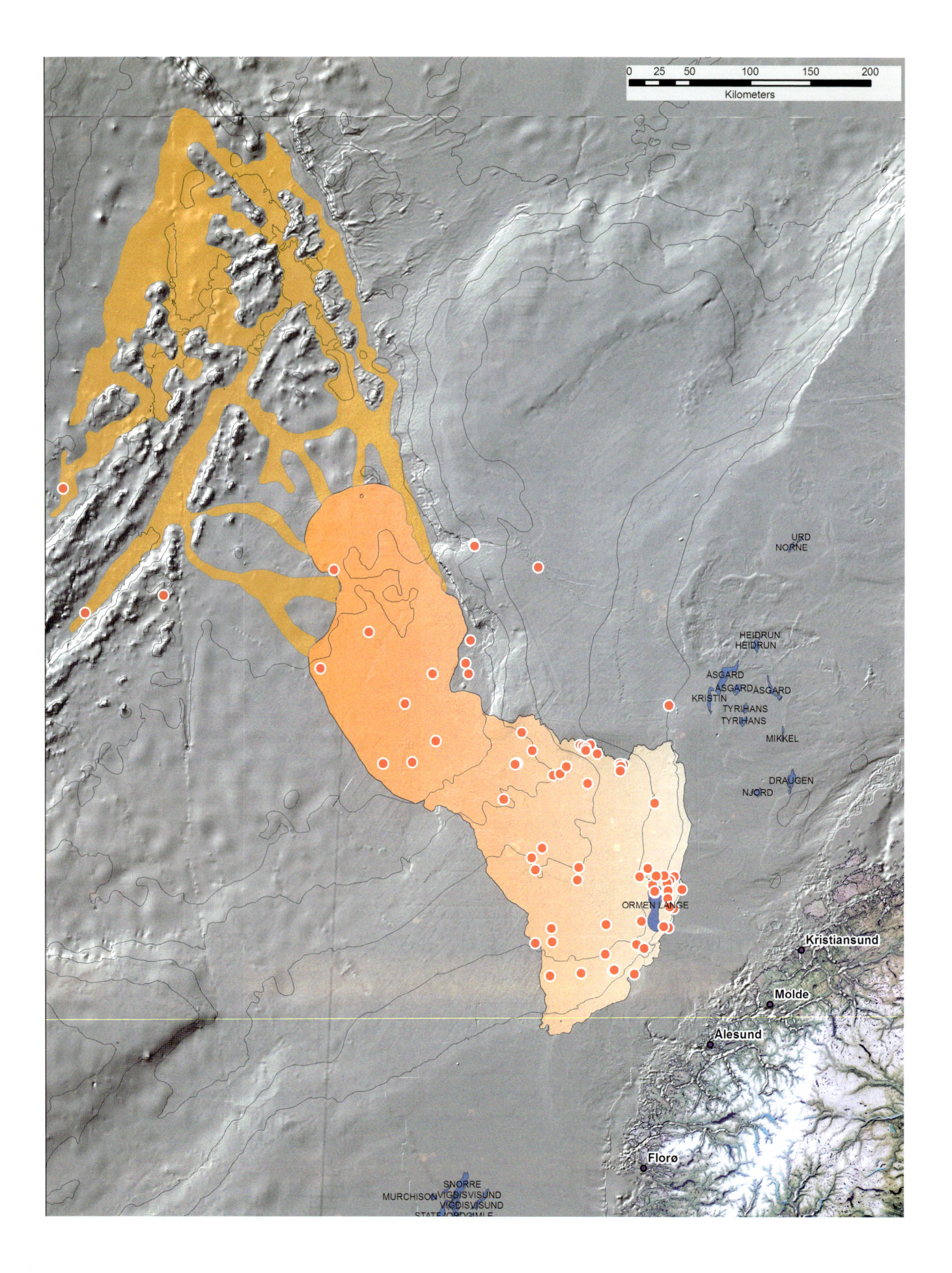

URD
NORNE

HEIDRUN
HEIDRUN

ÅSGARD
ÅSGARD ÅSGARD
KRISTIN
TYRIHANS
TYRIHANS
MIKKEL

DRAUGEN
NJORD

ORMEN LANGE

Kristiansund

Molde

Ålesund

Florø

SNORRE
MURCHISON VIGDIS VISUND
VIGDIS VISUND
STATFJORD GIMLE

Many sediment cores were collected to help date the Storegga slide. Detailed seafloor maps were required to select sites that would provide correct dates for the slide event. During this work a new depth record for ROV mapping in Norway was achieved by the survey company DeepOcean, with the deepest cores taken in water depths of more than 3,000 metres.

challenging the Hydro team in a tough but positive way. In the end there was mutual support for and agreement on the conclusions regarding slide risk. During this period Hydro was also audited by the Norwegian Petroleum Directorate, which is responsible for safety on the Norwegian continental shelf. Their three audits contributed to a safe conclusion on the slide risk issue. The outcome of the project as well as how the results were communicated internally and externally were significant issues.

The enormity of the Storegga slide made mapping the area a major challenge, as well as planning for sampling for dating and geotechnical boreholes needed for slope stability calculations.

The database was gradually developed through survey activities. Hydro and the Ormen Lange partners invested some EUR 90 million to determine slide risk and map the slide for pipeline routes prior to the decision to develop the field. An additional EUR 50–60 million was invested in studies and mapping related to the slide risk issues through EU projects.

RESULT OF THE SLIDE RISK PROJECT

The vast slide area was mapped using echo sounder, side scan sonar and seismic equipment. Analyses of more than 100 geological core samples confirmed the age of the slide, nearly all dating it to around 8,200 years. [2]

The technique used was to determine the age of the first sediments that had drifted along the slope on the Gulf stream current and been deposited in the depression left after the slide, much like drifts of snow. As much as 30 to 50 metres of soft clay has been deposited in this way over the last 8,200 years, thus dating the sediment layer directly above the slide surface.

The Ormen Lange structure is located in the central part of the slide scar close to the headwall of the slide, with the deepest cut in the shelf edge and the roughest terrain above the Ormen Lange reservoir.

Is this merely a coincidence or is there a connection between the failure of the sediments and the gas reservoir? Could gas have leaked slowly from the reservoir over several hundred thousand years and been trapped in the overlaying sediments and caused them to fail?

The question will remain unanswered as any potential evidence was lost in the slide 8,200 years ago. As the gas reservoir will be drained by the

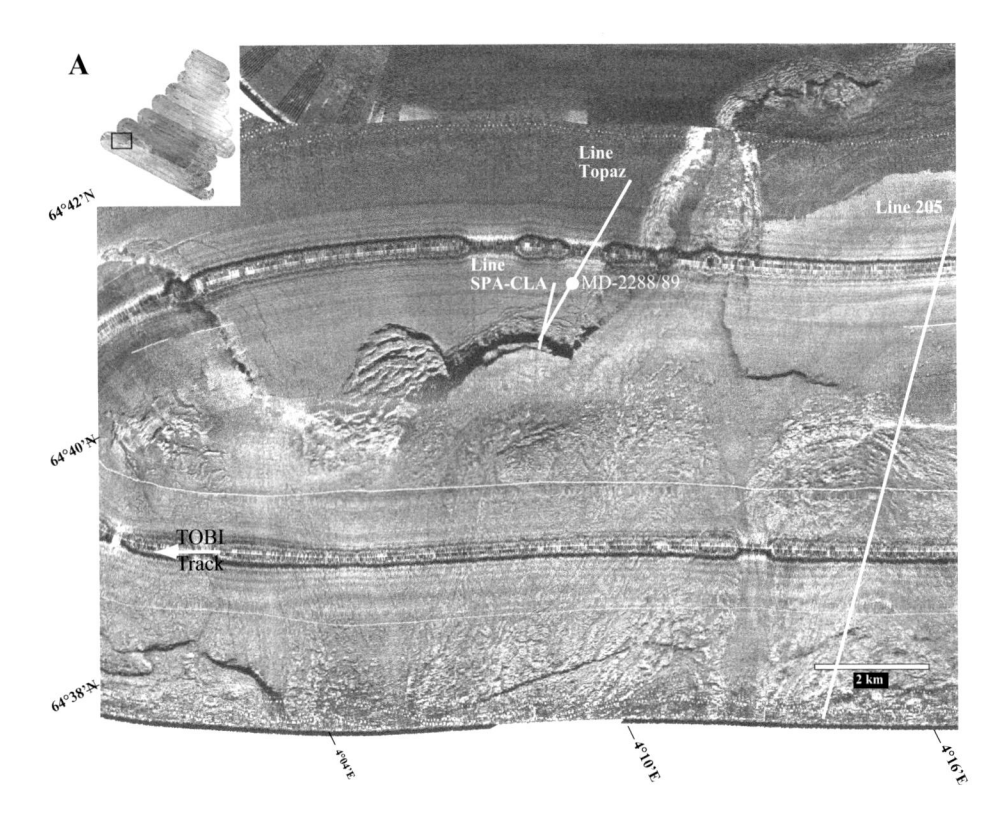

The University of Bergen performed a deepwater sonar survey of the northern sidewall of the Storegga slide in 1997. The sonar images indicated an ongoing failure of the northern sidewall. Local failures as well as cracks in the seafloor at the slide margin could be seen on the sonar records. Later work confirmed all failures to be 8,200 years old. [3]

planned gas production, it is assumed the gas will not be able to contribute to instability in the future as it may have before the slide took place.

Prior to the Storegga slide, the deep-water margin had a slope of around 1 degree, similar to the slope on a football field to let rain water run off. With such a low slope angle it was not easy to understand how the slope could fail – a question that puzzled the team working with the slide issue.

The project provided some remarkable results. Over the last 500,000 years, Scandinavia has experienced four to five major glaciations and been covered in ice for most of the period. Using seismic interpretation and a detailed geological model of Scandinavia as a whole, it was discovered that a major slope failure took place in the Storegga area during the last phase, or just after, each major glaciation. [4]

During interglacial periods, the Gulf Stream flowed across the slope depositing layers of soft clay. The glaciers pushed sediments out to the deepwater shelf break like a bulldozer. When the heavy boulder clay from the ice was loaded onto the soft clay layers on the slope, the soft clay became unstable and failed. These type of failures can occur even at very slight slope angles.

Once started, the failure quickly expanded causing a major submarine slide. As the slide caused a major tsunami, it would appear that a large volume failed over just a few hours.

The thaw lifted the nearly 3,000-metre thick ice cap over Scandinavia causing many major earthquakes – and finally triggering the Storegga slide.

Based on their comprehensive investigations and studies, Hydro geologists drew the following conclusion:

"All unstable sediment on the slope disappeared with the Storegga slide 8,200 years ago. A new ice age with glaciers bringing new glacial sediments across the shelf into the deepwater margin would be needed for new, large-scale instability to occur in the area. The steep slopes in the area with slope angles of 30 to 40 degrees were proven to be stable even in the event of major new earthquakes." [5][6][7]

When this conclusion was reached in 2003 it was a huge relief for the team, particularly as it was in mutual agreement with academia, the Norwegian Petroleum Directorate, the Ormen Lange partners and the international verification team.

Access to the area was granted!

For the Norwegian public it assured good pensions in the future. For Hydro and the Ormen Lange partners it meant development of the second largest gas field in Norway could commence.

From now on, the slide terrain would be the main challenge to the Ormen Lange development project.

In December 2004 when South East Asia was hit by a major tsunami, Hydro received a lot of media interest about the Storegga slide and the potential threat to the Ormen Lange development. As the conclusions from the slide risk project were so solid and well documented, media interest was limited to positive, informative articles about the Storegga slide and the work performed to document the area's stability.

There were however a number of setbacks during the slide project which affected the team's optimistic approach and its confidence in getting results that would support field development. Hydro backed a deepwater side scan sonar mapping survey of the northern headwall of the slide performed by the EU project ENAM and the University of Bergen. The conclusion was that the slide was most likely in an active failure situation. [3]

Sonar images indicated the headwall of the northern flank had experienced recent failure and that further failures could be expected. After two years of intense work including video inspections, geotechnical coring, dating and seismic interpretation it was, however, concluded that even the main part of the northern headwall was 8,200 years old, and the results from the initial survey could be set aside.

Results indicating failures close to the development area as recently as 1,800 years ago were also cause for concern. For some months the Hydro team were uncertain about how to progress. More work and additional cores were required to explain the results and correct errors. The conclusion: the slide is in fact 8,200 years old.

Illustration of seafloor mapping using an AUV. The small unmanned submarine is equipped with underwater positioning systems and a multibeam echo sounder for detailed mapping of the seafloor.

CHAPTER 4

MAPPING THE SEAFLOOR

Seafloor mapping technology has developed significantly in recent years. The Ormen Lange field development in extremely rough seafloor terrain has been a challenge, and new mapping technology was required to be able to plan pipeline routes and preparation of "roads" for the pipelines.

Hydro has been a frontrunner in its requirements for new technology and better tools for mapping. Few other projects around the world have required such sophisticated data to plan for a field development.

Since 1996, Hydro has worked closely with the survey industry to support and stimulate the development of innovative mapping technology for deepwater and high accuracy mapping. New or improved technology has been developed and tested each year from 1997, and the substantial experience this has given the Ormen Lange team and the industry as a whole has helped further advance mapping technology.

Seafloor maps and terrain models are generated using depth data from multibeam echo sounders which are mounted on the hull of a survey ship, on an ROV (remotely operated vehicle) or on an AUV (autonomous underwater vehicle) flying 20–25 metres above the seafloor during survey operations.

Echo sounders mounted on the hull of a ship cover a corridor of several hundred metres as they move along a predefined route. This sort of data provides good seafloor maps for the initial requirements of a development project like Ormen Lange, but far more detailed maps can be generated using the multibeam echo sounder mounted on an AUV or an ROV typically moving 20 metres above the seafloor.

During the mapping survey, the ROV is connected by cable to a survey ship through which it is powered and transmits seafloor data. The ROV pilot steers the underwater vehicle from the control room of the survey ship as it travels along the seafloor some hundred metres below the survey ship. High technology underwater positioning in combination with GPS is used to accurately position the ROV and the AUV, but the depths involved in Ormen Lange made underwater positioning more challenging. Upgraded technology was needed to improve the accuracy of positioning systems for mapping and installation work in Ormen Lange.

An AUV can fly freely under water like an unmanned submarine and is not connected to the survey ship by cable. The vehicle is powered by a

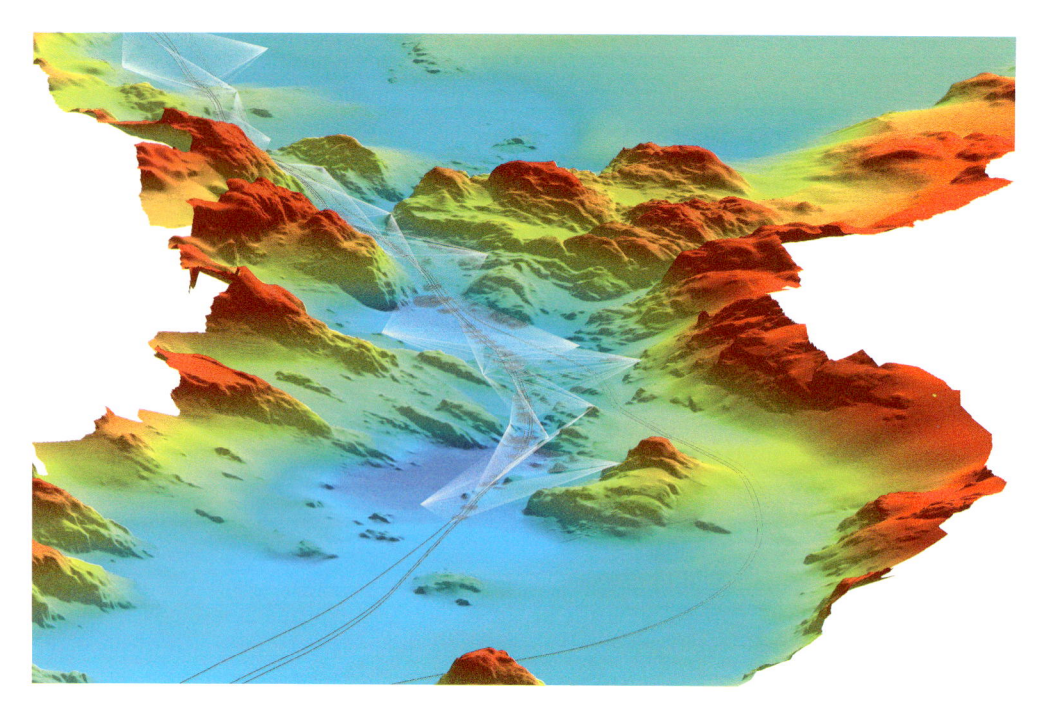

Underwater acoustic positioning networks were installed so the seafloor could be mapped as accurately as possible. The figure illustrates the narrow underwater valley in the near shore area with gas pipeline routes to the left, and the smaller diameter control cables and antifreeze (MEG) pipelines to the right.

battery that typically allows operation on the seafloor for two days before returning to the vessel to recharge its battery and transfer stored seafloor data.

The AUVs are programmed to follow a planned route along the seafloor while monitoring the distance to the seafloor. ROVs and AUVs can both collect multibeam depth data and shallow seismic data that provide information about sediment in the few metres directly beneath the seafloor, and also record video. The AUV has the advantage of being able to perform mapping at speeds of around 4 knots compared to the 1 to 2 knot speeds of the ROV. Doubling the speed halves the cost of data collection.

The ROV pilot sitting in his control cabin onboard the ship can stop the vehicle to look more closely at interesting items on the seafloor through the video cameras on the ROV. Video is digitally recorded with video grabs used to generate still photos. The pilot can also use manipulator arms to pick up items from the seafloor, which is why ROVs are often used although they are slower than AUVs.

AUVs have only been available for commercial use since 2001. The Ormen Lange project was the first commercial AUV mapping as well as the first deepwater AUV survey anywhere in the world. Hydro supported the final development of this technology from 1998 to 2000 through its Ormen Lange licence in preparation for use in the Ormen Lange project. Marine technology manufacturer Kongsberg and the Norwegian Defence Research Institute supported by Statoil had been active in developing the technology for many years. The major seafloor challenges in the slide area made it clear that better mapping tools were needed to complete the development of Ormen Lange.

Further development of multibeam echo sounders led to a huge increase in seafloor data density and in the total number of data points per area. This meant more data storage capacity was needed as well as new techniques to visualize the results. Standard contour maps have been complemented and partly replaced by 3D seafloor models as well as light and shadow techniques to visualize the seafloor.

The techniques developed in the Ormen Lange project in recent years have made it possible to map and classify objects as small as 10–20 centimetres. This has been key to successfully preparing pipeline and subsea structure installations, and

Multibeam echo sounder mapping using a hull-mounted echo sounder. The "light fan" underneath the vessel shows the area covered by a large number of acoustic beams measuring the depth to the seafloor.

This 3D image is generated using detailed bathymetric data gathered by the AUV at depths of 600 to 700 metres. The large slide block in the centre of the image is 900 metres long and 45 metres high. The smaller slide blocks seen here are partly covered by soft clay deposited in the Storegga slide area after the slide 8,200 years ago.

Brackets being loaded onto the survey vessel for installation on the seafloor where they will support transponders in the underwater acoustic network.

Small Lophelia coral reefs growing on hard rock outcrops in the near shore area close to the Ormen Lange pipeline route. Rocks as small as 20 centimetres in diameter can be seen on the photolike images of the seafloor using technology developed by Hydro for the Ormen Lange development project. An exciting new underwater world has come into view.

New data processing technology developed by the Hydro team has improved the accuracy of mapping rocks and other details on the seafloor.

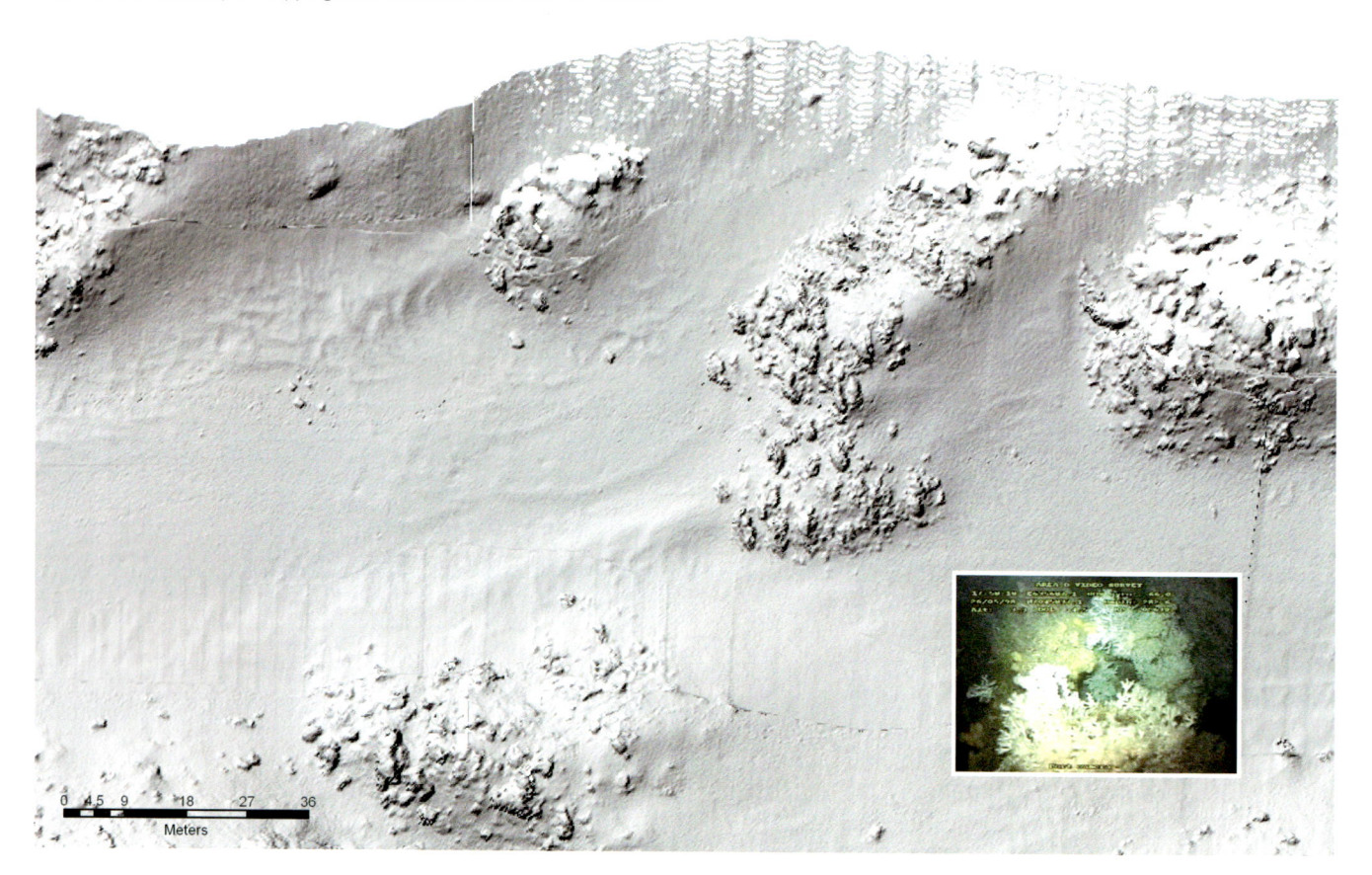

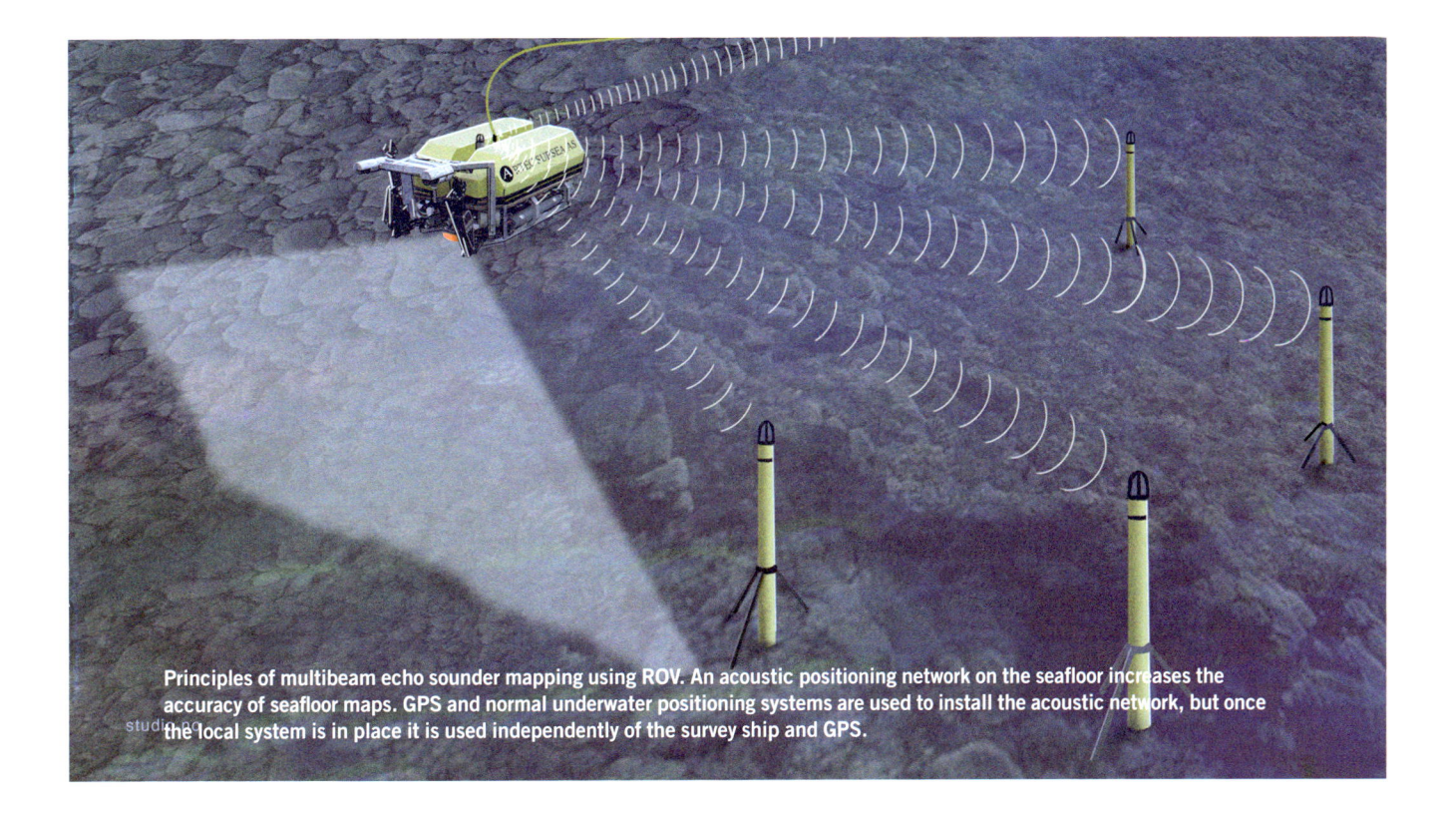

Principles of multibeam echo sounder mapping using ROV. An acoustic positioning network on the seafloor increases the accuracy of seafloor maps. GPS and normal underwater positioning systems are used to install the acoustic network, but once the local system is in place it is used independently of the survey ship and GPS.

particularly for seafloor preparation prior to pipeline installation.

Small coral reefs proliferated in the near shore area as coral tends to grow on hard rock outcrops and boulders on the seafloor. During the initial mapping phase, these reefs could only be seen on video. Mapping using multibeam echo sounder is a more efficient way of documenting the reefs, with video used to verify they are coral reefs. Coral reef preservation has been an important criteria during the selection of pipeline routes and was only possible due to recent development in mapping technology.

Hydro provided seafloor map data from the coral reefs to the Norwegian Petroleum Directorate (NPD) and the World Wildlife Foundation which was a much appreciated contribution to understanding of the occurrence of the coral reefs and the method of mapping them.

Bathymetric data to measure ocean depth has been complemented with high-resolution seismic data to map shallow soils. Geotechnical cores have been collected to verify the seismic interpretation and to analyze soil strength. Large supports of crushed rock were planned to support the pipeline, particularly in the near shore and slide area, and to ensure they would be stable, many soil samples were taken to evaluate soil condition.

A major seafloor mapping and drilling programme was also planned so the present stability of the Storegga slide headwall could be calculated, and to explain the Storegga event 8,200 years ago.

The mapping and investigation programmes performed for the Ormen Lange project have been very extensive and costly. It is most likely the largest programme of its type ever conducted, and has involved a major effort by the survey companies involved as well as the Hydro team.

The spectacular results have however generated a lot of enthusiasm and professionally, the process has been extremely interesting for the many specialists who have contributed to its successful implementation and results.

The Spider was tested from a barge at Jæløya in Oslo fjord in spring 2004. Dredging of sand, clay and boulders was tested and proved the technology proven to work as expected in soft soils. The system was adjusted slightly after the test before heading to the more challenging environment of the Ormen Lange field.

CHAPTER 5

BUILDING UNDERWATER "ROADS" FOR THE ORMEN LANGE PIPELINES

THE STOREGGA SLIDE AREA, FROM THE FIELD TO THE SHELF
The pipeline route from the Ormen Lange gas field to the processing plant at Aukra is some 120 kilometres long. The first 20 kilometres, from the field centre at a depth of 850 metres to the shelf edge at about 300 metres, passes through the upper part of the Storegga slide.

The terrain in the slide scar is extremely rough and in the project's first phase it was unclear whether it would be possible to find pipeline routes out of the slide scar. The first route mapped using detailed bathymetry was far from promising. Of the 20 kilometre mapped route, the pipeline would only have had seafloor contact for 4 per cent of its path across the slide area. Pipeline spans of several hundred metres at heights up to 30 metres above the seafloor were the best that pipeline engineers could come up with on paper.

The conclusion of pipeline engineers in the consulting company Reinertsen in Trondheim was quite blunt: it would not be possible to lay a pipeline in such rough terrain.

The next solution to the problem, evaluated for about a year, was a floating pipeline concept. The pipeline would have flotation elements and be tied with long ropes to concrete blocks on the seafloor. This concept was rejected outright by the fishing industry. It would make trawling along the slide edge difficult they claimed, as trawl boards would get tangled in the floating pipeline. So it was back to the drawing board for the Hydro engineers.

Several years of mapping and studying different route alternatives led to the selected pipeline route out of the slide scar. A floating pipeline was not needed. But even after the route was selected the route had to be optimised in detail. The terrain created by the slide event is chaotic with many large and small slide blocks up to 100 metres in height. Hydro managed to avoid the biggest slide blocks along the selected route but numerous slide blocks 10–15 metres high still presented a major challenge for pipeline engineers.

The last part of the route up to the shelf edge crosses the steep headwall of the Storegga Slide. The slope has an angle of 25–32 degrees, similar to that of the Holmenkollen ski jump in Oslo. During one project planning session, Hydro actually took the Ormen Lange team and its partners to the Holmenkollen ski jump to experience first hand the challenge of climbing such a steep and sharp slide edge.

Pipelines cannot have long free spans as the

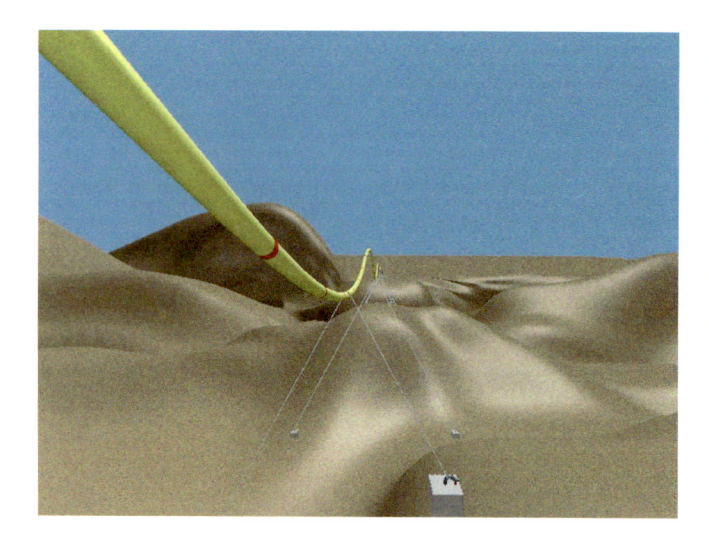

One of the potential solutions to traversing the rough topography in the slide area was a floating pipeline anchored in the seabed. Such a pipeline would be difficult to install and an expensive solution. Extensive mapping of the seafloor enabled better pipeline routes to be found and the floating pipeline concept was retired.

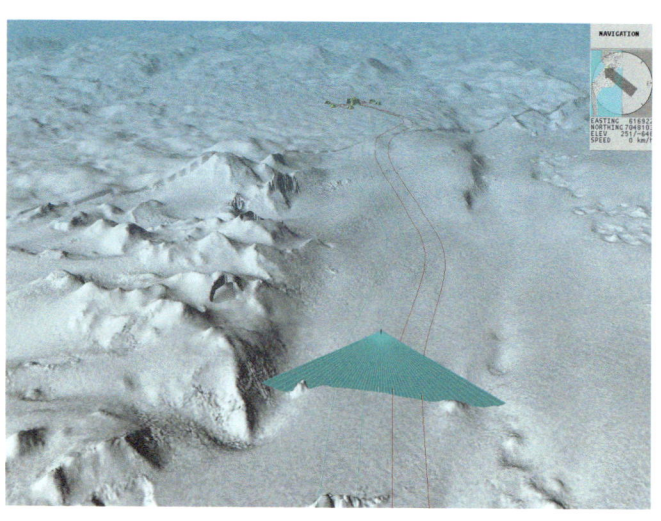

The AUV survey performed by the new developed Hugin AUV provided detailed new information about seafloor topography in the Ormen Lange field development area. Detailed field layout and pipeline route studies could be performed for the first time. The figure illustrates the AUV multibeam sweeping across the seafloor during mapping.

pipe would vibrate when current affects the spans. The vibrations would in time reduce the strength of the steel, potentially causing sudden failure. The other reason free spans are not acceptable is the risk of fishing trawl boards becoming entangled in the pipeline, damaging fishing gear as well as the pipeline.

Hydro engineers therefore had to plan "road construction" on the seafloor prior to pipeline installation. The underwater topography had to be levelled by cutting 5 metre wide trenches in the slide blocks and filling depressions between the slide blocks with crushed rock, in much the same way as roads are built on land. As the water is too deep for any diving operation it all had to be performed using remotely operated equipment controlled from vessels.

This type of work had never been done before at such depths and the technology was limited when Hydro started planning the Ormen Lange development.

Hydro challenged the dredging industry to come up with possible solutions, and Kristiansund-based dredging company GTO joined forces with Nexans in Halden to develop a concept for a new dredging machine for the challenging Ormen Lange terrain.

This was the start of the development of the "Spider", an underwater dredging machine designed to work in steep slopes in deep water with challenging soil conditions and rough topography. It was planned the machine would be operated from the ship using 3D models of the terrain and 3D animations of the machine. Soil cutting was to be done using high-pressure water jets and soil removed by suction, like a vacuum cleaner. Clay and boulders would be flushed through the machine and deposited on the other side.

Swiss forestry technology was used to develop terrain capability for steep slopes. Dredging was controlled using Play Station-like controllers, and sensors on the machine helped the operator follow the movements of the machine on the 3D screen.

After an intensive period building and testing the machine onshore, Nexans spent two weeks testing the machine in Oslo fjord in spring 2004.

The new machine was tested at Ormen Lange in summer 2004 and proved it could operate on slopes greater than 30 degrees. An exciting result for both Nexans and Hydro.

The Spider also proved it could cut trenches in the hard boulder clay which is some 30–50 times harder than the clay tested in Oslo fjord. The esti-

The Spider control room is equipped with 3D systems of the Spider and the seafloor to provide the operator full operational control even with no visibility on the seafloor.

Two Spiders worked in parallel for a while in 2005, controlled from the ship and monitored by the ROV where possible.

Nexans project manager David Rasmus, accompanied by Spider inventor Halvor Snellingen and Ragnvald Graff from Nexans management, during a visit onboard the vessel. The Spider system proved it was possible to dig trenches in the 30 degree slope at the slide edge.

To enable safe pipeline installation across the slide edge the Spider dug trenches 5 metres wide and up to 4 metres deep in the steep slide edge.

A 3D seafloor map showing planned pipelines. Some of the hard slide block tops have been cut to reduce the length of free spans, with the next step being to fill in depressions with rock prior to pipeline installation.

Video grabs of boulders on the seafloor left by retreating ice or dropped from floating icebergs. A great many boulders had to be removed before pipeline installation could start. Such boulders are frequently found both on the shelf and in the slide area.

A large vessel with a drilling tower was required to support the trench cutting and excavation operation.

3D illustration of trench cutting using a tool suspended in a pipe 450–850 metres under a large vessel during the excavation operation. High-pressure water jets underneath the frame cut the hard boulder clay while the large propeller above the yellow frame blows sediment away from the trench.

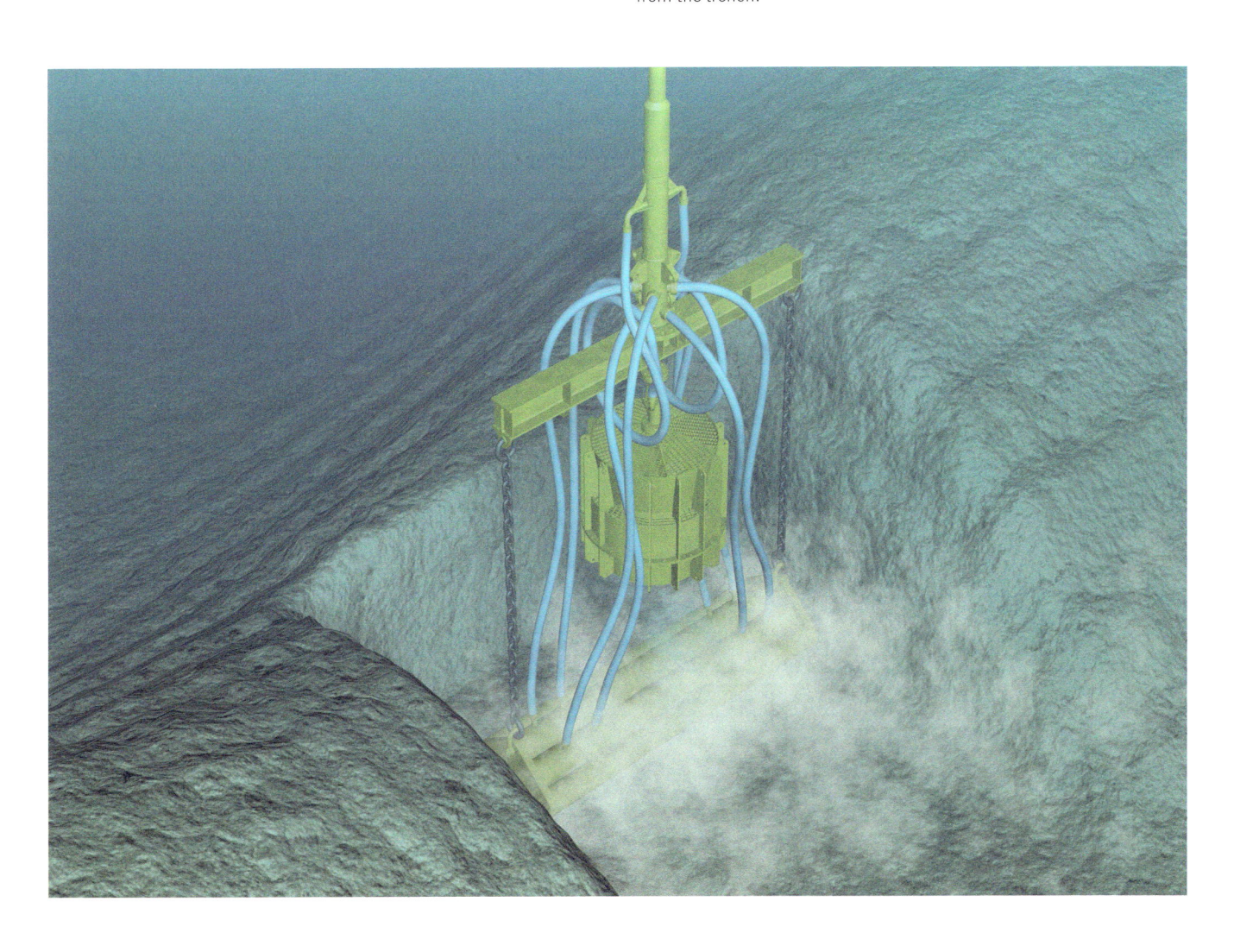

mated capacity was too optimistic, however. A lot of power is needed to cut soil that has been compressed by glaciers on the shelf for over 500,000 years. Dredging was a slow process.

An ROV with cameras and lights was used to watch the operation where possible, but the large dust clouds from the hard clay made it difficult to see anything at all for long periods. The operators were reliant on 3D terrain models and the Spider itself much of the time.

The Lego-like design of the machine was highly unusual and this in combination with the challenging tasks it was performing in rough terrain attracted a lot of interest from the media as well as from within the project organisation. A number of film teams that visited the Ormen Lange development project were particularly interested in the "Spider".

Following the 2004 test season an additional Spider was built to increase dredging capacity for the 2005 season. As the pipelines were to be installed in 2006, "road construction" had to be completed by early spring 2006. But even with two Spiders in operation, the capacity to cut and remove soil was not expected to be adequate for the huge Ormen Lange project.

Another cutting technology was tested in 2004 and used to cut seafloor soil in 2005. A frame with high-pressure nozzles combined with a large "fan" to blow away loose soil was lowered to the seafloor. The concept was efficient with 10,000 horsepower used to pump high-pressure water down through a pipe to the water jet cutting tool. The entire 2005 season into early 2006 was used to prepare the pipeline route using the two different dredging concepts.

As soon as the cutting of the slide block tops was completed, the large rock dump vessel *Nordnes* was sent in to fill depressions and build supports for the pipelines and the smaller diameter service lines. "Roads" for a total of six lines had to be prepared.

PIPELINE ROUTES ON THE SHELF
On the shelf, the pipeline route crosses areas of hard clay, soft clay as well as boulder clay, which is soil deposited directly under the glacier or at the glacier front. This type of soil is extremely hard to cut because it contains so many boulders. [1]

A major question for the Hydro team was how to protect pipelines from fishing and trawling operations. In soft clay and sand the small diam-

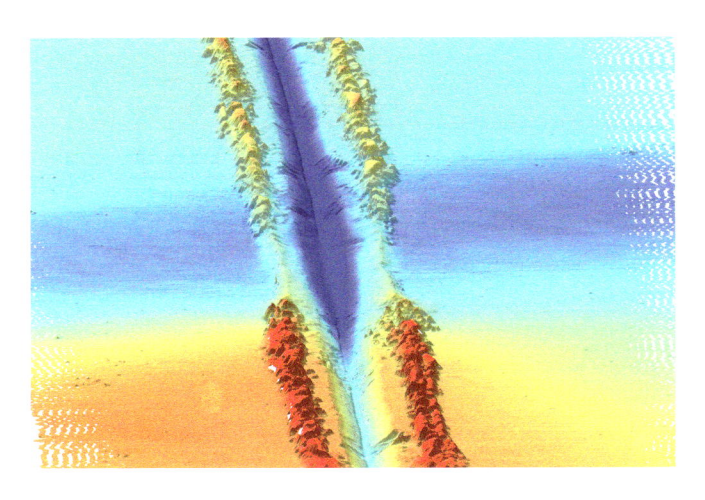

3D model of the seafloor on a ploughed area.

The pipeline plough used to create trenches on the shelf weighs 150 tonnes and is towed by the largest tug vessel available.

eter service lines could be trenched down after installation as in previous projects. But an area on the shelf some 30 kilometres long represented a challenge. There were a great many small and large boulders on the seafloor and the soil was up to 100 times harder than the normal clay found in the fjords and onshore in Norway. Normal trenching could not handle this type of sediment.

Hydro decided to pre-plough V-shaped trenches to install the lines in, protecting them with rock after installation. Even though a plough weighing 150 tonnes would be used, Hydro first had to remove boulders along the routes. The 30 inch gas pipelines could be laid on the seafloor and required no trenching or protection. However, as boulders along the routes could damage the pipes, all boulders more than half a metre wide had to be removed prior to pipeline installation – a total of more than 5,000 boulders. With a capacity of between 30 and 100 boulders per day, this work lasted for months. A large grab was lowered down to the seafloor guided by an ROV with cameras and each boulder was lifted up and moved away from the planned pipeline route.

Ploughing was an intense experience. In less than a month, 100 kilometres of trenches were ploughed and more than 500,000 cubic metres of soil removed. The strongest tug vessel in the world was used to pull the 150-tonne plough along the seafloor.

Closer to shore the pipeline route passes an area of large sand waves. The sand waves probably move slowly due to a very strong current in the area.

PIPELINE ROUTES IN THE NEAR SHORE AREA

The underwater landscape changes character some 21 kilometres from shore as it approaches the shore and the hard bedrock found throughout Norway is suddenly exposed on the seafloor. The underwater terrain resembles a valley landscape with sand and clay in the bottom of the valleys along with hard moraine and boulder clay. Exposed bedrock is also common in the narrowest parts of the valleys.

Cold water corals are common in the area, and the pipeline route had to be relocated when a large coral reef was discovered on the planned route. As coral reefs are protected by law, Hydro engineers had to find an alternative route through the area. This can bee seen on the 3D illustration on page 62.

The narrow valley through the area called Bjørnsundet was first ruled out as a potential pipe-

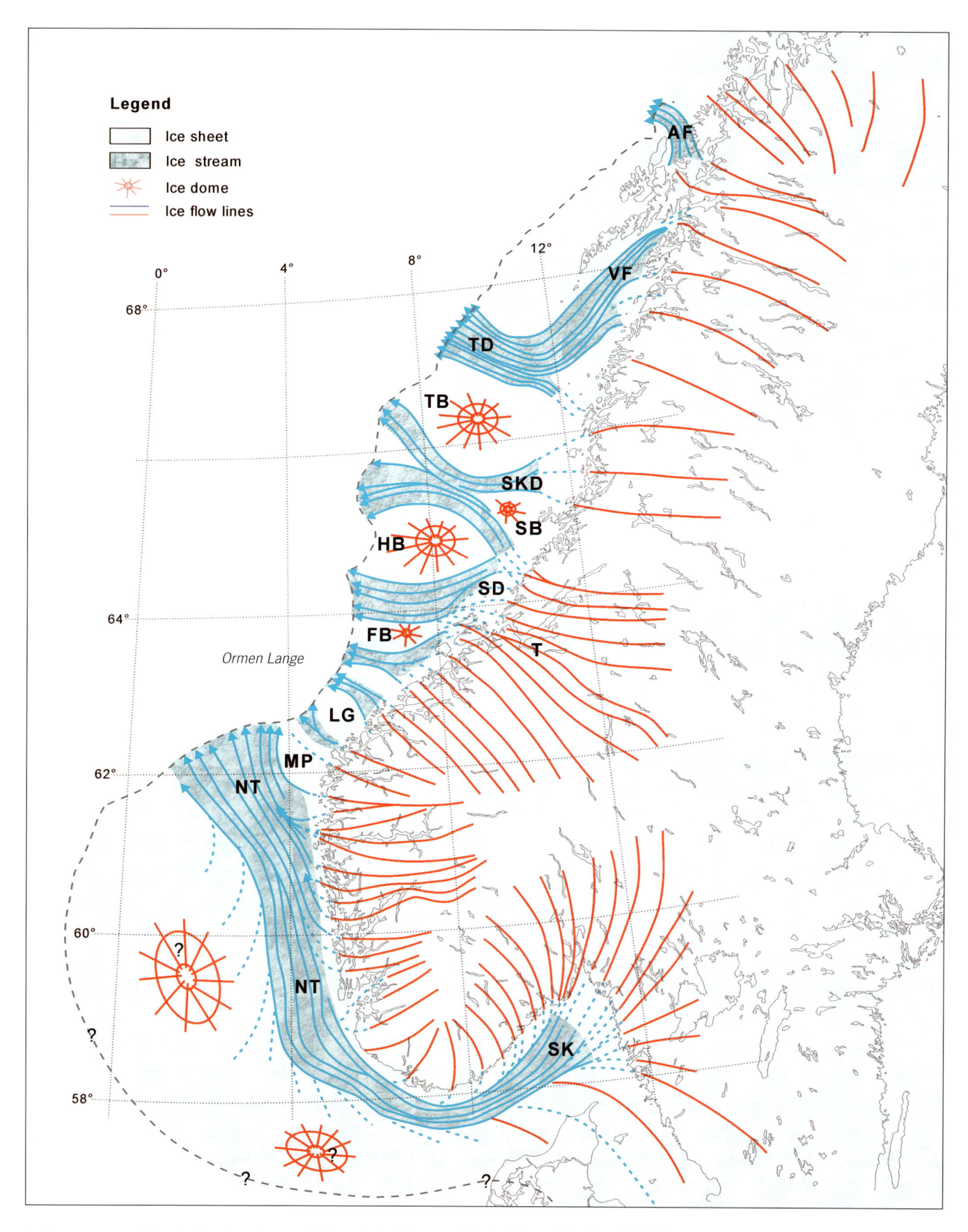

Ice has compressed the shelf sediments several times during the repeated glaciations of the last 500,000 years. The soils on the shelf are hard with many boulders strewn across the seafloor.

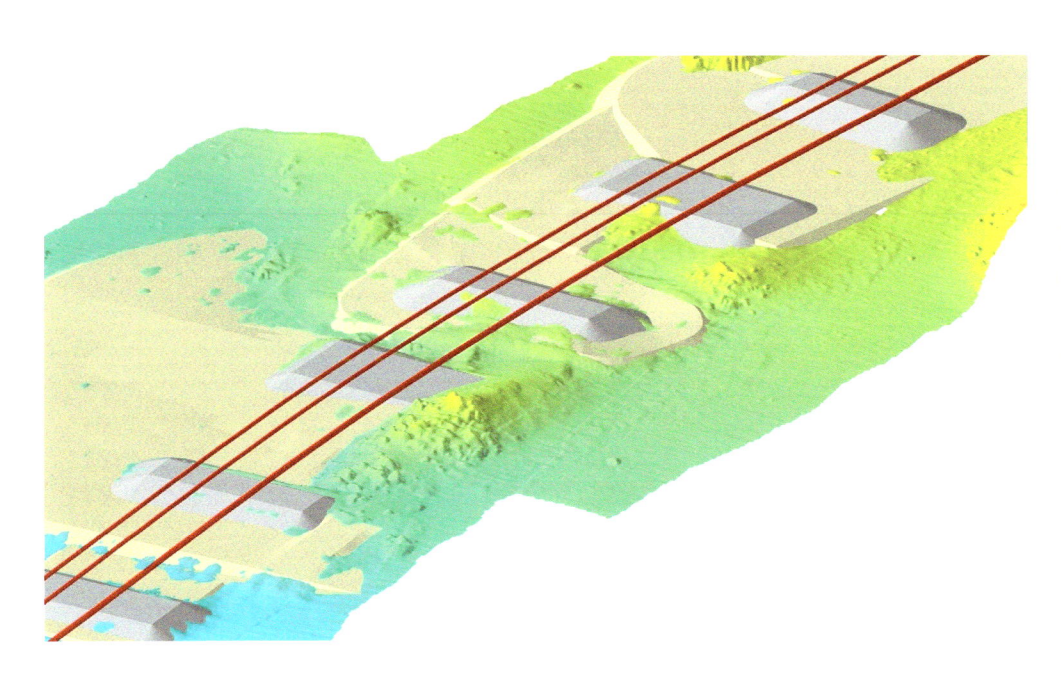

The pipeline routes in the near shore area pass through a narrow underwater valley, no more than 17 metres wide at its narrowest point close to Bjørnsundet. Seven lines pass through the area. A large number of pipeline supports were constructed by rock dumping prior to pipeline installation so the lines could be installed safely. The height of the supports was accurate to within 20 centimetres.

line route but following more detailed mapping a possible way was found through the area for the seven lines.

At its narrowest the valley is only 17 metres wide and the vertical topography was also a challenge. Many pipeline supports had to be designed and more than 500,000 tonnes of crushed rock installed to prepare roads for the lines. Rock supports had to be installed with a tolerance of plus or minus 20 centimetres to ensure the correct height of sleepers from one support to the next. Rock dumping vessels that can carry up to 25,000 tonnes of rock were used.

The rock dumping operation to prepare roads prior to pipeline installation started early in 2004 and was completed in spring 2006, a few weeks before pipeline installation started. Van Ord was awarded the rock dumping contract for Ormen Lange, a contract involving two rock dumping vessels and some three million tons of rock.

The vessel *Rocknes* was selected as the main vessel for rock dumping for Ormen Lange when the contract was awarded. However, the vessel had a tragic accident a few weeks before the Ormen Lange work was due to start, hitting some underwater skerries that were poorly marked on the maps. The vessel became unstable after running aground and capsized, with 18 lives lost.

A number of people were trapped alive inside the hull and a dramatic rescue operation commenced; three people were rescued from the vessel before it went down. The vessel was later raised and taken to Poland for reconstruction and repair, with the construction changed to make it more stable. The Ormen Lange team followed the reconstruction and redesign closely to ensure that if the vessel were to hit a skerry during the Ormen Lange work it would not capsize.

In the wake of the accident, Hydro was far from certain that Van Ord could install all the required rock supports as scheduled. The newest large rock dumping vessel in the market was no longer available. Hydro's project leader for the rock dumping scope, Stein Wendel, developed a new plan with Van Ord to use the smaller rock-dumping vessel *Tertnes* more or less continuously from spring 2004 to spring 2005. By summer 2005 the reconstructed *Rocknes* was back in operation under the new name *Nordnes* and the Ormen Lange rock dumping capacity requirement was secured.

The final part of the pipeline route to the shoreline is very steep and a large rock support was de-

The rock installation vessel *Nordnes* was used as the main rock installation vessel for the Ormen Lange project. A load of rock is approximately 25,000 tonnes and is transported down to the seafloor through a fall pipe. A large ROV, equipped with high technology mapping tools, is suspended at the end of the pipe and can be steered by propellers to precisely control the position of the rock flow.

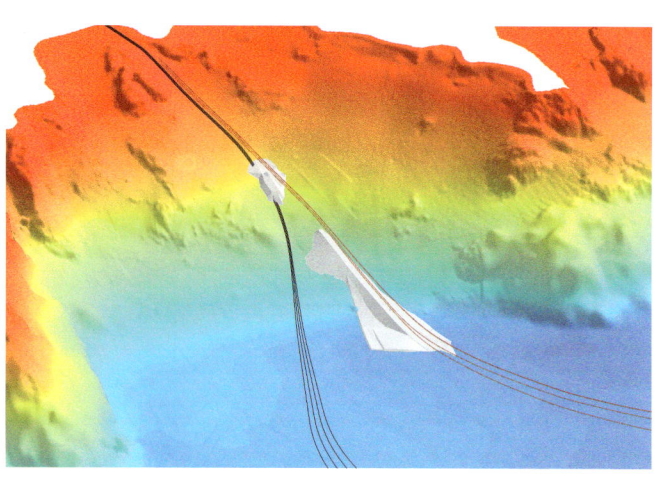

A large rock support of more than 100,000 tonnes was required to avoid free spans across the steep slope of the landfall. Local stability problems during installation of the support led to an urgent redesign prior to the pipe laying deadline in spring 2005 – a tense period for the Ormen Lange offshore team until a secure solution was found.

signed to avoid free spans in the lower part of the slope. The total volume of the support was close to 100,000 tonnes.

Soil conditions on the slope were investigated prior to the support being designed and as the slope consisted of hard boulder clay, no stability problems were expected. However, during installation of the support Hydro discovered some minor failures. Rock and soil were sliding down the slope on one side of the support. When this occurred in December 2004 it generated much activity in the Ormen Lange project, with a detailed new soil survey revealing a thin local layer of weak soil causing the failure.

The unpredictability of nature can't be underestimated.

The rock support was redesigned, some dredging was done to change the profile of the route, and the pipeline routes were changed slightly. With the pipeline installation scheduled to start in May, the Hydro team had little time to solve the problem, which involved winter work with four different vessels.

But by March 2005 the director for the offshore project Einar Kilde could finally relax; his team of seabed intervention engineers led by Trond Eklund had solved the problem. Rock dumping could be completed and the team was ready for the large pipe lay vessel *Solitaire* to come and start laying the pipeline.

PIPELINE ROUTE TO EASINGTON

Hydro was responsible for installation of the first 30 kilometres of the pipeline route to Sleipner and Easington, the 42 inch gas export line which follows the same route as the two 30 inch gas lines from Ormen Lange to shore. The rest of the 1,200 kilometre long Langeled pipeline was planned in detail by a joint Statoil and Hydro team. Statoil led all installation work on the Langeled project.

The Ormen Lange project required a lot of engineering capacity. For Hydro it was beneficial to take advantage of Statoil's extensive experience in the installation of long pipelines as well as their contracts for ordering steel pipelines and pipeline installation. Even before the Plan For Development was approved, steel was ordered for the world's longest pipeline. The Langeled pipeline would take a large part of the worlds steel capacity for two years and it was extremely important to secure steel supply to be able to keep the development schedule on track.

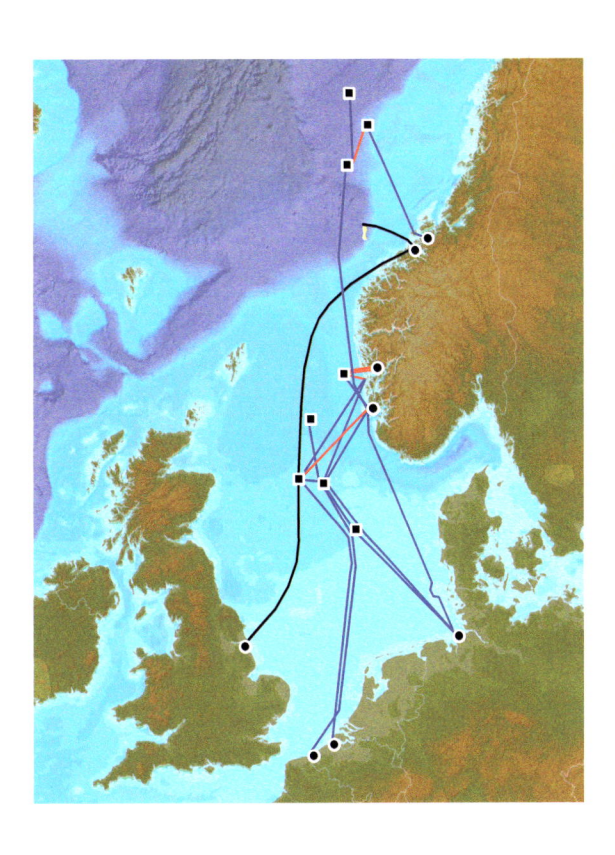

The Ormen Lange gas export line is connected to the European gas pipeline system at the Sleipner platform to allow gas export both to UK and central Europe.

After the first 30 kilometres, the export line turns south along the shelf. The seafloor is more gentle than the first 30 kilometres and didn't present any major challenges to the pipeline installation. Further south the route slopes gently down into the Norwegian trench in depths of up to 400 metres. The route passes the Gjøa field, the Troll field, the Brage field and others on its way to the Sleipner platform, approximately 800 kilometres from Aukra. It then turns westwards towards Easington.

The Langeled pipeline would cross a number of other pipelines and each crossing had to be prepared in terms of rock dumping and other protective measures in good time before the pipe was laid. Innumerable phone calls, letters and meetings were needed before all the crossing agreements could be signed with the different owners of the pipelines and cables. The near shore area and the landfall in Easington was also a challenge as it is a fishing-intensive area and agreements were needed so fishing vessels would stay clear of the laying route during preparation and pipe installation. It took a great deal of effort to find a good solution to these issues.

The final 70 kilometres of the pipe route towards shore passes a very shallow area where waves erode and transport sand on the seafloor during storms, changing the sand wave terrain over time. This means that after a storm, the pipe could end up with long new free spans, which are unacceptable. To avoid risks of this nature, a trench had to be constructed prior to pipeline installation.

Normal dredging techniques were used to create a trench running 30 kilometres out from shore. The next 70 kilometres of the route were made using the big pipeline plough used on the shelf between Aukra and the Ormen Lange field. However, there were areas where the plough struck hard carbonate rock which made trenching difficult, even with the strongest tug vessel in the world *Far Sovereign*. An additional tug vessel had to be brought in to help pull the plough. The planned trench was finally constructed and the laying of the 44 inch pipeline from Sleipner to Easington could start.

Gorgonocephalus cf. *lamarcki* using its long branched arms in search of food-particles.

CHAPTER 6

MARINE BIOLOGY IN THE PIPELINE ROUTES

The underwater world along the Norwegian west coast is home to many biological features. As part of its preparations for the Ormen Lange development, Hydro carried out biological reference, or baseline, studies close to the planned processing plant near Aukra and in deep water on the Ormen Lange field. Such surveys are performed as a biological reference prior to activities that may influence biological life and enable similar surveys to be performed later to monitor potential changes to the flora and fauna.

In the areas where proper biological surveys were performed, a rich flora and fauna was found and documented. A Van Veen grab was used to take samples at 11 stations near the Nyhamna area and 426 taxa, or species, were identified among the 15,906 individual samples.

A similar reference survey was carried out in deep water at the Ormen Lange field. The survey included 14 stations in depths ranging from 816 metres to 901 metres and three transects of video recording of benthic fauna. The sediment stations were placed in basins with thick sediment layers, and the video transects went through piles of slide blocks that form ridges between the basins.

These investigations at Ormen Lange revealed that the soft bottom fauna at Ormen Lange has relatively high diversity indices. A total of 39,898 individuals distributed amongst 212 species were sampled at the 14 stations. The greatest abundance of individuals across all samples was found among the mollusks and bristle worms (polychaeta), while Pogonophora species and bristle worms dominated in the deepest investigated layer.

The composition of the benthic macro fauna found in deep water at Ormen Lange is not significantly different from the composition or structure of the sediments at shallower offshore locations such as Snorre UPA, Visund, Norne, and Heidrun Nord.

The results reveal that many of the same species dominate the macro fauna community, with the ten most dominating species including bristle worms P. jeffreysii, C. setosa, Spiophanes and Tharyx species, the molluscs species Thyasira and Yoldiella and the Golfingia and Nemertea (varia).

The exceptions are the occurrence of sea spiders (Nymphon) in the top sediment and the large amount of beard worms (Pogonophora) in the bottom layer at Ormen Lange.

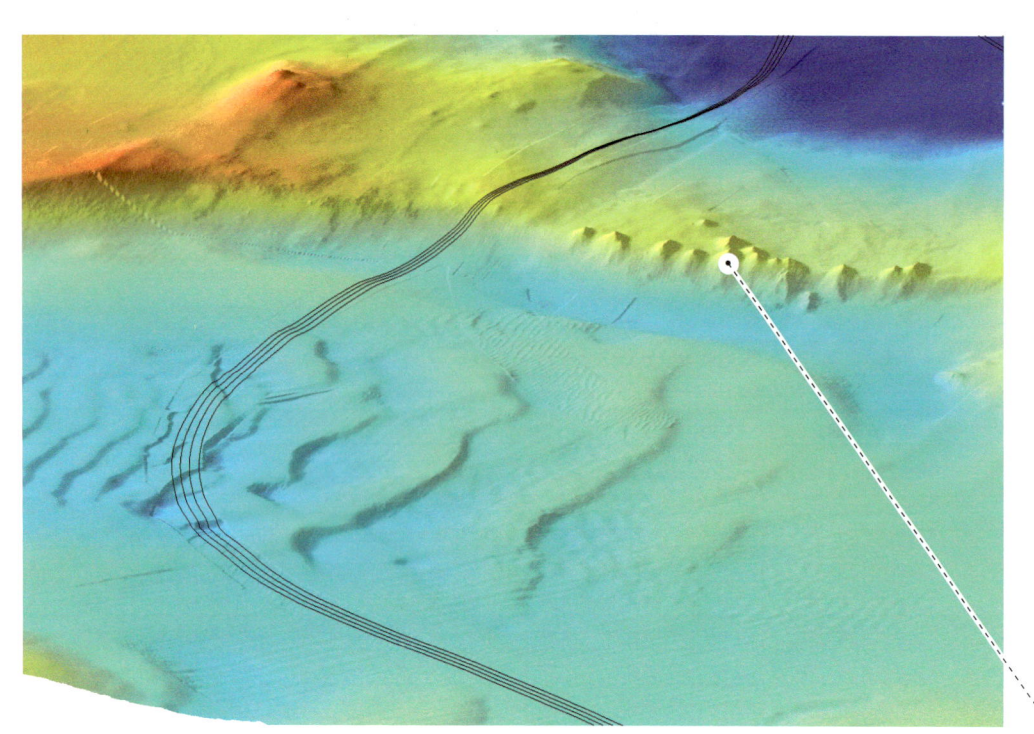

A 3D model showing how coral reefs occur on the seafloor, typically in areas of high current. These reefs are between 10 and 20 metres in height. Large, moving sand waves – often several metres in height – can also be seen on the seafloor and are another potential challenge to the long-term stability of the pipelines, even when trenched down.

Coral reef

There are, however, relatively large differences in the numbers of individuals from various deep sea localities. Many more individuals were found in the Ormen Lange survey than in for instance the Vøring and Ellida deep water surveys. These differences are probably a result of different sediment characteristics in the basins sampled at Ormen Lange, with slightly more organic matter and softer sediment. Sediment structure and organic material content appear more important than water depth for fauna composition

CORAL REEFS

The most prevalent type of coral in Norway is Lophelia pertusa, a stone coral which lives in cold water and grows on hard material like boulders, hard boulder clay and rock outcrops. As mapping technology has improved and more of the Norwegian shelf has been researched, increasingly many coral reefs have been identified. Corals can grow as single coral branches or as big or small reef structures.

Typically corals live for 250 years, but the living part of a reef grows on older dead coral structures and debris. A coral branch grows some 7–10 millimetres annually, and the largest reefs found in Norway are more than 5 kilometres long and can be up to 30–35 metres in height. Some of the reefs found on the Norwegian shelf are more than 8,000 years old.

Coral reefs are normally rich biotopes – up to 700 different species have been counted in the Lophelia reefs.

During investigations of potential pipeline routes in the early phase of the project, the Ormen Lange team had two coral-related objectives: the first was to gather as much knowledge as possible about the occurrence of coral reefs and where they typically occur, and the second was to try to avoid any conflict between the proposed routes and the legally-protected coral reefs.

Coral reefs were known to exist along the slide edge of the Storegga slide and had been investigated and mapped during ROV surveys and also during a manned submarine survey performed by American and Norwegian scientists. The mapping clearly indicated severe coral damage from bottom trawling, but in areas of preserved coral the ROV pilots could see quite spectacular coral reefs with a high level of biological activity. Coral reefs tend to attract a lot of fish, which is what makes them such attractive fishing areas.

Lophelia reef found in the area investigated to find pipeline routes to the different alternative shore sites for the processing plant. This picture is from the Breisundet area.

This knowledge helped Hydro avoid the reefs when selecting the final pipeline routes. Corals were also found in the near shore section of the route, typically on rock outcrops. A large coral reef was found in the route area approximately 18 kilometres from Nyhamna, and the pipeline was rerouted to avoid it. This is described further in Chapter 4.

The areas where corals have been mapped also correlate to areas of strong current which carry food to the stationary corals – a key condition for their survival.

Areas rich in coral reefs also provide good fish biotopes. A good example is the Storegga area, which is claimed to be one of the richest fishery areas in the world. Many fishing nets and fishing vessels were observed in the Storegga area during the Ormen Lange offshore activities and ROV pilots were left in no doubt about the multitude of fish. ROVs, dredgers and trenchers were frequently surrounded by fish during their operations on the seafloor, with the density of the fish sometimes bringing work to a stop as they flocked the light on the ROV, blocking its sight.

The amount of biological activity in the area is highly positive. The Gulf Stream, or the North Atlantic current, hits the steep slide edge and food for the fish wells up, explaining the presence of coral reefs as well as the rich fishery along the slide edge.

During ROV mapping survey the offshore team came across some strange biological features which were confirmed by a marine biologist to be Steletta Normani, a swamplike species living in deep water.

Different types of crabs and crawfish have also been observed as shown in the video grabs from the ROV during seafloor surveys.

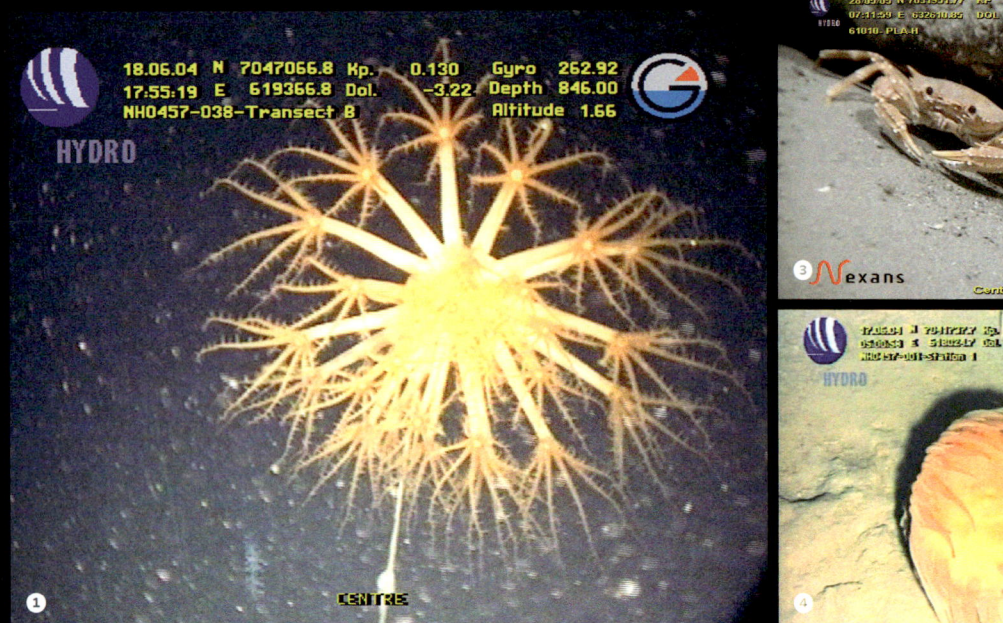

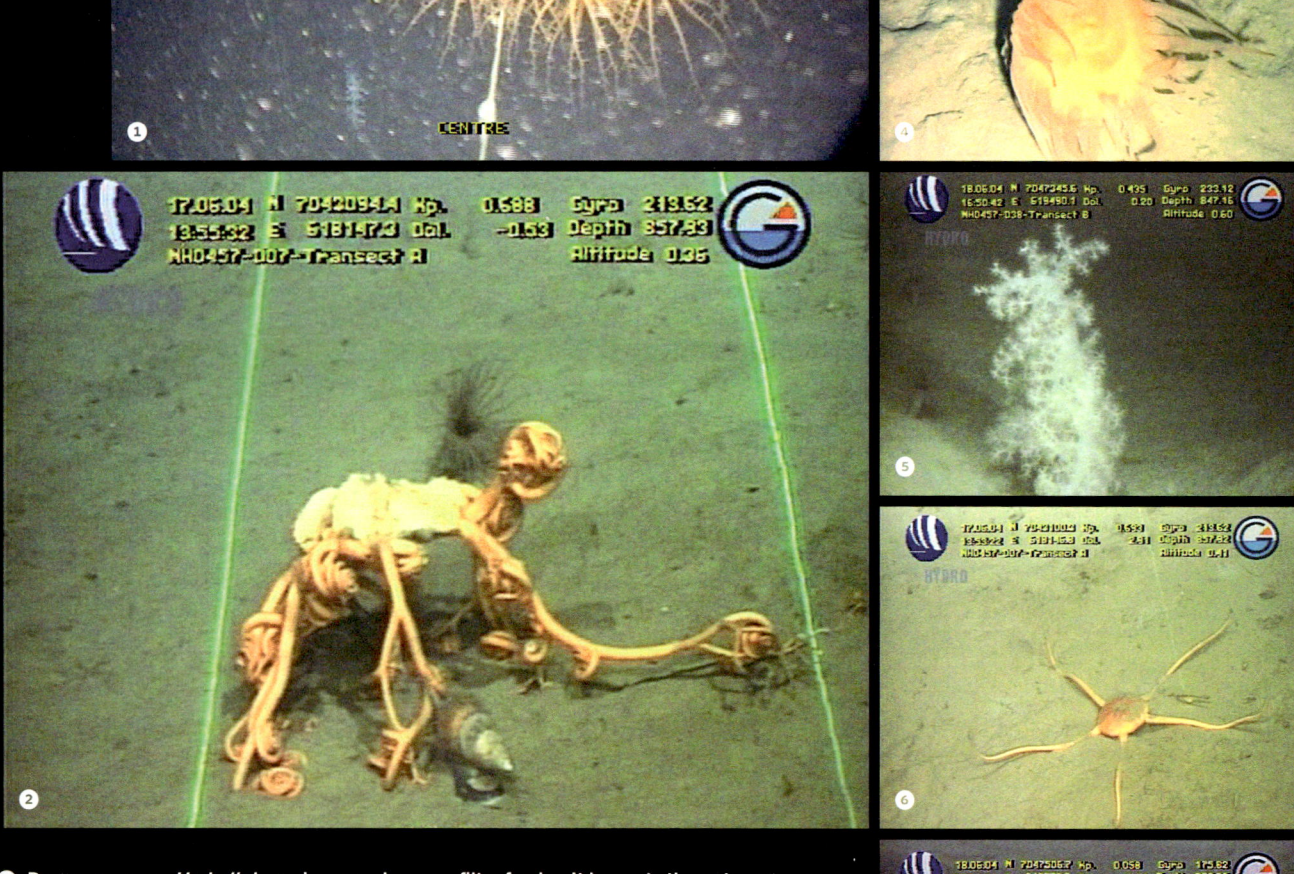

❶ Droopy sea pen, *Umbellula* sp. is a rare deep sea filter feeder. It harvests the water masses for detritus and plankton. ❷ A basketstar, *Gorgonocephalus* cf. *lamarcki,* accompanied by the common whelk *Buccinum undatum* and an anemone in the Ceriantharia family. Green lines are laser beams from the ROV. ❸ A multitude of crab species can be found in the Ormen Lange field, they are however quick to hide if disturbed. ❹ Sea anemones can get quite big and are undisputable predators, sometimes even catching fish and crustaceans with their sticky and poisonous tentacles. ❺ A soft coral probably belonging to the genus *Gersemia.* ❻ The brittle star *Ophiopleura borealis* is commonly found in the Ormen Lange field. ❼ Giant Club sponge, *Chondrocladia gigantea.* A deep water species with a rather peculiar appearance. Because of the fragility of their bodies collected specimens tend to be in poor condition, and are difficult to identify. [1]

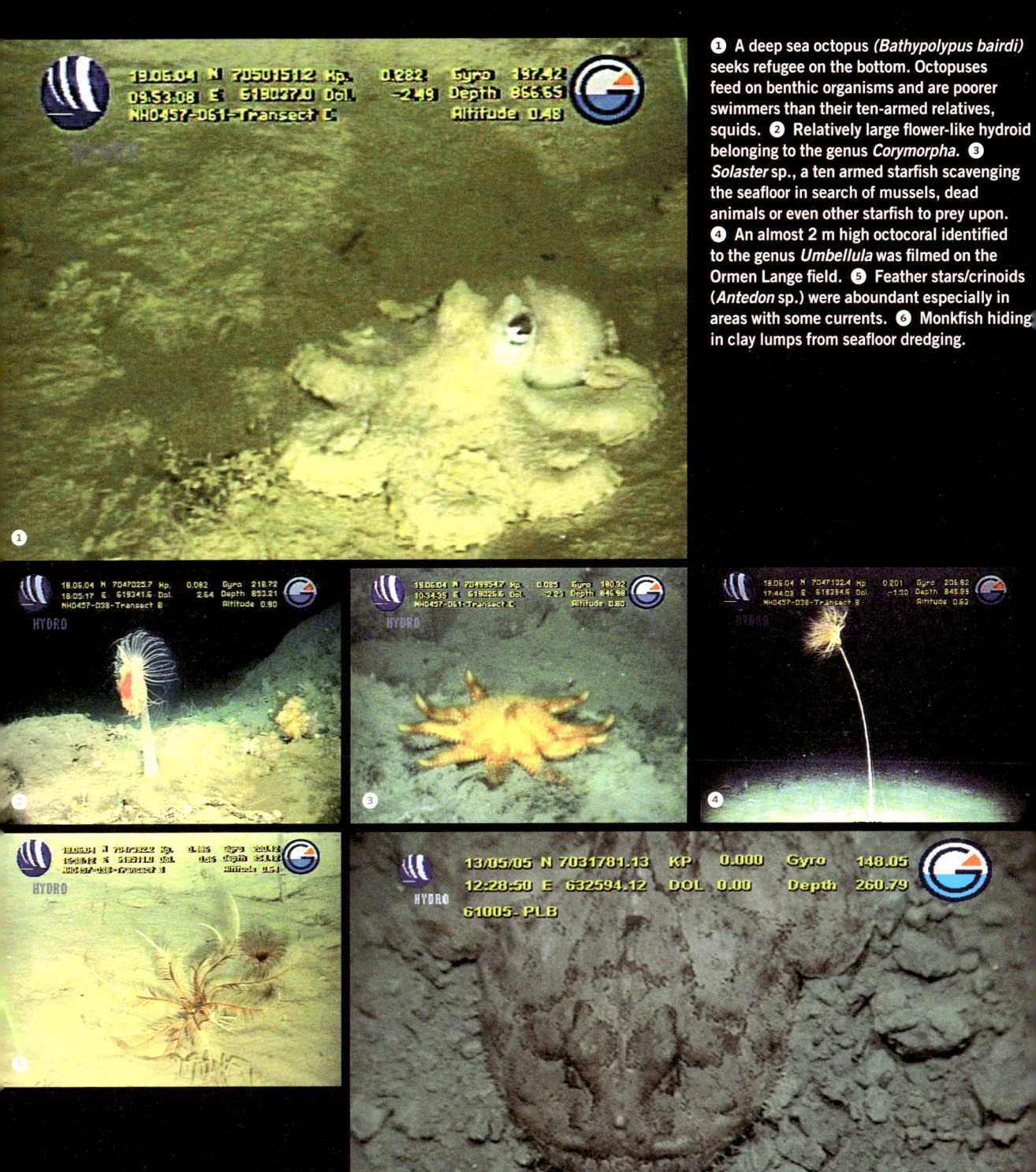

① A deep sea octopus *(Bathypolypus bairdi)* seeks refugee on the bottom. Octopuses feed on benthic organisms and are poorer swimmers than their ten-armed relatives, squids. ② Relatively large flower-like hydroid belonging to the genus *Corymorpha*. ③ *Solaster* sp., a ten armed starfish scavenging the seafloor in search of mussels, dead animals or even other starfish to prey upon. ④ An almost 2 m high octocoral identified to the genus *Umbellula* was filmed on the Ormen Lange field. ⑤ Feather stars/crinoids (*Antedon* sp.) were aboundant especially in areas with some currents. ⑥ Monkfish hiding in clay lumps from seafloor dredging.

FMC Technologies designed and built the well templates, the pipeline end-termination structure and the pipeline spools that form the main part of the Ormen Lange subsea production system.

CHAPTER 7

FROM THE ORMEN LANGE FIELD TO NYHAMNA – INSTALLING THE ORMEN LANGE PRODUCTION PIPELINE SYSTEM

Drilling of production wells has to start in time so the required production volume can be achieved when starting production from a gas field like Ormen Lange.

As Shell is the operator for the production phase, and responsible for gas production after production start in 2007, Hydro wanted Shell's involvement from an early stage in well planning and reservoir management.

Hydro also asked Shell to take responsibility for drilling the required wells prior to the start of production. Four to eight wells had to be completed before production start to achieve planned production volume, but before they could be drilled two subsea templates had to be designed, produced and installed.

FMC Technologies in Norway was awarded the contract to design and produce the subsea equipment including the two giant well templates and a pipeline end termination structure (PLET). It was an intense period for FMC who designed and built the templates in their yard in Tønsberg ready for installation in late summer 2005.

One of the world's largest lifting vessels, the *Thialf* operated by Herema, was awarded the installation job. Installing the world's largest templates at a depth of 850 metres was not considered an easy task. The templates weighed 1150 tonnes each and in the challenging seafloor terrain in the Ormen Lange field the installation had to be performed with less than 2 metres tolerance.

The templates have 8 metre long foundation skirts that will penetrate into the soft clay at the planned location. Outside the target area, the inclination of the terrain would be too great and the skirts would hit hard boulder clay. The most advanced underwater positioning systems available were used to control the installation. The Ormen Lange project helped further the development of underwater positioning technology to ensure successful control of the complicated template installation.

Everything was prepared in fine detail for installation of the structures in late August 2005. A wide-band long baseline acoustic network system had been installed by the Hydro survey vessel so the templates could be positioned accurately. The templates were towed out on big barges and were ready to be lifted from the barge for installation by the huge lifting vessel *Thialf*. However, the installation could not be performed in wave heights greater than 1.5 metres and in the second part of

The terrain in the development area represented a challenge for the design of the field. Flat template locations were required so the template could be safely installed, and the selected locations should ensure optimal draining of the reservoir as well as providing access for pipeline routes out of the area.

August the operation had to be postponed several times due to the weather.

The barge had to return to shore and wait time and time again; tensions mounted in the Hydro team as the days and weeks went by and the templates were still sitting on the barges.

Nobody in the Hydro team or at the meteorological institute could remember such bad weather in September before. Film teams waiting to film the installation became frustrated and impatient. Fortunately the installation was in the hands of the calm and collected project leader Torleif Sætervik from Møre; coming from this part of Norway means being used to bad weather and knowing that there is little that can be done to change the situation.

Finally some brief periods of good weather enabled the three structures to be installed in late September. But it was a short respite with bad weather then setting in for many weeks, seriously affecting seafloor preparation for the pipeline routes. All in all, Hydro was lucky to get the structures installed before this period of rough weather set in. It is hardly practical to have expensive vessels sitting offshore week after week with no progress to show for it, but nature is part of the game when developing a field in harsh environmental conditions.

The drill ship *West Navigator* could come and start drilling in late October 2005 as planned. Two major milestones in the project could be ticked off. The offshore development project was on track.

Pipeline installation from the field to Aukra was scheduled for 2005/2006. Installation was planned in reverse with the first 33 kilometres of the 42 inch export line and the first 33 kilometres of the two 30 inch gas production lines scheduled for installation in 2005. The seafloor was well prepared to ensure safe installation and stable conditions for the pipelines after installation. After so much preparation, it was an exciting day for the installation team when the giant pipe lay vessel *Solitaire* turned up in the narrow fjord area to start the pipe lay. The vessel occupied half the fjord and the coastal steamer *Hurtigruta* had to take another route for a while.

The *Solitaire* is the largest dynamically positioned pipelay vessel in the world, more than 300 metres in length with over than 300 people working on board. It is essentially a pipe factory, with smaller pipe carriers loading 12 metre pipe sections onto the vessel where they are welded together in a highly efficient precision process at eight welding stations.

The giant templates were transported from the yard in Tønsberg to the west coast of Norway for installation in the Ormen Lange field.

One of the largest lifting vessels in the world, the *Thialf*, lifted the 1,150 tonne templates from the barges and installed them on the seafloor at a depth of 850 metres. The barges transported the templates to the field from the Tønsberg yard.

The pipeline was safely pulled in to the shore facility system before laying could continue out to the fjord system. The team was unsure whether it would be able to lay the pipe as planned with an installation tolerance of no greater than one metre. Would it be possible to follow the curves so carefully planned by the Reinertsens pipeline engineers in Trondheim? Would the pipe land on the preinstalled rock supports?

The Hydro survey team had carefully prepared the pipeline installation during the spring. Counteracts had been installed to help feed the pipe around the sharpest curves. The survey vessel *Geofjord*, operated by Geoconsult, had prepared the underwater acoustic positioning system perfectly and an ROV on the survey vessel followed and positioned the pipeline touchdown as laying progressed. The team on board the pipe lay vessel *Solitaire* continuously received the corrections needed to hold the planned route. A 3D system guided the installation as it progressed. The turning points or counteracts installed on the seafloor prior to pipe installation helped curve the pipe along the route in the narrow fjord area.

The Project Director for the offshore project, Einar Kilde, was proud of his team's preparation and the superb teamwork between the different vessels during the installation work. Gunnar Paulsen, the team leader from Reinertsen who had led the planning and engineering team for pipeline installation, could breathe out after several years' intense work. The lead engineer for the work, Stig Arne Witsø, and Hydro team leader Geir Årflot, followed the installation from the vessel *Solitaire* and concluded all the effort had been well worthwhile.

The design of the rock supports and the preparation for the installation were a success. All three lines were installed with accuracy largely within the one metre tolerance and laid at 33 kilometres from Nyhamna.

The lay vessel *Solitaire* passed several times close to the vessel *Cehili* anchored seven kilometres from Nyhamna where marine excavation of the archaeological wreck on the planned route for the MEG and umbilical line was taking place. *Cehili's* owner, Tore Torsen, claimed he measured noise exceeding 90 decibels on the deck of his vessel. Being so close to *Solitaire* as it lay the pipe was like having the best seats at a football match, and a completely new experience for the archaeological team on board *Cehili*.

But after such a promising start, the pipe laying

The drill ship *West Navigator* arrived at the Ormen Lange field in late October 2005. Winter drilling in the Ormen Lange area with a dynamically positioned drill ship is a challenge and reduced the operational flexibility for the Shell team running the drilling operation. Although some well operations could not be performed in winter, production wells were drilled more or less continuously until production start in 2007.

process came to a sudden but expected halt. It was simply not possible to get more pipeline delivered that year. The enormous pipe requirements of the Ormen Lange project had affected the already overheated world steel market. Installation of the southern leg of the Langeled pipeline also required a huge amount of pipe in 2005, and the projects consumed much of the world supply of pipeline for the year.

By 2006 pipeline was once again available and installation could continue. *Solitaire* returned and picked up the 30 inch lines lying 33 kilometres from shore and recommenced laying towards the slide edge. *Solitaire* lays pipes in an S-shape which does not allow for any sharp curves. The plan was to lay the pipe a few kilometres down into the slide area, after which the huge installation and lay vessel *S7000* would pick up the pipe end and relay the pipe with sharper curves around slide blocks.

Hydro had installed networks of high technology underwater positioning systems throughout most of the slide area to control seabed preparation as well as the installation of pipelines and umbilicals, and this helped ensure the successful installation and final lay down of the 30 inch lines in the slide.

It was not believed the pipe end could be laid in the PLET structure within a one metre tolerance in a water depth of 850 metres. However, "Mission Impossible" became "Mission Possible" due to skilful positioning control and superb teamwork between the installation contractor Saipem, the survey contractor Geoconsult, Reinertsen Engineering and the Hydro team.

After laydown the lines were tied in and connected to the templates through pipeline spools. Spools are L or Z shaped pipes, 70–100 metres in length, used to connect subsea structures and pipelines. The length between the connection points must be accurately measured before the spools could be produced, installed and tied in. The lay vessel *S7000*, the tie-in vessel *Norman Cutter* and two survey vessels were involved in this complex task, which was performed in August and September 2006.

Due to the late arrival of the pipeline installation vessels in 2006, this work was on critical path in terms of completion. The rig was also due back to continue drilling and would prevent access to the templates should the work be much delayed. Fortunately the weather was superb in September 2006 compared to the very bad weather in September and October 2005.

The giant pipe lay vessel *Solitaire* arrived in Nyhamna in June 2005 to start laying the 42 inch gas export line and the two 30 inch gas production lines. The laying started with the lines being pulled in at Nyhamn, a challenging operation due to the steep slope and the sharp curves required in the narrow fjord.

The large-diameter pipeline lengths are welded together on board the vessel *Solitaire*, operated by Alseas. As soon as the welds are cured and the field joints coated the vessel can move forward slightly and the welded pipeline is installed.

The MEG (Mono Ethylene Glycol) lines and the umbilical were both carefully installed in the V-shaped trench ploughed by the 150-tonne Saipem-operated pipeline plough. They were then trenched down by the Capjet trencher and covered with rock to protect them from fishing gear.

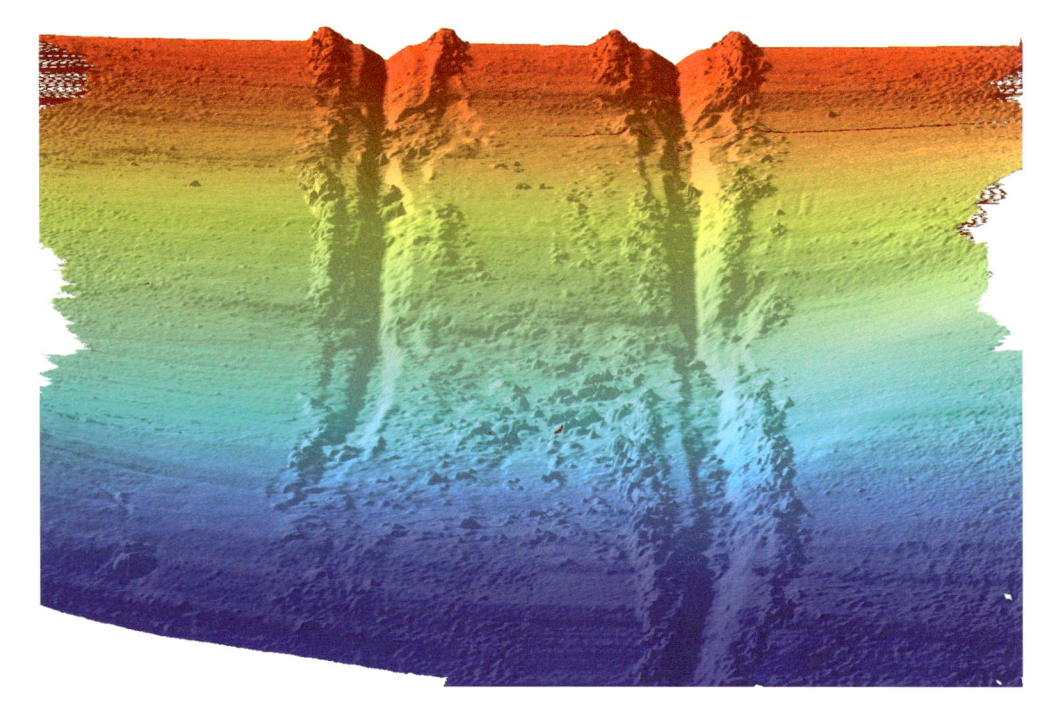

The lay vessel *Solitaire* met with the lay vessel *S7000* close to the slide edge. The *S7000* picked up the pipeline end as soon as *Solitaire* had completed lay down in the upper part of the slide and continued to lay through the challenging slide terrain down towards the field centre.

Lay vessel *Skandi Neptune* loaded with the 120 kilometre long umbilical on the large carousel, the maximum weight that could be safely carried by the vessel.

Three of the service lines were also installed in 2006. Stolt Offshore (which changed name to Agercy just before installation started) installed the two 6 inch MEG lines, a total length of almost 250 kilometres. It took the installation vessel *Seaway Falcon* some months to install the two MEG (Mono Ethylene Glycol, or antifreeze, to prevent gas hydrates) lines, a relatively slow process as the line is produced on board the vessel. Daily laying rates of five kilometres were reached; quite good considering this involves over 400 welds per day, and that all welds have to be carefully checked to ensure the 120 kilometre MEG line is tight and able to withstand the pressure and temperature of 25 years of operation.

Laying down the slide edge and in the challenging terrain in the slide area was the most exciting part of the MEG line installation. However, the slow and careful laying combined with the excellent preparation of the pipeline corridor paid off. The network of underwater acoustic positioning transponders helped control the laying operation and to hit the pre-excavated trenches and the rock supports with the pipe.

A survey ROV followed the laying at the pipe touch down position to check it was within the planned tolerances. The pipe has to be laid with as few free spans as possible, and so that it could be trenched down to protect it from trawling and other fishing gear.

V-shaped trenches had been prepared in the steep escarpment by the big pipeline plough, and the MEG lines were carefully installed to ensure the line was centred in the trench. The survey ROV monitored the position continuously during the laying operation.

During critical phases the project team onshore attended phone meetings to listen to the morning reports from the pipe lay vessel. Sigmund Lunde, the team manager responsible for MEG and umbilical installation, was pleased with the excellent results achieved by the Hydro and Agercy teams.

One of the two control umbilicals was also installed in 2006. It was produced by Nexans in Halden and loaded onto the installation vessel *Skandi Neptune* on a big carousel. The umbilical is 12 centimetres in diameter and, impressively, is produced and installed in a single length. Hydraulic lines, electrical lines and fibre optics are twisted together in a continuous spinning process with a high level of quality control. The big carousel could just take the planned 121 kilometre umbilical in one length,

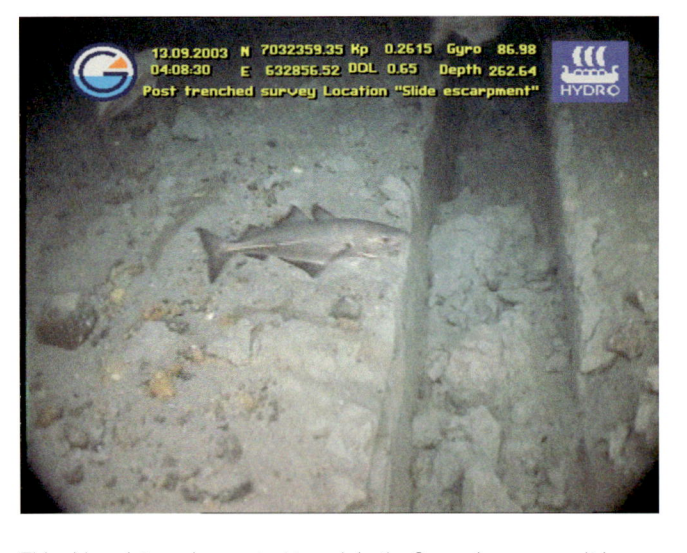

This video picture shows a test trench in the Ormen Lange area. It is typically 0.7 metres wide in firm or hard clay.

a total weight of some 2,200 tonnes.

Installation started as for the other lines, by pulling in the end of the umbilical to the shore facilities at Nyhamna. The daily laying speed for the umbilical was up to 8–10 kilometres.

As for the MEG line, the most exiting part of the umbilical laying was down the steep Storegga escarpment and the questions were many. Would the strong current drag the umbilical away from the planned route? Was it possible to hit the pre-ploughed trench down the escarpment with the relatively light umbilical? What about hitting the narrow trenches that had been prepared in the most challenging part of the deepwater area?

Once again the thorough planning and engineering paid off, and the laying engineers onboard *Scandi Neptune* had advanced the process of installing umbilical in steep slopes and complex areas with strong current and deep water.

After successfully connecting to the template, the shore-template connection was tested. It worked! All tests indicated the planned wells could be controlled from the control room at Nyhamna in 2007.

A few days after installation of the MEG lines and the umbilical had started, the survey vessel could document the position of the lines and check their condition. With such a small diameter, the lines cannot withstand the impact from trawling and had to be protected by trenching and rock dumping.

Nexans Norway was contracted to trench down the lines using their Capjet trenching systems. The trencher is docked on the line and uses a high-pressure sword system to cut a trench by fluidising the soil so the pipe sinks to the bottom of the trench. Fluidised soils settle on top of the line and provide protection. The lines were buried between one and two metres below the seafloor depending on soil conditions. Where the trenching results were inadequate Hydro increased the protection level by dumping rock in the trench.

In the slide area, a lot of hard slide blocks combined with soft infilled clay represented a challenge for the trenching operation. Side slopes of up to 15–20 degrees were common, with the escarpment slope being 25–30 degrees. No promises could be made regarding results in the most challenging part of the slide area, but the trenching team was optimistic nonetheless. The trenching system operators learned fast, and in the end nothing seemed impossible.

One of the field engineers from Reinertsen Engineering, Emma Moren, tries fishing during the trenching operation.

Rock dumping vessel filling rock in trenches.

Long and high free spans were trenched using the Capjet systems, and two support vessels and three trenchers used from late April to late October to trench 230 kilometres of MEG lines and umbilical. Slopes or very hard soils meant some sections were too difficult to trench and rock dumping was performed to protect the lines. Additional rock cover was installed for protection in high intensity trawling areas. Reinertsen engineering advised Hydro on the best technical solutions for each area and phase of the work. Finally, all the MEG lines and umbilicals were corrected for free spans and were efficiently and well protected.

It appeared the complex and highly challenging scope in 2006 would end with 100 per cent success. However, after testing the umbilical for some weeks, a pressure drop in one of the hydraulic lines was detected. This initiated a long investigation to find the leak, no easy task given that the umbilical was buried 1.5–2 metres deep and covered in 0.5–1.2 metres of soil. However, after some weeks of modelling, pressure testing and physical tests at the template, the pressure drop was shown to be some 40 kilometres from shore. During search for the leak, the ROV team noted a change in sonar reflectivity in the trench in one particular area; when they landed the ROV in the trench it was like a small mud volcano with MEG bubbling up from the soft soil. It was a combination of good work and good luck that helped the team find the leak.

The Hydro team wanted to establish the cause of the leak. Could the umbilical still be used, or was the quality not good enough? Trond Eklund in the Hydro team led the investigation which involved closely checking the quality of the umbilical production, its loading onto the installation vessel, and the actual installation. Could trenching have damaged the umbilical? The video recording of the inspection prior to trenching was checked to verify no damage was evident. The guard vessels that had protected the umbilical from trawling until it was trenched and rock dumped confirmed no exposed line had been impacted by trawlers.

Capjet trencher used to trench the MEG and umbilical lines. The trencher was redesigned for the Ormen Lange project to trench in the steep slopes and in the rough slide terrain.

The leak area was partially uncovered to investigate the leak but the cause of the problem was not fully understood. However, the confidence in the quality of the umbilical was re-established as a result of the thorough investigation. A spare hydraulic line in the umbilical will be used during the operation. An additional umbilical has been installed as planned during the 2007 season to provide redundancy and flexibility when controlling the large gas field. A high level of robustness is critical when supplying 20 per cent of the UK's gas consumption. For engineers however, it is frustrating not to identify the cause.

The problem with the umbilical was one of very few problems experienced by the offshore team during four years of installation. All the challenges and uncertainties that arose were handled extremely well by the Hydro team and the many construction and installation contractors.

The entire system has been tested and prepared for production start in 2007. The pipeline has been filled with gas from the Sleipner platform so as many of the processing plant functions as possible can be tested. As soon as the wells in the field were completed they were connected to the template and pipeline system in readiness for production start. All valves and functions on the templates and the well systems have been tested from shore, using the control system in the processing plant.

Slowly but surely, the Hydro team is preparing for the start of production from the second largest gas field in Norway. It is a goal and in fact a tradition in Hydro to try to start production from a field prior to the planned schedule. During 2007 gas production through the entire system was started. Such early starts creates additional value for the owners, but more important for the Hydro team is the satisfaction of this achievement.

ROV picture of a trencher during work in Ormen Lange.

Boulders in the ground prevented trenching in the most difficult areas. The ROV inspected the pipe in the trench after trenching, in this case to investigate the boulder area.

Picture of the gas terminal in Easington.

CHAPTER 8

FROM NYHAMNA TO EASINGTON – INSTALLING THE LANGELED GAS EXPORT LINE SYSTEM

Langeled is the world's longest subsea gas pipeline and a complex project. 1,200 kilometres of pipe connects the processing plant at Aukra with the Sleipner platform and the gas terminal in Easington. A challenging shore approach towards Nyhamna, midline subsea welding, tie in to the Sleipner platform, a challenging shore approach in Easington, and the design and construction of the gas terminal in Easington are all aspects of this complex project.

Hydro completed installation of the 42 inch gas export line the first 33 kilometres from Nyhamna in 2005 using the lay vessel *Solitaire* as described in Chapter 7. Statoil's main task in 2005 was to install the southern leg of Langeled from Sleipner to Easington. *LB 200* started pipeline installation in late April 2005 at the Sleipner platform and laying commenced towards Easington. In the near shore shallow area close to Easington, pipeline installation was performed by Allseas using the vessel *Tug Mor*. *LB 200* (renamed to *Agercy Piper*) continued laying out to approximately 70 kilometres from shore where the to 44 inch pipeline ends were connected by a subsea welding system. The two pipeline ends have to fit exactly to be able to weld them together. The welding operation is supported by divers and ROV.

One million tonnes of steel were used for the Langeled line; the southern leg alone is almost 600 kilometres long. In the 1,200 kilometre pipeline from Nyhamna via the Sleipner platform to Easington, 96,600 pipe sections, each 12.5 metres long, were welded together. Every welded joint is carefully checked using ultrasonic tests to verify welding quality, and before the pipe leaves the vessel the joints are coated with concrete. This makes the pipe heavier, which makes installation easier and the pipe more stable during gas production. It also protects the pipe from trawl board impact.

One million tonnes of concrete were used to coat the lines, more than was used to construct the enormous Troll A platform.

Pipe production in Japan and Germany started two years before the installation to ensure sufficient pipe would be on hand for the lay seasons.

Bredero coated the pipes in their coating yard in Farsund. The job increased activity in Farsund for a long time with 600 people working in the pipe preparation plant to coat the pipes with asphalt and concrete. The inside of the pipes were cleaned, polished and painted to avoid corrosion.

A total of 12 pipe carriers were used to transport pipes to the lay vessels. During the lay season the

Agercy Piper laying the 44 inch gas export line from the Sleipner platform towards Easington.

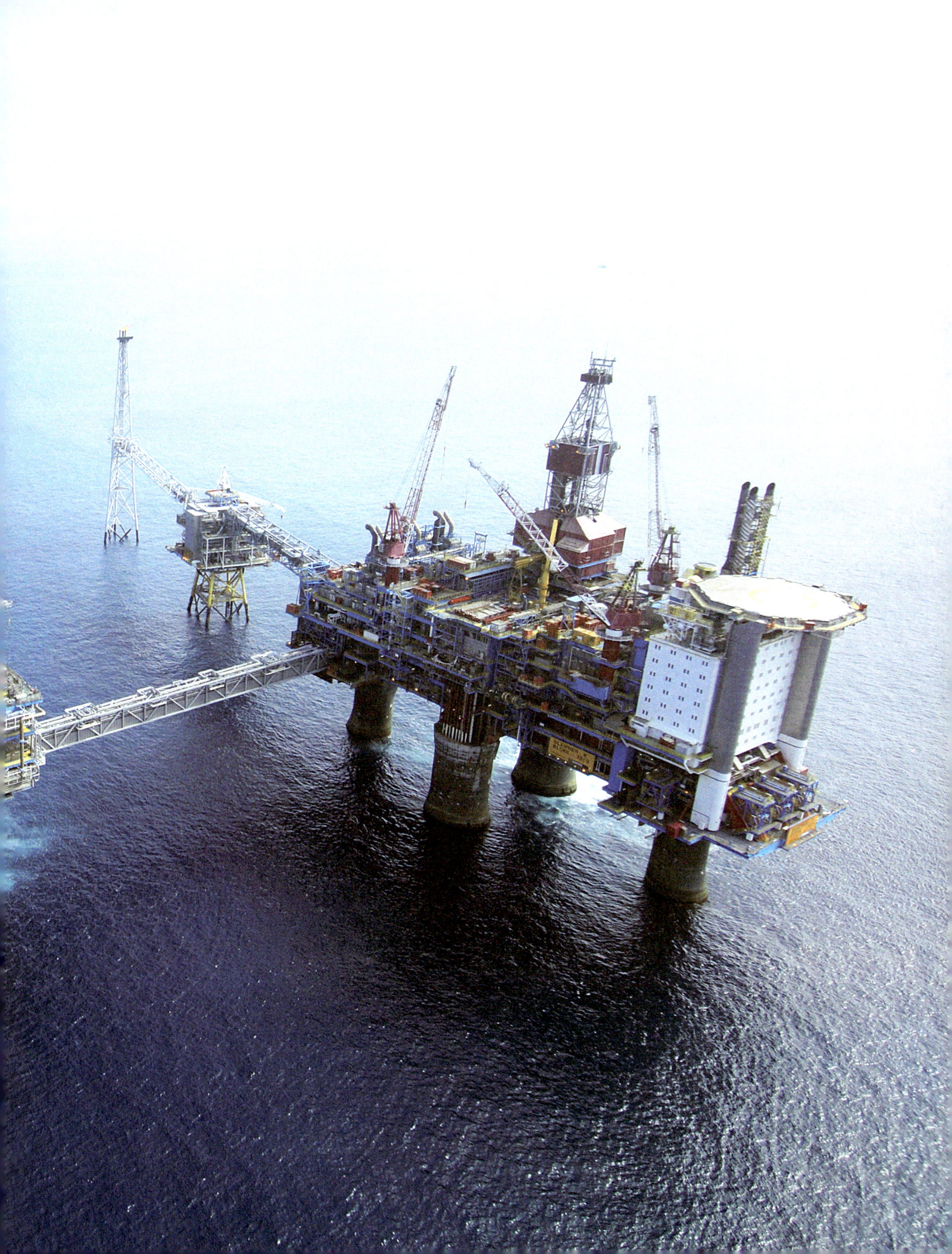

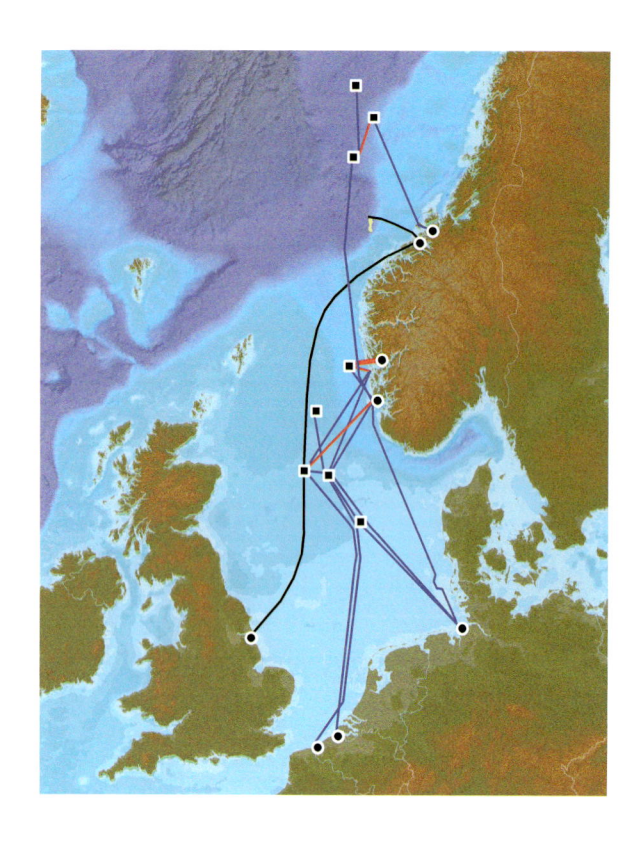

The Langeled line is connected to the Sleipner platform through a riser platform. The Sleipner platform enables gas to be exported directly to Holland and France.

Pipeline corridor preparation in the shore approach towards Easington.

Reiten, Blair and Stoltenberg attended the official inauguration of Langeled South in London.

lay barges and lay vessels are "welded" or tied to the pipe on the seafloor and cannot sail to port. Supply ships carry materials to the vessels and personnel are transported by helicopter.

The northern leg of Langeled was installed in 2006. On 19 March the lay barge *Agercy Piper* picked up the pipeline end left 33 kilometres from Nyhamna in 2005, and after some technical problems laying progressed well during the season. However, even with a lay speed of 3–4 kilometres per day it takes months to complete such an enormous operation, so to maintain the schedule, the *Solitaire* was also brought in to lay 80 kilometres of the Northern leg.

The preparations at the Sleipner platform and the construction of the gas terminal in Easington were both large subprojects with critical schedules. It was planned the Langeled southern line would open for gas transport from the Sleipner platform in October 2006. The inauguration of Langeled South was held on 16 October, a successful achievement for the Statoil and the Hydro teams.

The first gas was transported through the system as early as September 2006; a critical milestone for the Ormen Lange project which had only 30 months earlier been approved by the Norwegian parliament. Project director Tom Røtjer heartily congratulated all the contractors involved along with the joint Statoil and Hydro team. A successful co-operation that could possibly even be considered on a more permanent basis.

The mayor of Aukra municipality, Aud Mork, turns the first spade for the processing plant site in April 2004. Project director prior to construction start, Bengt Lie Hansen, and Terje Uthus, project director responsible for the design and construction of the Ormen Lange gas processing plant, witnessed this historic event.

CHAPTER 9

CONSTRUCTING THE ORMEN LANGE PROCESSING PLANT AT AUKRA

The stories behind the offshore project and the marine archaeology project are the main themes in this book. But what makes the Ormen Lange project special is its huge size and the broad spectrum of challenges involved in its development.

Ormen Lange is the largest gas development in Europe and the processing plant is the heart of the project. That it each day will treat 70 million cubic metres of gas indicates the sheer scale needed for the processing facilities. The processing plant is 120 football fields in size. Every hour 10,000 cubic metres of seawater are pumped through the seawater tunnel to cool the gas.

The Ormen Lange project team became familiar early on with the design of the processing plant at Aukra through photomontages of the planned facilities in the terrain, prior to any physical development activity. However, it is quite a different matter when blasting and transport starts and it becomes clear what 120 football fields really represent.

Hydro spent the period between concept selection in 2002/2003 until the development plan was approved by the Norwegian parliament on 2 April 2004 preparing building contracts for the processing plants. One of the main ones was the civil contract for preparation of the plant area. It included excavation, blasting, excavation of rock caverns, mass transport, road building, building of deepwater quay for shipping of condensate and a construction quay for other transport of material to the plant, water supply and other parts of the infrastructure required for the plant and for the construction activity to take place.

Although physical development could not be started until the Plan For Development (PDO) was approved by the Parliament, Hydro ensured that contractors were ready to start more or less immediately when the PDO was approved. The strategy was successful and by May 2004 digging and blasting was underway. This was the start of three years of intensive construction at Aukra.

The land archaeology team was just completing two years of excavation and for a short time worked in parallel with the civil work. Blasting, big excavators and dumpers replaced the meticulous excavation by the archaeologists. Two completely different cultures had to coexist for a while. Even though the archaeologists were prepared and well informed about the plans, they were surprised by the rapid progress and amount of change.

The archaeologists could now continue their work at the university facilities – a lot of material

The archaeological excavation in the processing plant area took two years and could continue uninterrupted during the winter under heated tents above the excavation areas.

Blasting and transportation in Nyhamna in 2004. As much as 3.4 million cubic metres of rock were blasted during the civil work preparing the plant area.

had been gathered by up to 70 terrestrial archaeologists during two years of extensive excavation. More than 300,000 objects from Stone Age and Bronze Age settlements were recorded of which around 180,000 were carefully photographed, packed and stored for research and exhibitions.

During the first year, the terrain gradually changed with several hundred thousand cubic metres of excavated soil stored onshore or deposited in a small offshore basin. 2.3 million cubic metres of rock were excavated. The plant site gradually started to resemble the design drawings.

The largest "hotel" in Norway, and one of the largest in the world, was built at Aukra to accommodate the people involved in construction of the plant at Nyhamn, often up to 3,500 at a time. Close to 9,000 people were employed on a shift basis. When more beds were needed Hydro brought in two of the *Hurtigruta* coastal steamers as floating hotels.

As the civil construction approached completion, construction of the plant facilities gradually took over.

The gas that arrives from the field is not treated in any way. The hydrocarbons arrive at Nyhamna in a multiphase flow which means the gas also contains light oil components. It also contains antifreeze fluid, Methyl Ethylene Glycole (MEG), which is injected into the gas flow at the wells to prevent gas hydrate forming. Gas hydrates are methane gas and water that form an icy mass that can plug the gas pipeline and MEG absorbs water produced with the gas from the reservoir. In the gas processing plant, the gas is processed and transformed into a dry sales gas ready for use in industry and normal heating and cooking. Just the thing if you want to put the kettle on for a cup of tea…

The plant consists of the following main facilities:

- Gas treatment system to separate gas from the light fluids (condensate)
- MEG separation system to separate the MEG from the gas
- MEG treatment system to separate water from the MEG and to clean the MEG
- Caverns for storage of condensate
- Seawater intake for cooling the gas
- Deepwater key for shipping of condensate in tankers
- A flare system for the gas when venting of gas is required

More than 180,000 artefacts from Stone Age and Bronze Age settlements at the Nyhamna location were collected during the archaeological excavation prior to the plant being built. They included a Stone Age axe which is estimated to be 9,500 years old.

Tom Røtjer, project director for the Ormen Lange development project, during one of his many presentations of the Ormen Lange project.

- Gas export system
- Well control system for steering of the production through the control umbilicals.

Skanska won the main civil contract. Aker Kværner and Vetco Abil were awarded the contacts to design and construct the processing facilities. Many other contractors were involved in smaller contracts or as subcontractors to Aker Kværner, Vetco Abil and Skanska. It was positive that Norwegian contractors were able to play such an important role in the design and construction of the gas processing plant, a task they performed well.

The work progressed as planned, with project director Tom Røtjer nearly always reporting "on schedule and on budget" during the project execution phase. His team and the contractors involved managed to speed up any project activity that fell behind schedule and solve all the technical problems that occurred during the building of Ormen Lange.

And in such a large and complex project as Ormen Lange, problems will always occur. It is a matter of recognising them as early as possible and being prepared and able to handle them.

When the processing plant is completed in 2007 more than 20,000 people have been involved in the construction work at Aukra. Workers from 50 nations have contributed directly and indirectly through subcontracts. The team of workers can be justifiably proud of being part of one of the largest industrial projects in Norway's history.

More than 15,000 visitors have been guided around the construction site, which also illustrates the huge public interest in this impressive industrial project.

Nyhamna in Aukra prior to the Ormen Lange development.

Up to 3,500 workers were accommodated in the largest hotel in Norway during the construction of the Ormen Lange gas processing plant. Many of the visitors who came to see the impressive construction work also stayed in the Ormen Lange hotel.

The construction site in June 2005, 13 months after construction start. The tie-in of the first gas pipeline is seen in the near shore area.

The processing plant close to completion in 2007. Testing of the facilities with gas from the Sleipner platform was one of the verification tests to prove the readiness of the system before production start from the Ormen Lange field in 2007.

PART TWO
SHIPWRECKS

Bjørnsund, Bud and part of Hustadvika.

CHAPTER 10

MARITIME FRÆNA – A SHIP'S GRAVEYARD

In the early 19th century an unknown ship was wrecked near the entrance of Harøysund, between Bjørnsund and Bud in Fræna Municipality, close to a large islet at the mouth of Hustadvika. A more classic shipwreck site than this would be hard to find in Norwegian waters.

The area around Nyhamna – Aukra Island, Bjørnsund and Bud – is a classic Norwegian maritime cultural landscape with mountains, islets, and islands where the open sea meets the complex fjord system. The many archaeological sites on either side of Bjørnsund, going back to prehistoric and historic times, indicate the area has been important to the cultural development of Central Norway. [1]

The sheltered and topographically varied bodies of water have always been attractive fishing and hunting grounds, and terrestrial and maritime resources have been well used in the area throughout the ages. The area represents a cross section of key terrestrial and maritime transport zones.

The Fræna region and islands around were populated as early as the Stone Age by settlements based on fishing and sea mammal hunting. In the Bronze Age, numerous monumental coastal cairns were built in the area, marking the development of a local aristocracy. During the Iron, Viking, Medieval and post-Medieval periods an entire network of maritime infrastructure was developed, including local harbours, beacons and other sailing marks, boathouses, and supported by other maritime elements such as place names, sagas, etc.

Archaeological finds from Bolsøya [2] and Veøya show the area was a politically and economically powerful regional centre during the Iron and Medieval Ages. Historical processes created a rich maritime cultural environment with many important archaeological and historical sites dated to the Stone, Bronze, Iron, Medieval and post-Medieval periods.

The main maritime elements in the cultural landscape in the vicinity of the wreckage site are:

- Hustadvika – one of the most treacherous sailing routes along the Norwegian coast
- The old fishing and transition harbour at Bud
- Fishing settlement and harbour at Bjørnsund.

The area constitutes an important stretch of the main sailing route along the Norwegian coast with longstanding tradition and great significance for the maritime cultural development at a regional, national and international level.

NORVEGIA REGNUM, vulgo NOR-RYKE.

SERENISSIMO PRINCIPI
CHRISTIANO,
DANIÆ, NORVEGIÆ,
VANDALORVM, GOTHORVMQ; PRINCIPI,
Duci Slefvici, Holfatiæ, Stormariæ, & Ditmarfiæ,
Comiti in Oldenburgh & Delmenhorst.
Tab. hanc D.D.D.   I. Blaeu.

Norvegia regnum. 1662 by Johan Blaeu, showing location of Bud in Central Norway.

FRA BUD FISKEVÆR MOLOEN. Eneret A. B.

Parti fra Bud - Romsdal.

Archive photos of Bud.

The waters in the Hustadvika area outside Fræna are very difficult to navigate, particularly the three kilometres out from land due to skerries and rocks. The sailing route between the towns of Molde and Kristiansund, along Hustadvika, is considered one of the most dangerous parts of the Norwegian coast with over twenty historical shipwrecks registered and innumerable legends and stories of shipwrecks over the centuries.

The harbour at Bud has always played an important role in the area's maritime cultural landscape. It has long been a fishing settlement and trade harbour for timber and dried fish, and an important regional harbour for other maritime activities. Bud was for some centuries also the most important marketplace in the entire region between Bergen and Trondheim.

The settlement was host to some of the most significant events in the history of Norwegian independence. On 15 August 1533 the last Catholic archbishop of Norway, Olav Engelbrektsson, called for what should be the last meeting of the State Council (Riksrådet) before the Reformation. He chose Bud because it was close to the main sailing route and because the land route over Lesja through the valley of Romsdal was the most accessible route between eastern and western Norway.

Since the 17th century the harbour at Bud has played an important role in fishery, both local and regional. The sea close to Bud has always been rich in fish, with 18th century texts mentioning blue ling, cusk, cod, coalfish, flounder, mackerel, haddock, pollock and other less common varieties. In the years 1740–1760 the region experienced extremely rich herring fishing, and in the mid-18th century Bud was actually one of the largest fishing settlements in Norway, with 400 to 500 local fishing boats. Fishermen used a number of different types of local boats [3] including *sambøringer*, *åttringer*, *fjørefaringer*, *seksringer* and *færinger*.

The town of Molde, some 40 kilometres south of Bud, was granted trading privileges in 1742 despite strong opposition from Bergen and Trondheim. Foreign ships soon started anchoring in the Molde harbour and in subsequent years up to 40 visits were registered from foreign ships: Danish, English, Scottish, Dutch and Spanish. Apart from fish, commodities such as timber, iron, leather, smoked meat, cheese and berries were traded.

Bjørnsund village on an island in the vicinity of Bud has existed as a local fishing settlement at least since the Iron Age. In conjunction with Bud it

Molde harbour c. 1830.

provided a system of safe harbours; a final chance for vessels heading north across Hustadvika to stop or turn back. The Bjørnsund harbour provided shelter from strong winds for boats and ships. However, there are numerous stories of hurricanes that dragged boats from the harbour in Bjørnsund, causing many wreckages between Bud and Aukra Island.

Consequently, there are many written references to Bjørnsund, Bud and Hustadvika as places where maritime tragedies have occurred due to storms or navigation errors. Written sources also refer to auctions of equipment from wrecked ships in the area, which was regularly visited by foreign vessels as early as the Middle Ages in connection with rich herring fisheries, timber trade, general trade, and naval operations.

Along the coastline, the Ormen Lange pipelines therefore cross a rugged seabed with numerous shipwrecks. To help select the potential pipeline routes which would meet the least obstacles, Hydro conducted sonar and topographical seabed surveys over a number of seasons. No less than eight shipwrecks were found close to the planned pipeline routes, all of them modern. Much of the seafloor in the area has been used as a dumping ground in recent years and these shipwrecks are in fact mainly obsolete fishing vessels that have been abandoned in modern times.

Because of the rich maritime history and its geographical location, the area is also on the Norwegian Directorate for Cultural Heritage's (Riksantikvaren) list of regions with special priority for marine archaeology and protection of underwater heritage in Norway. The Norwegian Cultural Heritage Act requires detailed surveys to be carried out before starting industrial projects in order to prevent damage to potential marine archaeological sites.

To ensure the pipeline would not damage any archaeological remains, Hydro presented existing survey data from their proposed pipeline routes.

Molde harbour c. 1803.

However, this survey data could not adequately detect the presence of archaeological material in the proposed pipeline corridors so it was decided the Norwegian University of Science and Technology should carry out a new investigation.

NTNU archaeologists have unique experience in detecting shipwrecks, and have developed marine archaeological methods and performed similar projects in Norway and abroad since the early 1990s [4]. Over the past decade NTNU has participated in or directed marine archaeological projects in Norway, USA, Greece, Malta, Bulgaria, Portugal, Greenland, United Arab Emirates, Argentina, Chile and Mexico. This work has resulted in the discovery and documentation of numerous historic shipwrecks.

By using advanced archaeological survey methods and equipment developed for these projects, the archaeologists can detect objects that escape the attention of the oil industry surveyors. When the archaeologists performed a new and higher resolution sonar and visual survey of the seafloor in the Bud area, additional shipwrecks appeared.

The first of these was a steel-hulled vessel in the middle of the pipeline route. Another wooden wreck has been identified as the wreck of the vessel *Nordsund* (1918), which was lost off Bud in 1941 while carrying a stone cargo. The area was also littered by waste such as tangles of wire, fishing equipment and steel frames. There are more than 50 kitchen appliances, a complete kitchen, oil drums and even a 1950s car, none of which were shown on the seafloor maps produced by Hydro. Years of experience in developing technology and methods to detect even the smallest features on the seabed paid off and the archaeologists' detection capability proved to be more accurate and more effective than the industry standard.

Then overnight the survey became more exciting than anyone would ever have imagined.

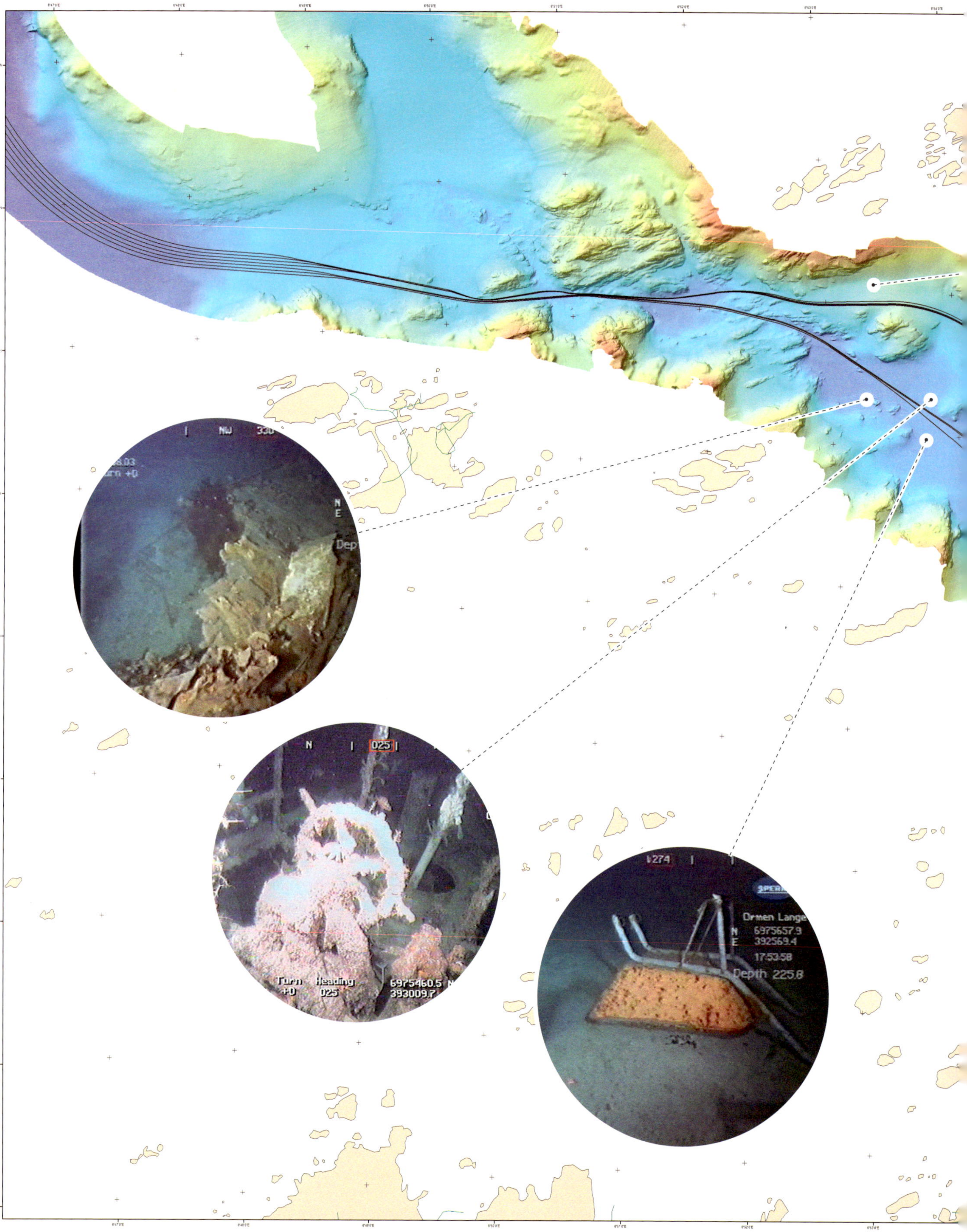

NW 330
N 025
Turn +0
Heading 025
6975460.5
393009.7
274
Ormen Lange
N 6975657.9
E 392569.4
17:53:58
Depth 225.8

103

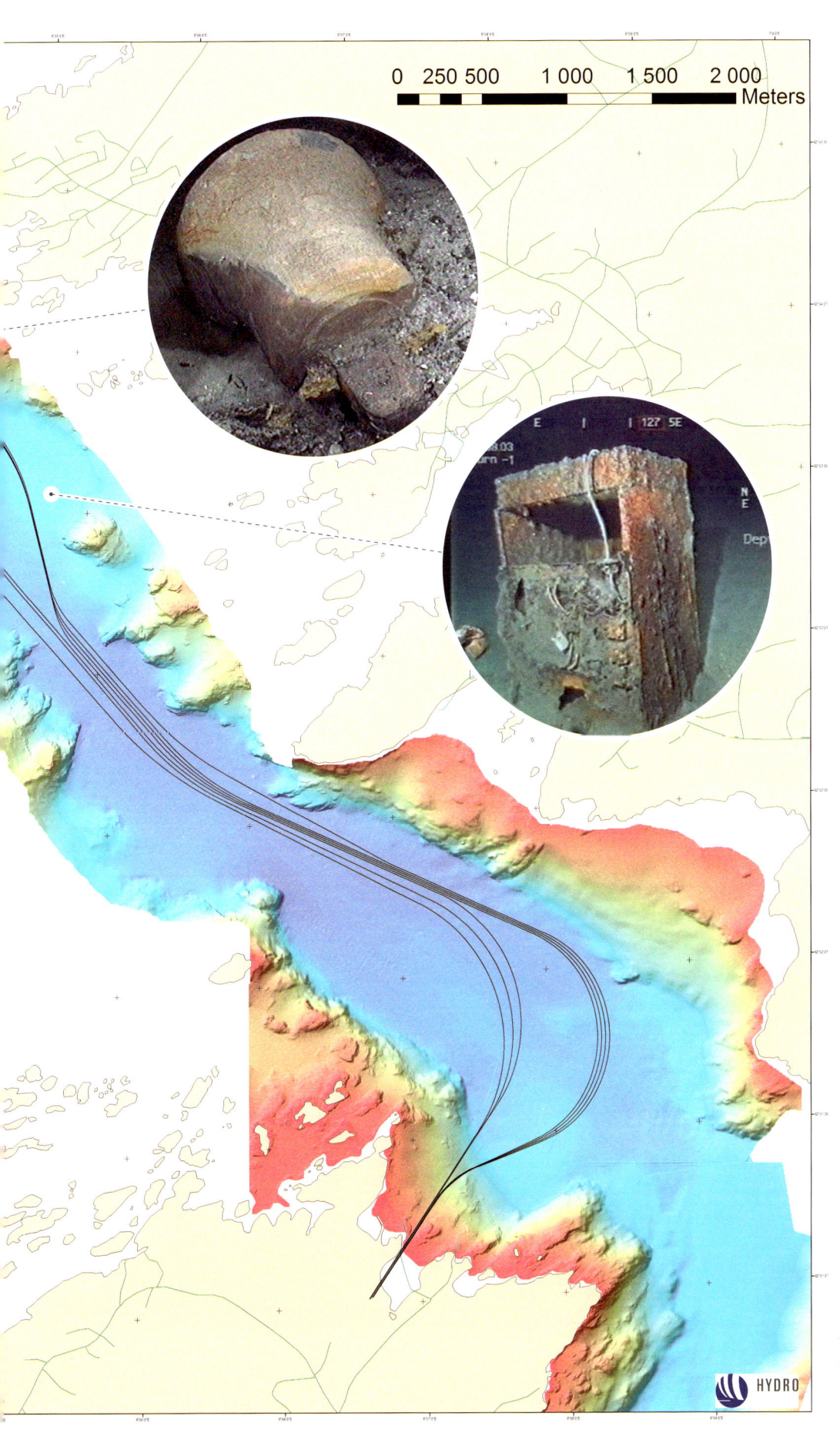

The underwater terrain and pipelines from Aukra to Bjørnsund with some of the many artefacts discovered along the pipeline route.

Preserved elements of the bow
section of the shipwreck.

CHAPTER 11

SHIPWRECK!

Members of the marine archaeological crew are not likely to forget the date, 25 August 2003. Earlier that month they had initiated the marine archaeological survey of the planned pipeline route for Ormen Lange. [1]

As they boarded the survey vessel that particular August morning, the team had no idea this day would shape their professional lives for several years to come. The working day started as usual: the boat sailed into position, the captain switched on the Dynamic Positioning System, the team sent the ROV to the seabed, and started slowly following the planned pipeline routes.

Around noon the first man-made objects started to appear on the monitors of the sonars and ROV cameras that were used to map and visually inspect the seafloor and seafloor anomalies. The first objects were modern.

Later that afternoon an anomaly was detected on the right channel of the side-scan sonar system. The sonar monitors showed an image seen so many times before – hundreds of bright spots on the dark red background of the monitor, forming a shape that would indicate an archaeological site. The team was familiar with images like this from Greece where it had spent five seasons surveying the bottom of Aegean and Ionian seas in search of ancient shipwrecks. [2] Bright spots like this in Mediterranean conditions are often caused by piles of ancient amphoras – the hard pottery which reflects acoustic signals very well. But here in Norway?

The camera-equipped ROV was steered closer to the target – and there it was! The picture showed a sandy mound covered with hundreds of wine bottles at a depth of 170 metres. A giant underwater party, someone joked up in the control room of the research vessel. Sadly, it couldn't have been further from the truth; the bottles were the remains of a tragedy at sea long ago. The ROV soon revealed more: wooden structures covered in a thin layer of sand, more bottles, stoneware plates, iron objects in the shape of cannons, and even a ship bell lying on the side and partly visible over the sand layer. The team had discovered a historic shipwreck site.

The atmosphere that filled the control room in the minutes after the discovery can hardly be described. The team was facing the first deep-water historic wooden shipwreck discovered by archaeologists in Norwegian waters. After a break to calm down, filming of the site continued and

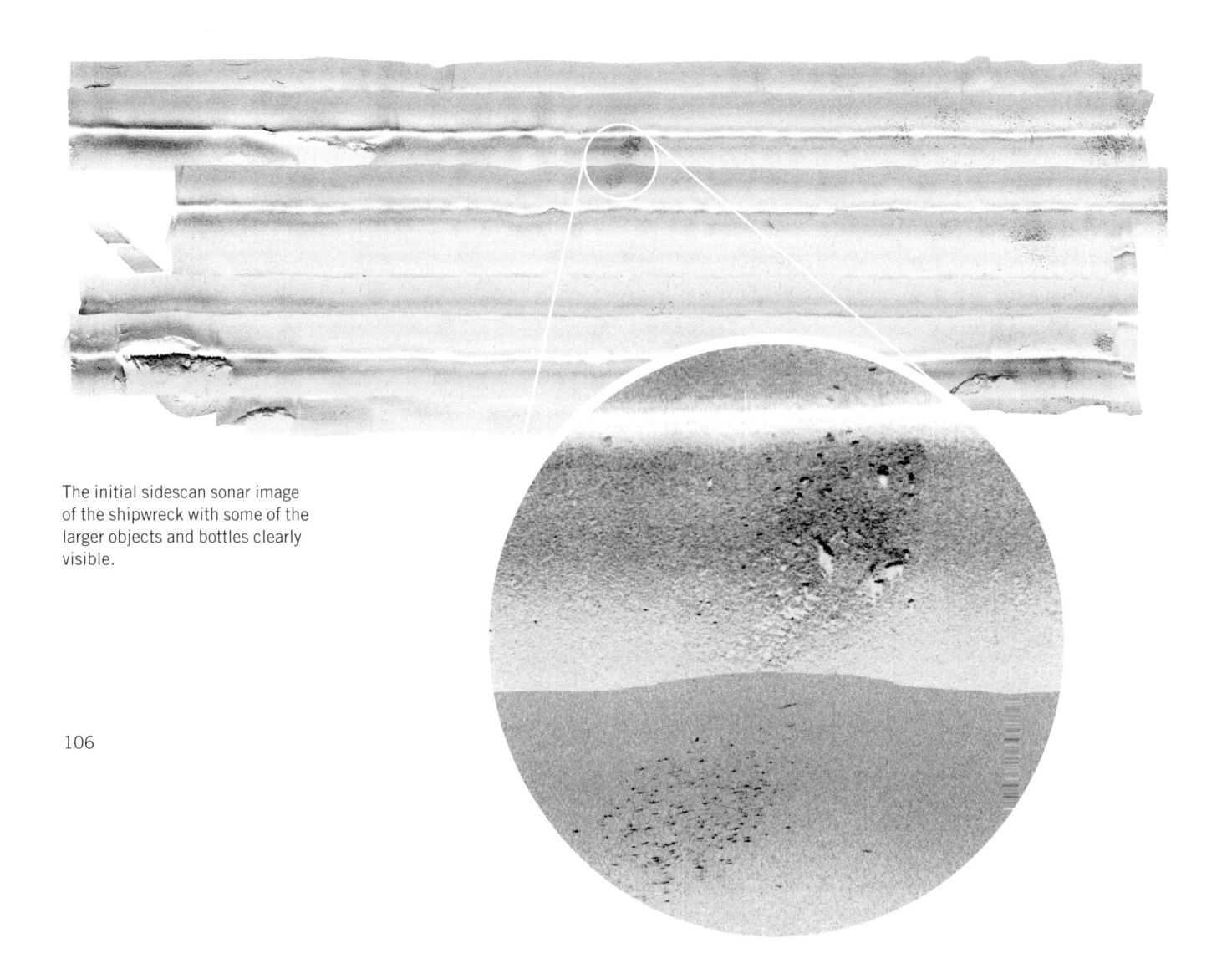

The initial sidescan sonar image of the shipwreck with some of the larger objects and bottles clearly visible.

hundreds of still photos were taken.

The team returned to the site the following day to look more closely at the artefacts. Pictures of bottles, china and ceramics transmitted from the ROV clearly showed items typical of the late 18th century. The initial investigations of the site established that it was a historically significant and undisturbed shipwreck.

A cursory examination of the bottle pile revealed there were probably more than 1,000 bottles of varying morphology visible on the surface, with many more partially or completely buried to the south-southwest of the main site. The bottles were most likely ship's cargo, along with stoneware containers that may have carried wine, champagne, cognac and brandy.

The visible wooden structure was approximately 30–40 metres long. It was situated on the seafloor along a line running northeast to southwest. The natural terrain of the site ranged in depth from approximately 165 to 170 metres. [3]

The shipwreck appeared to be splayed open due to decay of the deck timbers and upper parts of the ship. The bow section was recognisable by the presence of four lead hawse-pipes through which anchor lines would have passed and which would have been at the very bow of the ship, to the starboard and port of the bowsprit and pulpit. Clearly visible in the bow were the massive cant-frames and stem-timber and possibly the remnants of major timbers such as the apron and keelson in a good state of preservation.

The bottle scatter from the first video recording of the shipwreck site.

The archaeologists studied the finds as they appeared on the monitors: rigging blocks of hard wood, Selters bottles of stoneware, some china, elements of hull constructions, and even coins. Literally thousands of artefacts were visible on the surface of the seabed. Who knew what was hidden under the sediment?

The next couple of days were spent making preliminary measurements and descriptions. According to the observations from the initial period the site, numbered as 059 in the target list, appeared to be some 30–40 metres in length. However, since there were clearly more artefacts buried beneath the sediment the overall length of the site could be as much as 50–60 metres; most likely the site also extended quite a distance to the south and southwest.

The sinking ship reached its final position on the seabed only 700 metres from the harbour at Bud. The team was immediately aware of the closeness of the central part of the site with its wooden hull structures to the planned route for the pipeline and additional gas installations. The proximity alone, combined with the significant spread of the archaeological material around the central part of the site, could well cause Hydro problems in developing the gas field due to the protection provided by the Norwegian Law for Protection of Cultural Heritage.

This was very quickly proven to be the case.

The Oseberg ship on display at
the Viking Ship Museum in Oslo.

CHAPTER 12

WHY DID WE DO IT? – THE NORWEGIAN CULTURAL HERITAGE ACT

All European and most Western countries have more or less effective laws protecting their national cultural heritage. This legislation differs greatly from country to country and provides varying degrees of protection for monuments and archaeological sites on land as well as in territorial waters, but generally aims to protect and administer them for present and future generations.

Cultural heritage is seen as both a material manifestation of earlier national and international traditions, of importance to the general public, and also as a key source of data for archaeological and historical studies. [1]

The Norwegian Cultural Heritage Act has a clear maritime genesis. The discovery of the famous Viking Age ship *Oseberg* was the catalyst that initiated the development of the initial cultural heritage legislation in Norway as early as 1905.

On 8 August 1903, a Norwegian farmer Knut Rom informed Professor Gabriel Gustafson of the University Museum of Antiquities in Oslo that he had come across the remnants of a ship while digging in a large burial mound on his farm, Lille Oseberg in Slagen in Vestfold.

The following summer and autumn of 1904, an excavation team led by Gustafson carried out archaeological excavations of this spectacular ship.

Under the Norwegian law current in 1903 the *Oseberg* site, including ship remnants and artefacts, belonged to the landowner Knut Rom who could sell it to anyone he wanted to, foreign buyers included. The problem was finally resolved when the rich landowner Fritz Treschow purchased the find from Knut Rom for NOK 12,000 and donated it to the Norwegian State. Shortly after, Norway imposed a law prohibiting the export of antiquities and in 1905 the first Norwegian Law on Cultural Heritage was passed. This law automatically protected all cultural monuments, including archaeological sites, dated before 1537 (the year of Reformation in Norway) on land and underwater.

1905 was also the year that Norway regained independence after five centuries of unions with Denmark and Sweden, and the new law intended to emphasize that the Norwegian nation had its own, significant cultural heritage. This was clearly also a political marker, in the domestic as well as international arenas.

Since 1905 the Law has undergone several major transformations to modernise it and extend its areas of application. On 9 June 1978 the Norwe-

The grave chamber of the Oseberg ship during excavations.

gian parliament passed the Norwegian Cultural Heritage Act (Kulturminnelov) which replaced the 1905 Law and changed some key attitudes towards cultural monuments.

In terms of maritime heritage, the 1905 Law protected all submerged sites earlier than the Reformation, including boat remnants, shipwrecks, harbour constructions etc. This was a highly important aspect of the law for a maritime nation such as Norway and meant that many sites of European significance were protected from destruction.

Two significant changes in the Norwegian legal framework for maritime heritage took place in 1963 and 1974. The 1963 change included marine, or submerged, shipwreck sites later than 1537 but more than 100 years old (counted from the year of their construction), in the heritage management system (section 14 of the Act). The 1974 change extended section 14 to also include shipwreck cargo, equipment and accessories on board at the time of the wreckage.

The reason for the 1974 extension was the discovery of the 'Runde' shipwreck site by sport divers in 1972. The wreck of the Dutch ship *Akerendam* that sank near Runde on the western coast of Norway in 1725 appeared to contain a huge amount of gold and silver coins, and legal conflicts between divers and the Norwegian state after the discovery led to the Act being amended.

Unlike most western countries which manage cultural heritage under their respective ministries of culture, Norway considers cultural heritage to be a key environmental issue and has placed it under the Ministry of the Environment. The National Heritage Board (*Riksantikvaren*) is a governmental directorate under the Ministry.

This unique Norwegian solution is not merely an administrative arrangement but primarily an expression of philosophical, political, and social attitudes towards cultural heritage and its status in Norway. The Norwegian system sees monuments of cultural heritage not only as cultural manifestations of the past, but also as important natural elements in our everyday environment.

Consequently, historical monuments are looked after to the same extent as other subjects of environmental protection such as water, air and other natural aspects. Cultural heritage is also seen in Norwegian national policy as an important environmental resource and subject to sustainable development policy.

The Norwegian Cultural Heritage Act imposes specific obligations on private or governmental organisations that plan to carry out any construction work on land or on the seabed.

First, project developers, in this case Hydro, are obliged to finance the surveys by state institutions to find out whether the planned project interferes with cultural heritage in the area. If a conflict is confirmed by a specific archaeological survey or based on studies of existing databases, the entrepreneur must redesign the project to eliminate the interference. If the conflict cannot be avoided, the authorities deny permission for the project to be carried out in that particular area as the Act forbids any cultural heritage being disturbed or devastated. [2]

However in cases of projects with a high level of national significance, a special dispensation from the Act may be granted by the Ministry of Environment on the condition that the developer fully covers the costs of the investigations needed to save archaeological data from the site for further studies [3]. As described in the following chapter this was exactly the situation that arose when the shipwreck site was discovered in the pipeline route for the Ormen Lange gas field project.

❶ The ship's bell on the seafloor ❷ during recovery ❸ and safely on deck

CHAPTER 13

ACHIEVING A WIN-WIN SOLUTION

The Norwegian Cultural Heritage Act imposed certain demands and limitations on further development of the pipeline installations after the newly discovered shipwreck was reported to the authorities.

The first, in autumn 2003, was a request from The Norwegian Directorate for Cultural Heritage (Riksantikvaren) for more detailed information. They (heritage authorities) needed to know more about the actual shipwreck and the closeness of the wreck to the planned pipeline route before they could make any further decisions. They also needed to evaluate the value of the shipwreck as an object of historical heritage and a source of historical and archaeological data.

As soon as Hydro was informed about the shipwreck discovery, it started to evaluate alternative pipeline routes in the area to avoid conflict with the shipwreck and with section 14 of the Norwegian Cultural Heritage Act. Since the main problem was the closeness of the shipwreck site to the planned secondary pipeline route, the Norwegian company Reinertsen prepared a plan for an alternative route. This route also had to be inspected by the marine archaeological team to ensure there were no cultural remains on the seafloor of this route.

The team therefore went back to sea in October 2003 with the same research vessel and ROV equipment used in the August survey. Its first task was to collect additional information from the wreck site. During the inspection the team could observe and document on film new details of the ship remnants as well as the artefacts scattered in the area. French wine bottles, English table plates, Chinese porcelain, and German and Dutch pottery were sighted; many of the images were breathtaking. Two sonars installed in the front of the ROV provided new acoustic images of the site and its surroundings.

The seabed topography around the wreck appeared to be complex with narrow open corridors between elevations and huge rocky outcrops. It would soon become clear that one of these in particular would create significant problems for the project.

Finally the exciting day arrived when the ship's bell would be raised. It was hoped the bell would unveil crucial information about the ship's chronology, nationality, perhaps even its name. Special equipment was installed on the ROV early in the morning including digging equipment and a frame with strong plastic netting in which to lift the bell up to the surface.

The discovery of a second shipwreck prevented the alternative pipeline route being used. ❶ + ❷ Two anchors were located close to the shipwreck. ❸ Bottle and dinner plate close to the stone mound.

The operation was complicated, but after several hectic hours the bronze ship bell was lifted from the water onto the deck of the research boat. The entire crew gathered around the bell, searching it for clues: an inscription could be seen, and ornamentation covered in marine organisms and patina. Gradually the inscription emerged: SOLI DEO GLORIA Å 1745. The rim of the bell was highly ornamental and the bell showed a female figure wearing a rococo style dress

Once again the atmosphere was charged with emotion. The raising of the bell from the wreck 170 metres below was almost as exciting as the discovery of the wreck in August. The team involved in the project and this particular operation were congratulating each other, hundreds of photos were taken, and interpretations of the three Latin words in the inscription became increasingly imaginative. The latin term actually means "Glory to God alone". Documentation of the bell commenced, with measurements made on deck showing it to have a maximum diameter of 41.5 centimetres, height of 45 centimetres and weight of 55 kilograms.

Further studies revealed the bell to be of Dutch origin but although it is a beautiful specimen it did not provide the information the team had hoped for.

The 1745 date supported earlier assumptions that the ship was probably built around the middle of the 18th century. But sadly there was no ship's name on the bell; information that would have made it much easier to later research the ship and its story.

The fact that the bell was produced in the Netherlands says a lot about the bell itself, but gives no indication as to the nationality of the ship. In the second half of the 18th century there was much international trade in ship equipment and Dutch bells were among the most popular on the European maritime market. A Dutch bell might be used or even reused on more or less any European ship of this period.

The second main task of the October 2003 survey was to inspect the alternative pipeline route in the area developed by Reinertsen. The procedure was the same as during the earlier survey, involving an ROV with cameras, lights and sonars flying just above the seabed along the planned lines. New objects appeared on the monitors – modern dumped rubbish, huge boulders, etc.

One stormy afternoon a few days into the survey, when the ship was battered by driving rain and the first snow of the season, an electrifying image appeared on the screen. A mound of stones with a boat like shape and two iron anchors on the sides.

Cehili at the site in 2004.

A closer look with the cameras revealed a bottle and a couple of dinner plates close to the mound.

The sight was unmistakeable: the stones were ballast from a historic wooden vessel. A second historic wreck had been discovered, lying on the seabed in the alternative route for the pipelines. [1]

There was silence in the control room. The team stared at the monitors, at one another, back to the monitors. Not only was it unmistakeable, it was unbelievable. In the world of marine archaeology, situations like this don't happen often. Two routes, two survey cruises, and two historic wrecks obstructing the routes.

The second wreck was much smaller than the first, most likely a local fishing vessel. Judging by the typology of the anchors and the few visible artefacts the boat would most likely be dated to the late 19th century and thus protected under the Cultural Heritage Act.

The discovery had to be reported to Hydro immediately, not a pleasant task. The voice on the other end of the line was far from happy: it appeared that all the time, effort and money put into developing a new route to avoid conflict with the first wreck had not achieved a thing.

The alternative route was also obstructed by an historic wreck. Worse, the seabed topography in the area excluded new alternatives, and the rocky outcrop mentioned earlier made it impossible to move the original route further away from the first wreck.

The project had landed in a major crisis.

Several days later the team returned to Trondheim and started preparing its report. Hydro and the other partners in the Ormen Lange consortium were debating what should be done. Intensive discussions, meetings and attempts to find a solution went on throughout the winter of 2003 and early spring 2004. Finally it became apparent that the consortium could see no alternative to going back to the initial route and taking the financial consequences. It would cover the cost of further archaeological investigation at the 18th century shipwreck site, assuming the Norwegian cultural heritage authorities would accept the application for permission to disturb the site.

The next step was to define how big a disturbance it would involve and subsequently what kind of archaeological exploration was needed at the site to fulfil the requirements of the Act.

In May 2004, Hydro needed to do additional surveying in the area and the archaeological team was invited to join the survey vessel Geobay for a few days to conduct a more detailed survey. The objective was to determine the size of the entire

Historic shipwreck 1

Historic shipwreck 2

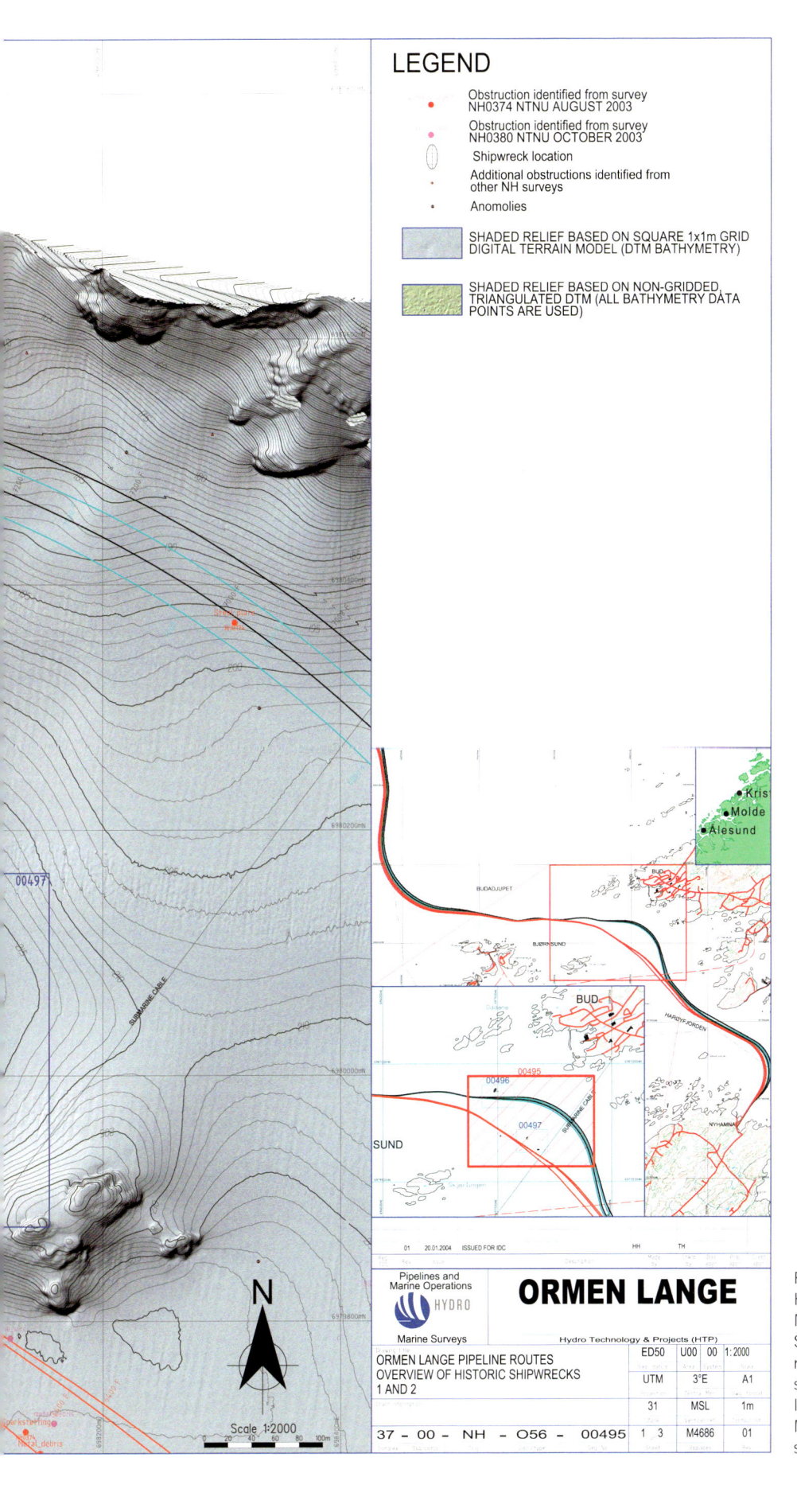

Pipelines and shipwrecks on the seafloor. Historic Shipwreck 1 is in conflict with the MEG lines and umbilicals, while Historic Shipwreck 2 blocked the alternative pipeline route. There are an additional 3 modern shipwrecks in close proximity to these locations. Red lines: Gas pipelines, Green: MEG lines, Black: Umbilicals; a total of seven pipelines.

3D terrain model showing the underwater terrain and shipwreck.

Shipwreck

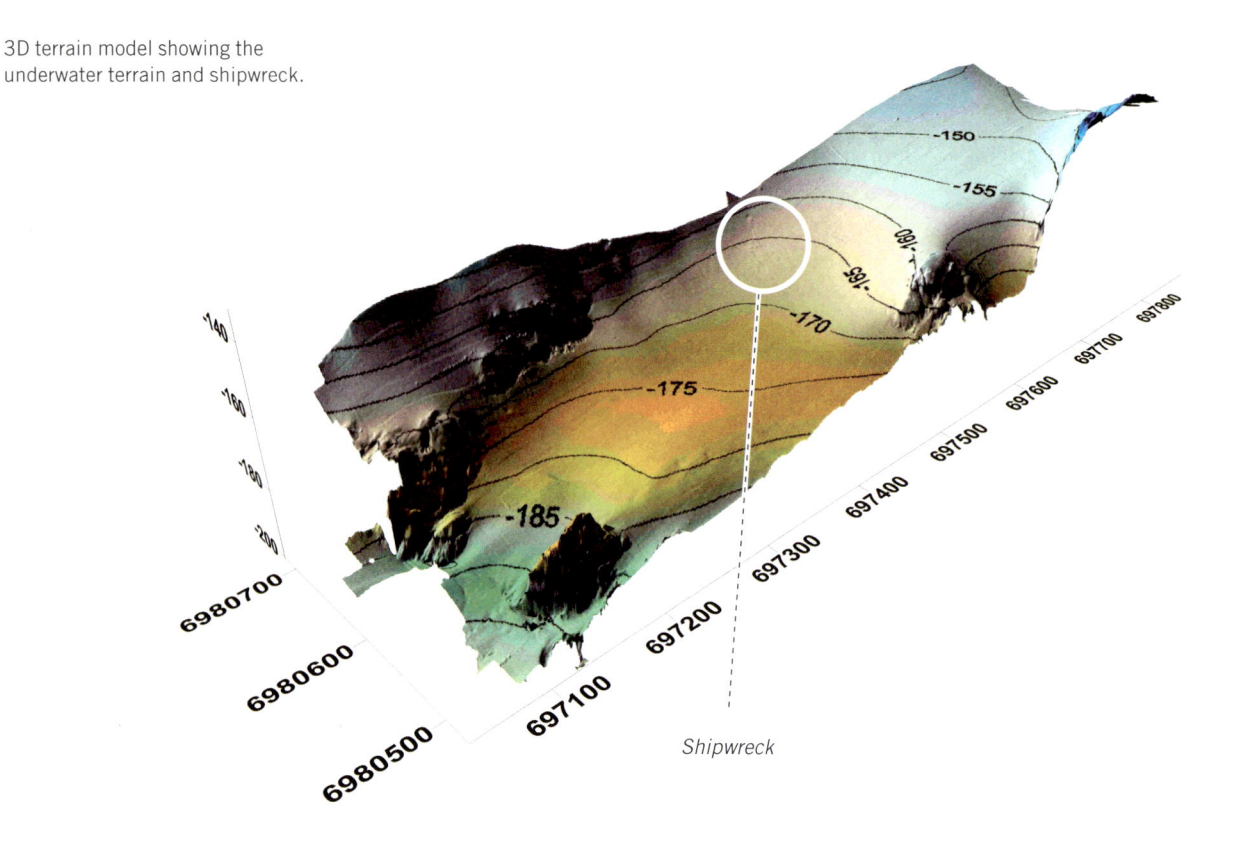

site, including the area of the wreck itself and the spread of artefacts and other archaeological material in the underwater terrain. The survey used multi-beam sonars, side-scan sonar and sub-bottom profiler as well as visual observations from ROV cameras to document the shipwreck and surrounding seafloor.

The few hectic days on board *Geobay* showed the entire site to be quite big in size, some 700 x 200 metres, as the archaeological material was spread widely around the wooden remnants of the hull structure at the centre of the site [2]. Even though the main wooden structure would not be directly influenced by the pipeline routes, the spread of artefacts clearly extended through the planned pipeline route corridors quite substantially.

An additional issue was that it was unclear whether or not the stern of the ship, which would be situated closest to the pipelines, was hidden by sediment. Without excavating this part of the site it would be impossible to determine if the stern section was in situ or alternatively had broken off and been deposited elsewhere, possibly even on a pipeline route.

Results from the survey in May 2004 therefore helped little in finding a way to avoid the conflict with the Act and time was running out. The installation schedule for the pipelines was starting to become jeopardised by the marine archaeological discoveries.

On 22 July 2004, the Norwegian Directorate for Cultural Heritage (Riksantikvaren) made an interim decision. Data collected during the 2003 season and in May 2004 were inadequate for the Directorate to process Hydro's application and define the scope of archaeological excavations needed before the pipeline could be installed in the wreck area. The Directorate wanted other sub-bottom profiler systems and trial pits to be used to establish whether more archaeological material was covered by sediment in the pipeline route.

It also required the southern part of the wreck to be excavated to resolve the stern part dilemma. If the stern part of the wreck was deposited in situ with the rest of the hull remnants, and the sediments inside the pipeline corridor in the wreck area did not contain more archaeological surprises, Hydro would receive permission to proceed.

Under the schedule for the Ormen Lange gas project, the work could begin in the 2004 season and continue in 2005. This was a win-win agreement that both parties could live with and preparations began for the two major cruises of the marine archaeological project.

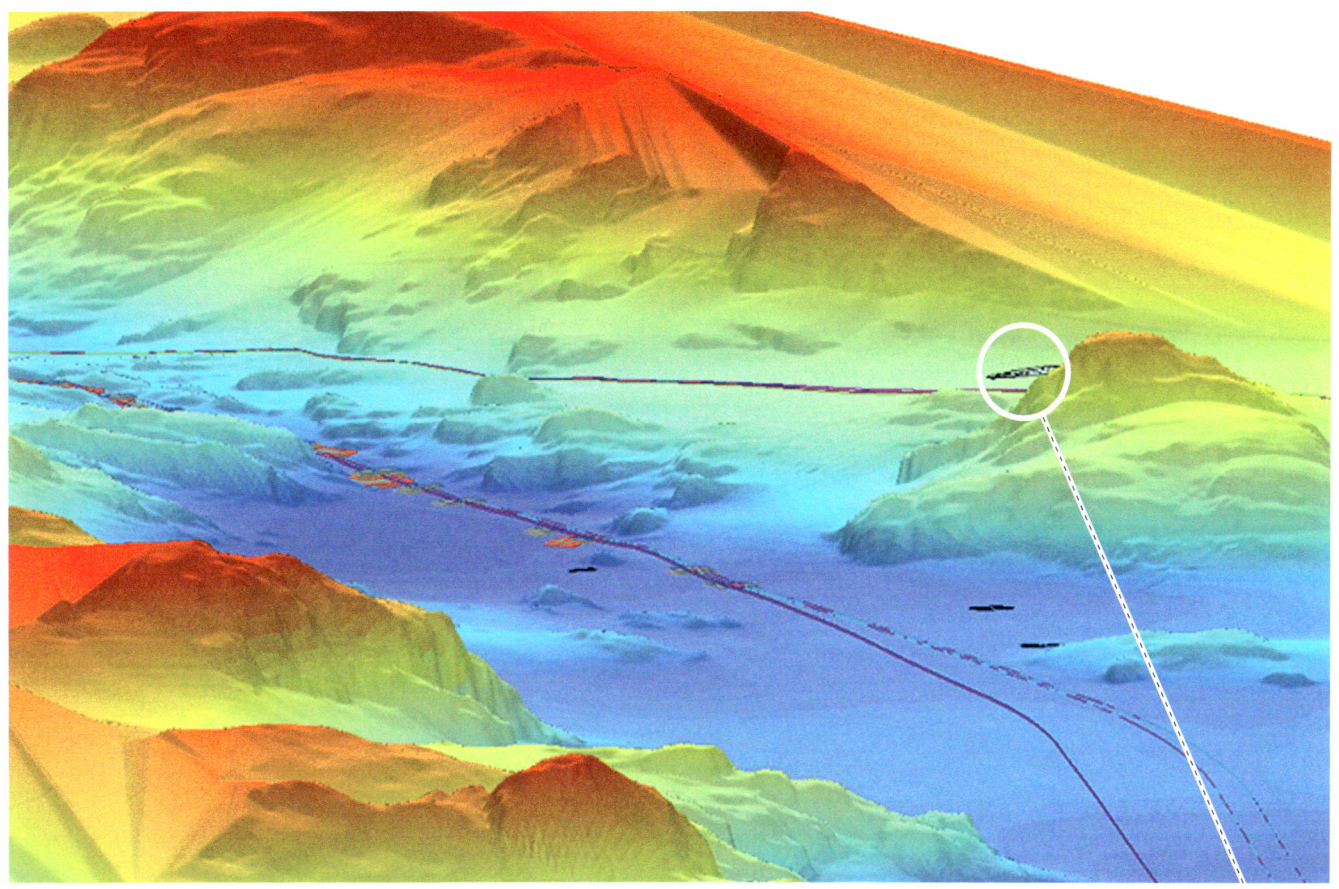

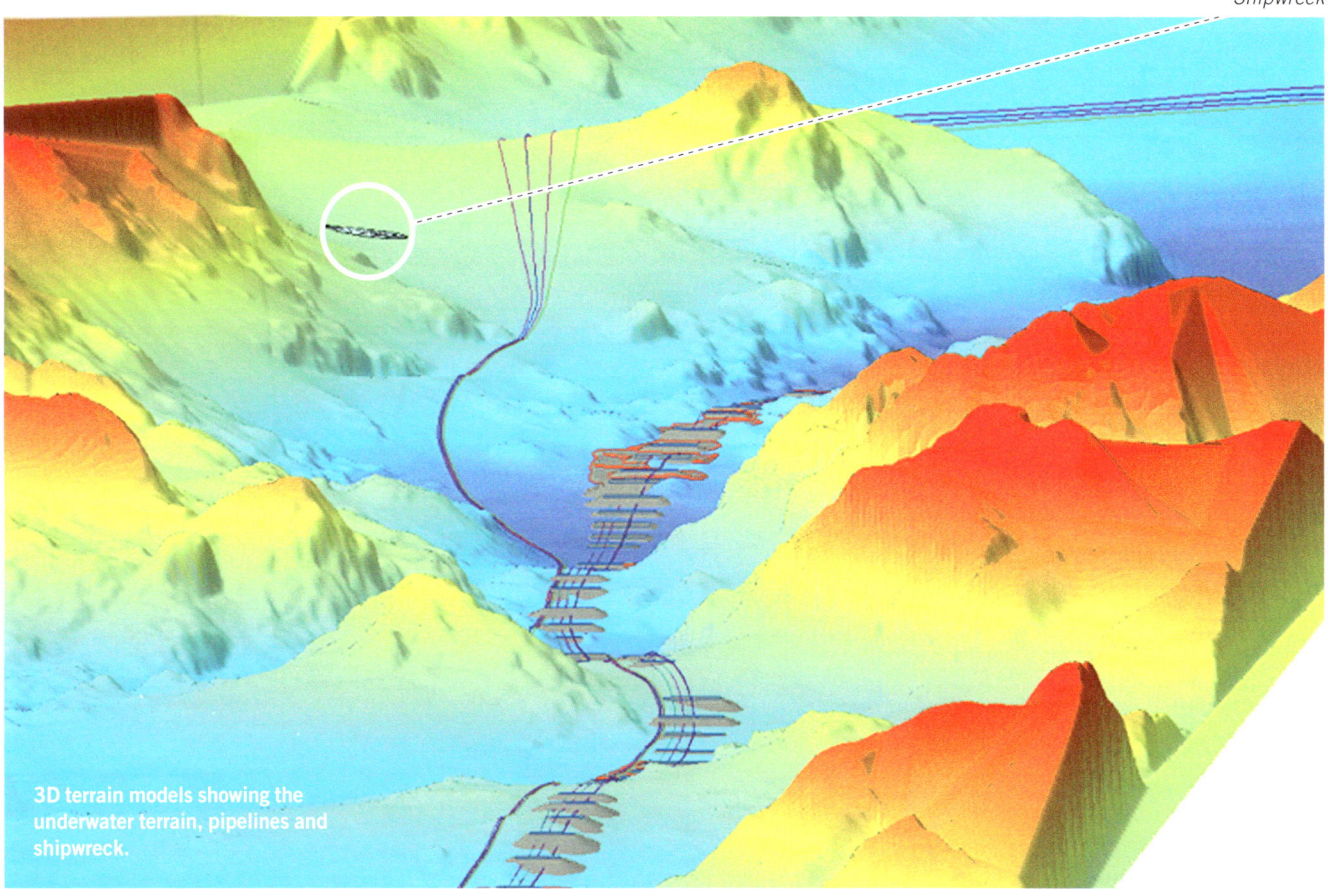

Shipwreck

3D terrain models showing the underwater terrain, pipelines and shipwreck.

The ROV has been launched and is descending towards the shipwreck site deep below the research vessel *Cehili*.

CHAPTER 14

THE DEEPEST DIG

The team had to use advanced technology and new methods to document and excavate the site, making it the most technologically advanced underwater archaeology project ever undertaken in the world [1]. Scuba diving was impossible due to the site being at a depth of 165–170 metres and so all mapping, surveying, sampling and excavation was conducted by remotely operated vehicles (ROVs).

ROVs are well-known tools in marine archaeology. Less advanced versions, mostly designed for the oil industry, have been used by archaeologists to locate wrecks and collect objects for many years. However, these bulky devices have often disturbed the very sites they were sent to investigate. They were simply never designed for marine archaeological tasks, and thus deep sea archaeological operations have traditionally been limited to documentation and sampling.

When it became clear that extensive documentation and even excavation of the site would be necessary prior to installation of the pipelines, it was decided that NTNU's unique experience would be used to develop a special ROV for marine archaeology.

The system was designed in close co-operation with Norwegian ROV manufacturer Sperre AS who subsequently also built and operated the ROV. The two-tonne electrical work-class ROV is capable of carrying the special tooling needed to document and even excavate deepwater sites. Another smaller ROV was used as a backup system, for film documentation, and for tasks that required simultaneous use of two ROV systems.

This set-up successfully enabled the project to perform all the tasks that previously could only be done by divers in shallow waters. The ROV systems were operated from the research vessel *Cehili* which was anchored with a 4-point mooring system over the shipwreck site.

DETAILED DOCUMENTATION
The shipwreck site and the area surrounding the wreck were surveyed using video cameras to establish the full extent of the site, and to locate objects that may have become separated from the main wreck site over time. Detailed visual inspection of a 400 by 800 metre area surrounding the main shipwreck structure revealed 179 man-made artefacts in the vicinity of the shipwreck. The inspection also revealed a spread of shipwreck-related artefacts to the south and southwest of the wreck – down-

The purpose-built ROV was designed to complete even the most advanced marine archaeological tasks in deep water.

hill from the main wooden structure towards the planned pipeline routes.

This visual inspection used seven high-resolution video cameras, including broadcast cameras on the ROV. Special designed gas lamps were used to give far better wide area illumination than traditional lights. [2]

Other cameras were used to collect videomosaics and photomosaics of the main shipwreck site. Due to rapid attenuation of light underwater, the only way to get a large scale view of a large site is to build up a mosaic of smaller local images. The mosaic technique was used to construct an image with a far larger field of view and level of resolution than could be obtained with a single photograph.

The photomosaics were created by flying the ROV over the site at a constant altitude with the camera pointed parallel to the site. After the site had been completely photographed, the collected images were processed in a software program that joins images so the borders are not visible.

The delicate work of collecting data with sufficient accuracy required the ROV to be equipped with closed-loop control. This enables it to operate in an automatic mode and to run dense survey patterns over the site along pre-programmed survey lines, at constant altitude. This is a task that a human operator cannot do with the required accuracy.

An array of acoustic Kongsberg LBL transponders was installed around the wreck site and used to position the ROV, and to provide the main control parameter for closed-loop control along with a doppler log and other motion sensors. The data was entered into a specially-developed software package developed in co-operation with EIVA to output the necessary control signals for the ROV. The ROV therefore became a hybrid between ROV and AUV (Autonomus Underwater Vehicle), the first ROV of its kind.

It was expected that archaeological material may be completely buried underneath sediment and could not be located by visual aids or sonar. The area surrounding the wreck site was therefore surveyed with additional state-of-the-art subbottom profilers and magnetometres to determine the full extent of the site buried beneath the sediment.

Three different subbottom sets were collected. The data was reviewed in its raw format without conversion to prevent any degradation in resolution. Targets were only selected if they were single

Before *After*

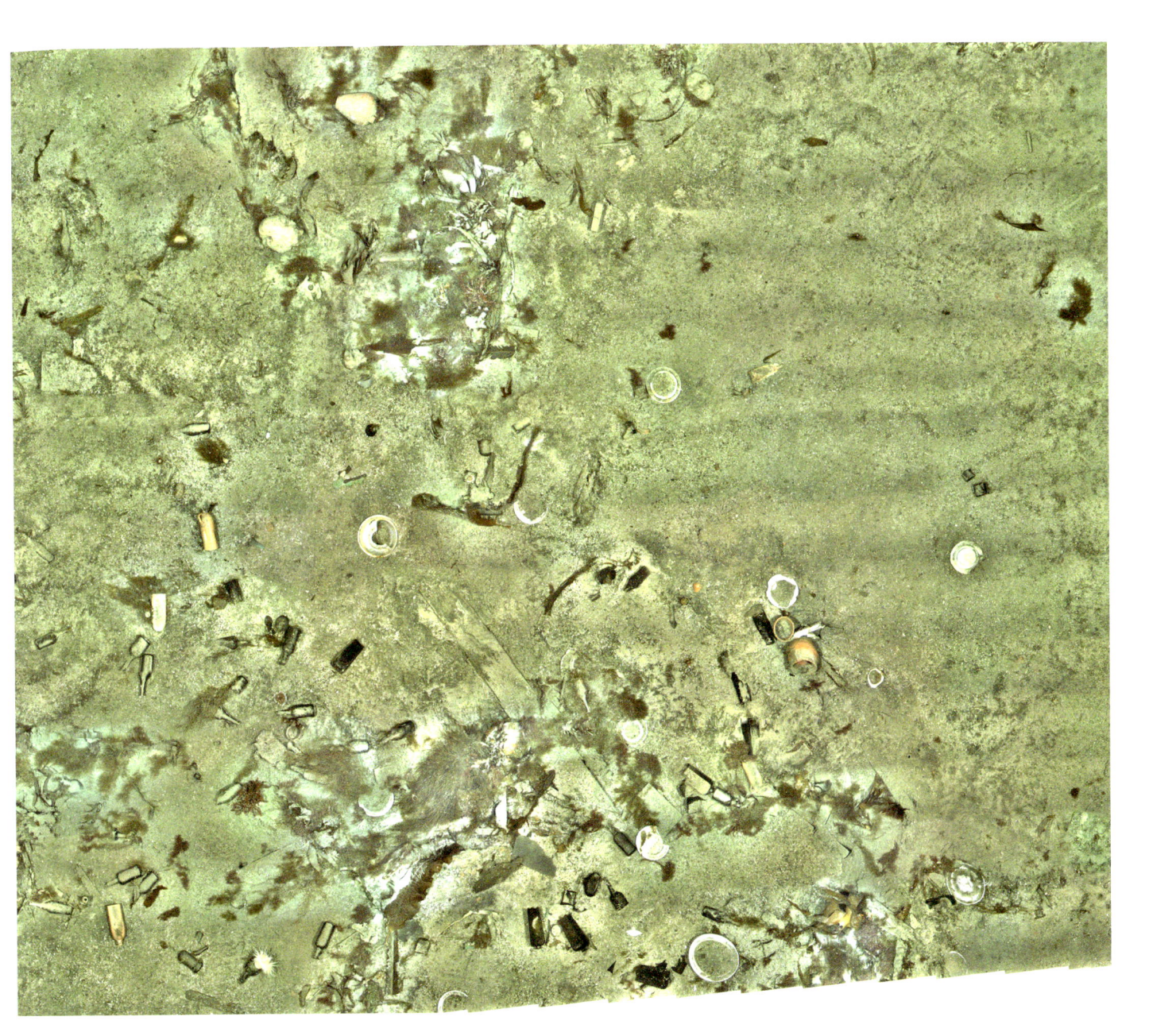

Site plans of the shipwreck site before and after the investigations

Underwater images from the project. The ROV is docked on the excavation frame to investigate artefacts on the seabed.

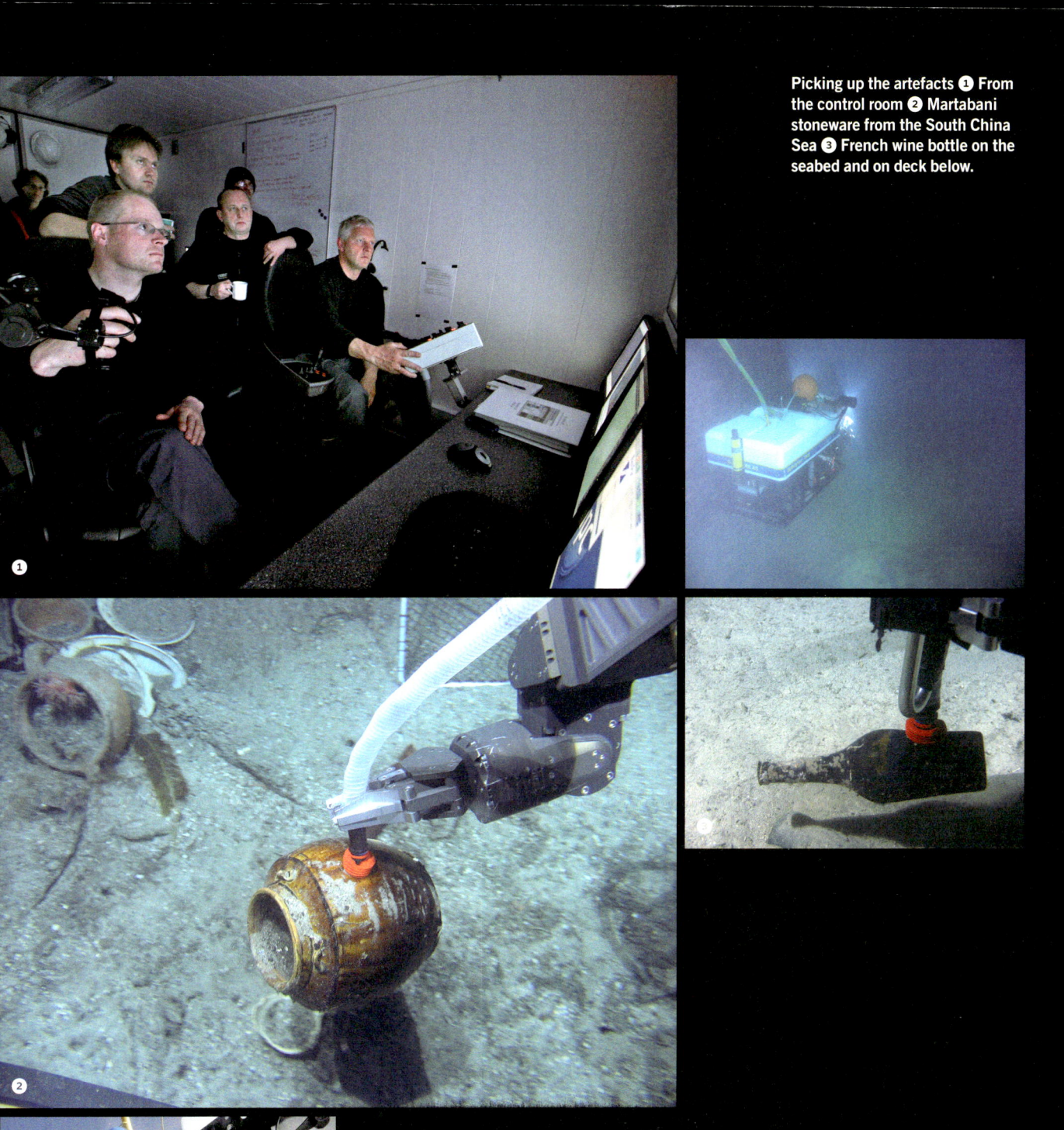

Picking up the artefacts ❶ From the control room ❷ Martabani stoneware from the South China Sea ❸ French wine bottle on the seabed and on deck below.

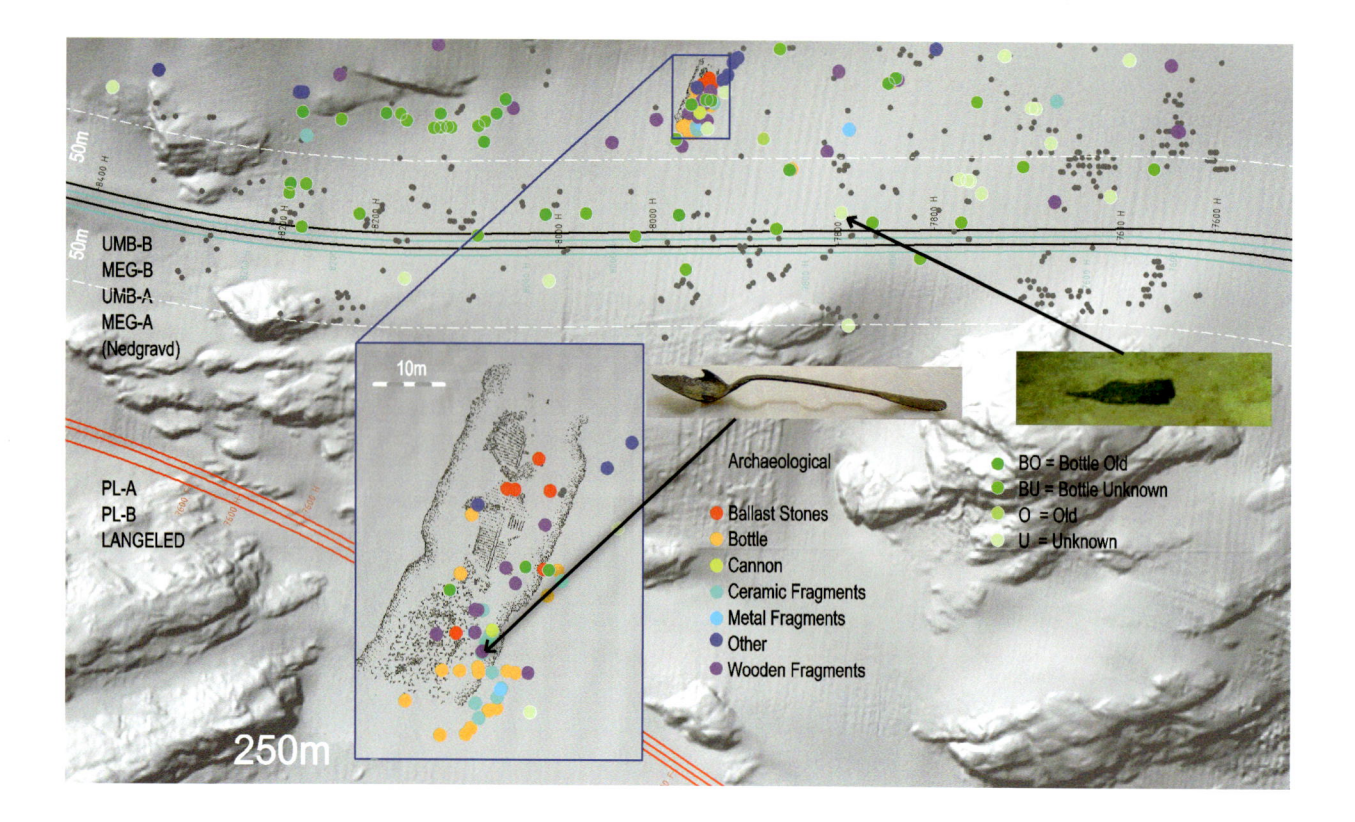

'point-source' or a contiguous series of anomalies and/or diffractions, regardless of amplitude, in the near surface sediment and not deeper than the pre-post glacial sediment boundary. Any features/anomalies that were obviously of geological origin, with or without seafloor expression, were not selected as targets.

Any anomalies due to acoustic, electric and/or environmental noise in the data were also excluded from selection as a target whenever possible. The data was plotted in maps and compared with the available bathymetry, side-scan sonar and photo-mosaics, and correlated with cultural material and modern debris to determine the origin of the anomaly in its respective data set.

Based on the subbottom results, the extent of the main shipwreck site beneath the sediment with no seafloor expression and not visual by ROV inspection were postulated to extend south-southwest from the southernmost visible artefact on the seafloor, and the site extent was also enlarged to the west and east.

The results of the subbottom surveys further away from the main shipwreck site proved more difficult. A few areas were selected for further study based on the distribution of clusters of subbottom anomalies, where all subbottom data coincided. These areas were located to the southwest of the wreck and along the pipeline routes, with priority given to anomalies lying along the pipeline route corridors, and between the corridor and the wreck. In this way, any anomalies/artefacts at risk of disturbance or damage due to their proximity to the route of the pipeline corridors would be examined.

A series of test pits were dug to try and correlate the occurrence of targets in the subbottom data to buried artefacts and/or sediment type. Within the wreck site there was an apparent correlation between the higher density of localised higher amplitude reflectors and disturbed sub-seabed sediments, which correlate with the location of the wreck.

An extension of the main wreck site was evident through the excavation as several metres of wooden construction were uncovered to the west, east and south of the visible structure.

Further from the wreck, the clusters were less obvious, and there was limited evidence of a direct relationship between the presence of a higher amplitude reflector on the subbottom data and any buried artefact. Instead, the results of the excavations indicate a relationship between the presence of higher amplitude reflectors and sediment

The detailed surveys enabled the archaeologists to map every man-made artefact on the seafloor in the area, represented by dots on this map.

variation, particularly the presence of fauna-rich sediments and areas with higher densities of shell fragments and small clasts. The results suggest that for small clusters of anomalies, it is difficult to determine from the subbottom data whether the anomalies are indicative of a buried artefact or a soil attribute (high organic content, shell fragments and clastic material).

PRE-EXCAVATION CONCLUSION

The results of the initial fieldwork were not sufficient to answer important questions about the shipwreck and the extent to which the shipwreck site would be damaged by the planned pipelines. Additional fieldwork was therefore initiated in 2005 to partially excavate the stern section of the shipwreck.

The pre-excavation documentation formed the basis for a preliminary site analysis and site plan. The results of the multibeam survey, sidescan survey, detailed visual inspection, sub-bottom survey, magnetometer survey and test pits indicated that there was limited spread of material from the shipwreck, visible on the surface and buried beneath the sediments.

However, large sections of the main shipwreck site were believed to be buried beneath a thicker layer of sediment. It was therefore decided that these parts of the site should be uncovered and partially excavated to establish the extent to which it would be damaged by the pipeline construction and to learn more about the shipwreck site itself.

EXCAVATION

An archaeological excavation of a sunken historic ship is difficult, even at shallow depths. Doing it at 170 metres was extremely complex.

Groundbreaking technology made the world's first deepwater archaeological excavation possible.

Most importantly the project team designed a unique excavation support frame to investigate in detail and partially excavate the shipwreck. The 10 x 10 metre steel frame was made by Sperre AS in Notodden and taken to Bud where it was put together. Hanging from the stern of the local support ship *Rambo* it was successfully lowered to the seafloor and placed over the shipwreck site, its legs resting just outside the wreck site. The ROV would then dock onto a platform on the steel frame. From the control room of the research vessel, the ROV pilot could move the docking platform in

The revolutionary subsea excavation frame developed for the project combined with the purpose built ROV enabled archaeologists for the first time ever to excavate a deep water shipwreck with the same precision as land-based archaeology.

all directions on the frame using motorized cogwheels. Sitting still on the docking platform just above the shipwreck, the ROV would pose no risk to the thousands of fragile artefacts scattered on the seabed, and could be used to document, excavate and recover artefacts.

The only problem was that when the ROV docked onto the platform the first time, nothing happened. The system did not work. All the hours that had gone into construction and installation had come to nothing. The next week was spent recovering, repairing and then installing the frame once more. This time everything worked perfectly.

Positioning of the ROV platform is based on rotation sensors on the frame, backed by high resolution directional sonar sensors with accuracy of less than a centimetre. Position input from the LBL system was also recorded. The frame allowed the archaeologists to excavate the seafloor with great precision so the maximum amount of data could be extracted while carefully handling any objects to be recovered.

The combination of the specially designed ROV and the excavation frame enabled the team to conduct a systematic excavation, equivalent to a land-based excavation, at a greater depth than ever before.

A specially designed marine archaeology dredge was developed by GTO Sediment to remove sediment and uncover fragile items. An altimeter was used to measure trench depth. Excavated sediments were filtered through a sediment collection basket. Two hundred and fifty small artefacts were later collected from this device.

When an artefact had been uncovered from a cultural layer it was picked up using a 7-function

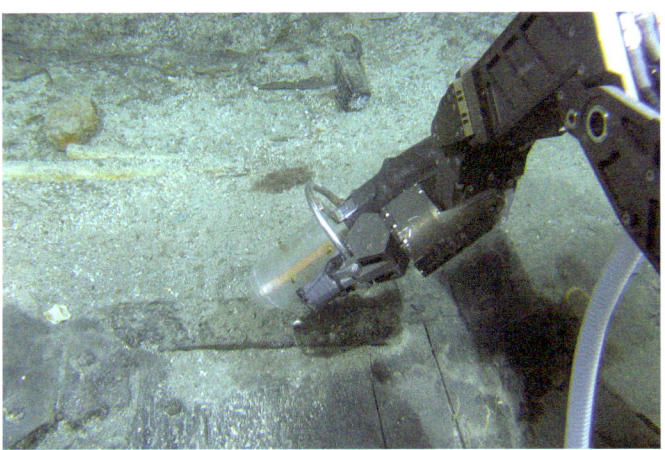

Excavating, picking up and placing an artefact in the recovery basket.

Kraft Raptor force feedback manipulator arm. The force feedback function enabled it to pick up fragile artefacts, but the main recovery tool for artefacts was a specially developed suction picker that picks up artefacts using a small suction cup connected to a pump by a hose. When the pump is started the suction cup can be used to pick up even the most fragile artefacts. More than 200 artefacts were recovered without any damage. Some artefacts were also lifted using specially developed tools that were constructed onsite.

Artefacts were stored in internal collection baskets in the ROV or lifted in external collection baskets. They ranged from tiny buttons to large ceramic vessels and stone plates more than 50 kilograms in weight.

The project also developed a software module to record images and data on artefacts as they were excavated from the shipwreck. All significant data was recorded in real time, while video from the ROV-mounted cameras were stored using a digital video recording system.

This technology enabled the team to successfully complete the first ever deepwater archaeological shipwreck excavation. Nearly 500 artefacts were recovered from the site, making it the most comprehensive and detailed excavation ever carried out by an archaeological institution in deep water. The project was successful in developing equipment and methods that made it possible to perform tasks that could previously only be done by scuba divers in shallow waters. Archaeologists can now investigate and excavate cultural heritage sites in deep water with the same precision and standards as on land, something that has not previously been possible. [3]

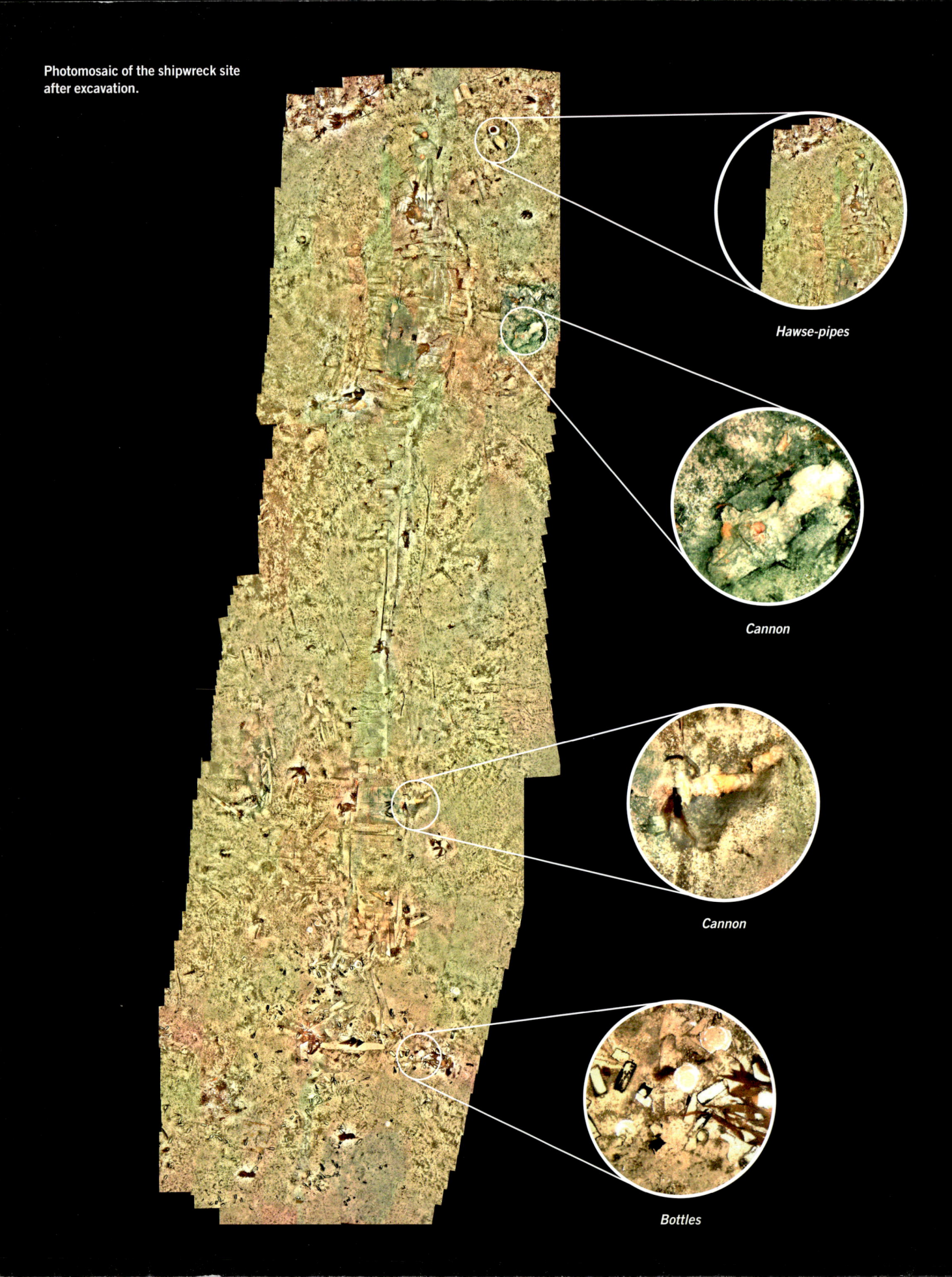

Photomosaic of the shipwreck site after excavation.

Hawse-pipes

Cannon

Cannon

Bottles

CHAPTER 15   THE SITE BELOW

Months of surveying and excavating during the 2003–2005 seasons generated an impressive set of data and information about the 18th century shipwreck site of Bud.

Archaeology is like doing a puzzle. Archaeologists collect the data as systematically as possible, using their eyes, hands and in the case of deepwater archaeology, using sensors on technologically advanced equipment. Yet all the while, little is known about what information all this data represents.

After the fieldwork is done, there is a long, demanding, and highly complex process to sort, study and interpret the data – to try and put the pieces of the puzzle together. Interpretations and theories developed onboard a research vessel during the fieldwork phase are often confronted, changed, or even rejected during the intensive research back at the office and in the lab.

"Mission accomplished" is a phrase not heard in the world of archaeology. Archaeologists are often left with the feeling that there is more that could have been done, or that things could have been done differently. There is however, always a day that marks the end of fieldwork on a project, at least for the time being.

Thoughts of this sort were in the heads of the archaeological team as it prepared to leave the site in August 2005. The equipment was packed; artefacts from the shipwreck were prepared for transport to the conservation laboratory of the University Museum. Goodbyes were said to the Russian, Indonesian, Indian and Norwegian crewmembers on the *Cehili* that had taken such good care of the team and become good friends, and to research colleagues from the US, Britain and Norway.

But the story was not over, and this particular shipwreck with its history and hidden secrets will remain an important part of several people's lives in years to come.

While writing this book the data is still being studied, although the information gained so far has been shared with colleagues in the marine archaeological community through introductory articles and outline presentations at international conferences and seminars.

What do we know now, regarding the site and shipwreck itself in regard to its state of preservation?

Regarding the state of preservation of the wreck, the most important influence has been a small creature: the shipworm (*teredinidae*). Shipworms are the biggest enemy of shipwrecks in the Atlantic waters of the northern hemisphere. These tiny but ravenous creatures eat all but the hardest wood found on the seabed. Wood borers are clams that bore into wood with a rasping action of their clam shell grinders. When borer larvae touch wood they quickly bore in. Once inside, the organism follows the wood grain, creating a tunnel about 0.8 centimetres in diameter. Research data from the US Navy shows that an entire wooden wreck could be devoured within 25–50 years.

It has long been believed that deepwater shipwrecks escape this fate and rest in a perfect state of preservation but this project dispelled that idea. Shipworms also thrive as deep as 170 metres, and other biological and chemical processes assist in disintegrating sunken ship hulls. Most of the wood has dissappeared, and the data left for marine archaeologists is from elements that were immediately buried in the seabed when the wreck occurred and/or were protected by non-organic ship cargo.

The team also conducted a marine biology investigation to provide a brief overview of the benthic macrofauna and biology of the wreck site. These also influence wreck sites by burrowing and other destructive processes. The delicacy of the site and location of the wreck when the investigation was carried out ruled out the use of destructive sampling equipment. The investigation was therefore designed as a more superficial qualitative inspection rather than the "qualitative initial inspection" normally required for environmental investigations.

The collected material indicated a normal number of species. However, two species were found that have only been identified a few times before (Amphiura griegi and Hero formosa). They are little known in Norwegian waters and have scattered distribution, so the find is an important contribution to knowledge about their distribution in the area. While these two species could be considered rare given the number of investigations in shelf waters, the areas around Bud and Hustadvika are among the least investigated along the coast. [1]

Wrecks typically become artificial reefs and provide hiding and feeding areas for a range of organisms. A diverse mobile fauna is often documented on wrecks in places where there is typically less mobile fauna, such as wrecks located on muddy bottoms. This is clearly visible when wrecks are filmed. By creating an artificial reef, a wreck will attract mobile species of benthic macro fauna from nearby areas with similar habitats such as bedrock and kelp, gravel and stones.

Normally the species occupying a wreck site

Photomosaic of the excavated area after excavation.

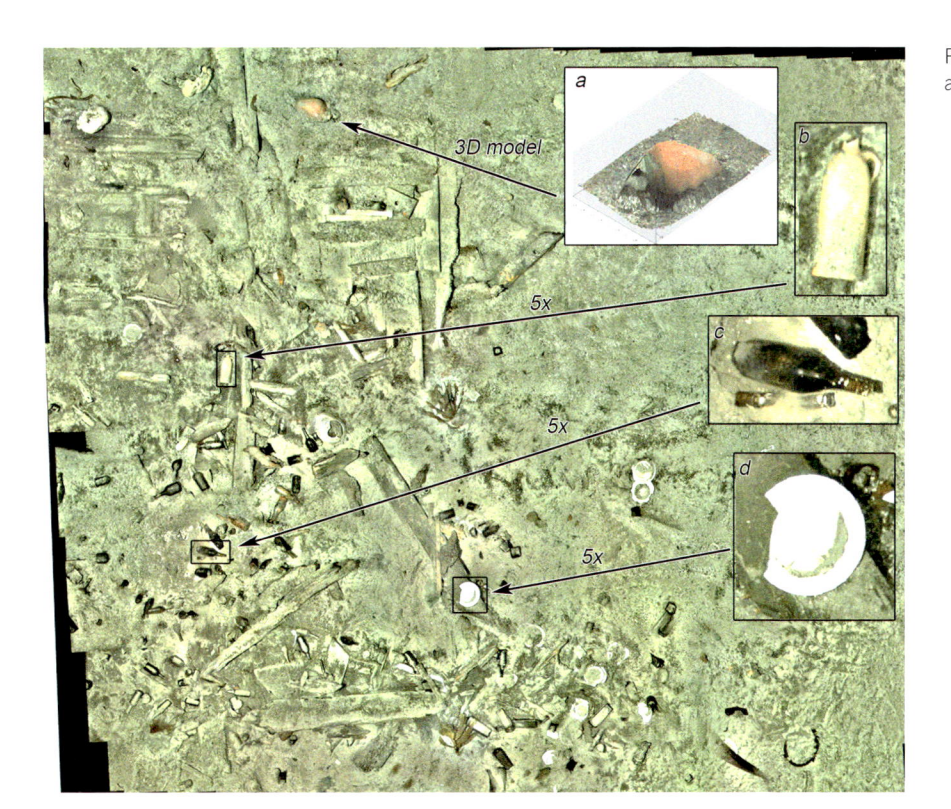

would be similar to those found in surrounding areas, assuming healthy environmental conditions.

Artefacts provide hard substrate for organisms to attach, and several specimens were actually found attached to artefacts. [2]

However, the investigation showed that the overall marine life in the area has returned to normal and that the initial effect of the shipwreck on marine life as a source of nutrients for woodborers and an artificial reef has ended and that normal conditions once again dominate the wreck site.

During the 2004 and 2005 field seasons, much effort was put into determining if the *unseen* stern section of the ship was still in situ but covered by thicker layers of sediment, or if it had separated from the rest of the ship and was in another area, possibly creating an even greater conflict between the pipeline and cultural heritage requirements.

As the survey methods (sonar, subbottom profilers and magnetometer) failed to provide conclusive answers to this critical question, trial excavations of the stern area needed to be made. The excavations revealed that although much disintegrated, the stern section of the hull was in situ and covered by a thick layer of sediments.

The high degree of disintegration could be due to damage caused before the ship went down (impact with rocks on shore for example), or by the stern section hitting the seabed first while sinking.

The trial excavations in the stern area disturbed the thin sediment covering parts of the midship and bow sections and exposed the preserved remnant of the lowest part of the hull, including keel, skin and lower fragments of ribs throughout the length of the shipwreck.

The best-preserved section of the hull was found to be the round/oval shaped bow-section with a declining state of preservation along the hull structure towards the stern section.

The measurements and other preserved details of the hull lead the archaeologists to conclude the wreck was once a large and impressive full-rigged merchant sailing ship that sailed gracefully over the seas. The well-made hull was built in oak with some pine elements. The construction is undoubtedly of northwestern European origin, but due to the ship's state of preservation the team has not so far been able to determine its origin or what type of ship it was. More detailed comparative studies are required, but an educated guess is that it may be a barque. [3]

Iberian pottery, two hawse-pipes in the bow section, measurements of the hull constructions, Dutch gold coin, a wooden frame, and a small collection of artefacts.

Details of the wooden structure, with the inscription "SBII" and artefacts.

Documentation drawing of a Canton
China plate with double bottom.

CHAPTER 16

ONCE ON BOARD, NOW IN OUR COLLECTION

The major elements of the hull structures have been studied remotely via film, photo, and other images sent from the seabed to the control room from equipment installed on the ROV. The hull will remain forever in its final resting place. However, the many artefacts collected during the excavations provided a completely different experience when they could be studied in real life. When they were lifted onboard and the team could look at them close up and even touch them, the real story behind the wreckage and of the people onboard during those final hours was brought closer. The tools, utensils, navigational instruments and personal belongings now on deck were the very same the crew had been using onboard the fated ship.

Emotions were at a peak each time a new container filled with artefacts surfaced from the seafloor. Excitement and anticipation was in the air as the container was opened and the team gathered round to see what it held. Could the new artefacts answer any of the many questions? Could they help throw light on the story behind the wreck?

Archaeologists tend not to sort artefacts as being more or less important: every piece of archaeological material is a carrier of data and information that is an important part of the whole story. Often a tiny and apparently unspectacular item can later make a major contribution to studies and interpretations in the project.

When all containers were unloaded and sorted, a total of 489 artefacts in different categories and sub-categories had been collected from the shipwreck site over the three years of fieldwork from 2003 to 2005. Of these, 239 artefacts were specifically selected to be brought up by the ROV. The other 250 small artefacts were retrieved from the sediment collection box filled through plastic pipes by the excavation equipment while exploring the sediment.

The database of artefacts developed specifically for the project includes a set of recording categories for artefacts with their positions, photo images, and short descriptions. Each category is divided into sub-categories.

The nine main artefact categories are: Ship Components, Glass, Metal, Ceramic, Organic, Stone, Wood, Laboratory Samples, and Unknown. The distribution was as follows:

- 27 registrations of ship components with 7 in the sub-category of *planks*, 6 *frames*, 10 *rigging elements* and 4 in the sub-category *other*.

- 93 registrations of glass artefacts, with 43 in the sub-category *bottles-round*, 1 *drinking glass*, 14 *bottles-square* and 35 *other*.
- 185 registrations of metal artefacts, with 22 in sub-category *utensils* including navigational instruments, 52 *coins*, 1 *fastener-nail*, 87 in sub-category *other*, and 25 *unknown*, i.e. artefacts with functions that were not determined during field work.
- 67 registrations of ceramics, with 19 in the sub-category *porcelain/china plates*, 4 of *porcelain/china dishes*, 3 *porcelain/china cups*, 6 *porcelain/china teapots*, 7 *porcelain/china other*, 9 *stoneware bottles*, 7 *stoneware jugs*, 4 *stoneware cups* and 8 *stoneware other*.
- 16 registrations of organic material, with 1 in the sub-category *leather shoe* and 15 *other*.
- 9 registrations of stone artefacts, consisting of 1 in the sub-category *ballast* and 8 in the category *other*.
- 90 registrations of wooden artefacts, all within the sub-category *other*.

CERAMICS

This is the category analysed in most detail to date, predominantly by the archaeologist Ian Reed after the field work was completed. The following is based on his ceramics report from the project.

A total of 62 whole or partial ceramic vessels were recovered from the wreck site. Most of these are from Germany, England and China, with some from Holland, the Iberian Peninsula and South-East Asia. Some of the items, notably tableware, show obvious signs of use, but no attempt has been made here to distinguish cargo items from those used on board.

According to Ian Reed, the recovered vessels include Westerwald mineral water stoneware bottles from Germany, Frechen stoneware from Germany, North German and South Scandinavian redware, Delft tin-glazed earthenware (Holland), English Creamware, English Pearlware, Chinese porcelain (Canton wares and Nanking wares), Martabani stoneware (South China, Indo-China, Burma or Siam), diverse under-glaze blue wares (China), European porcelain, and Iberian wares (Catalonia and Portugal) [1]. Reeds report describes several categories of ceramics:

Westerwald mineral water bottles

A total of 9 cylindrical bottles were recovered. These bottles were produced at various workshops

A stoneware jug.

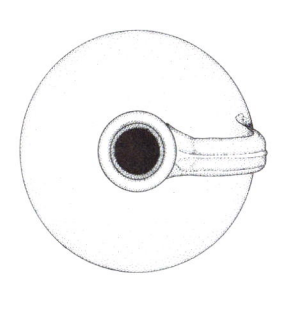

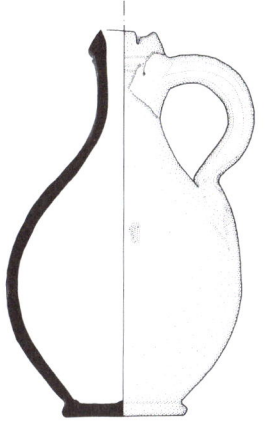

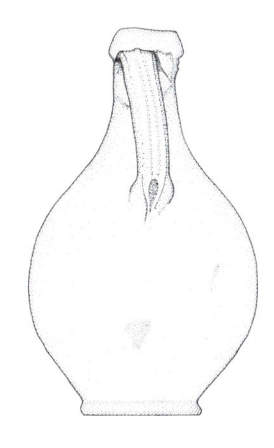

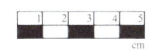

in the Westerwald, an area to the east of the Rhine between the Rivers Sieg and Lahn in Germany. The bottles are in a pale grey to cream stoneware and have a salt-glazed exterior varying in colour from greyish white to brown. The bottles were initially made by hand, with the form becoming more cylindrical towards the end of the 18th century. By the 19th century machine-made cylindrical bottles were produced and by 1745 the annual production of these bottles had reached 600,000. The bottles bear the stamp of the wells where they were filled.

All the bottles in this collection bear the seal of the mineral water well at Selters, and several have a dark blue circle painted around the seal. The name appears in a circle which contains either a cross with the initials CT in the lower two quarters on seven of the vessels, or a crown over the initials NW on two of the vessels. The first stands for Kur Trier who had a monopoly on the Selters walls from 1775, and the second for Nassau-Weilburg. In December 1802 Friederich, Fürst of Nassau-Weilburg took control of the wells at Selters and held it until September 1806 when the Duchy of Nassau was established.

The bottles are also marked with a letter and a number referring to the pottery town where they were produced and the number refers to the individual potter. Five of the bottles bear the letter 'B' indicating they were produced in Baumbach, one bears the letter 'H' probably for Hilscheid, two bear the letter 'N' for Nauert, and one bears the letter 'R' for Ransbach. Not all the potters' numbers are recorded and they did change occasionally. From Baumbach two of the vessels bear the number '3' used either by Johann Wingender or Peter Gerharz, and three bear the number '9', probably used by Jackob Krumeich. The marks from the other towns are less certain.

Frechen stoneware

Only three vessels of this type, all ceramic bottles, were collected. Frechen is a small town some 10 kilometres west of Cologne, Germany which produced pottery and stoneware from the 13th until the late 19th century. The most common vessels were jugs and bottles. From the second half of the 16th century, Frechen coarseware began to dominate the export market and became the most widely traded of all German stoneware. The fabric of the finds is a reduced grey stoneware and the exterior is covered with a salt glaze, usually brown.

Dutch square case bottle.

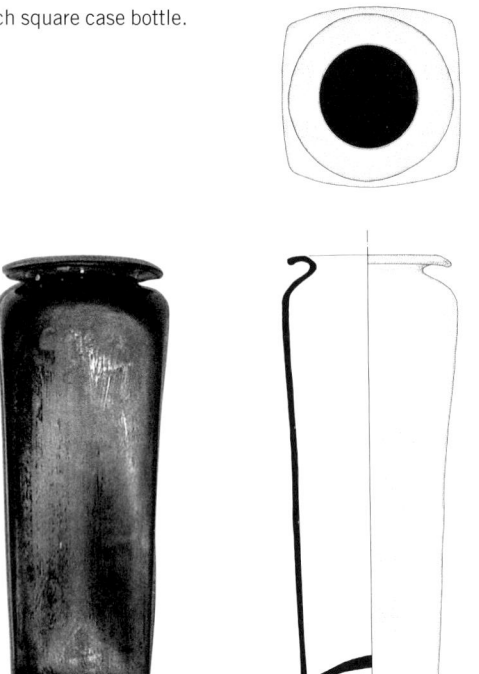

Other German stonewares

Utilitarian vessels were produced at a large number of potteries in Germany, including Westerwald and Frechen. These are generally very similar in fabric and form and have no diagnostic features to associate them with one production centre or another. Two of the vessels collected are small bottles while the third is an ointment jar. It is possible that the bottles are products of the Frechen kilns.

North German and South Scandinavian redware

This group of redware includes products from a number of different centres across a broad geographical area. Vessels produced in similar fabrics to those recovered here have been found in north Germany where they are believed to have been produced, but wasters found in Copenhagen and Stockholm show they were also produced in Scandinavia. The fabric is generally hard and ranges in colour from orange-red to brick-red. The glaze, which normally only occurs on the inside, varies from bright orange to dark green-brown and even blackish-green. Many of the vessels produced have pronounced external rilling.

Five vessels of this type ware recovered, four of these are jars of various shapes and sizes and the fifth is part of a plate. One of the vessels is a double-handled jar with an internal light-brown glaze and the characteristic external rilling. A smaller jar without handles is in a slightly darker fabric and unglazed. There is also a small slightly flared jar which is also completely unglazed. The last jar is flared and has a dark brown internal glaze which also covers the upper part of the exterior. The plate fragment has a brick-red fabric and traces of a slip-coating and decoration in yellow and green.

The vessels here are difficult to date as these types of wares were produced over a period of at least 300 years. The shape of the double-handle jar and the fragment of plate however suggest a date not earlier than the 18th century.

Delft tin-glazed earthenware

The fabric of these wares is usually soft, whitish or pinkish-buff or cream with occasional red iron oxide inclusions. The most famous of the production centres is Delft, Holland. The four items recovered have a white tin glaze internally and externally and were drug jars or ointment pots. Three have a standard shape from the early 17th century; the fourth does not have the waisted base.

Field conservation of artefacts.

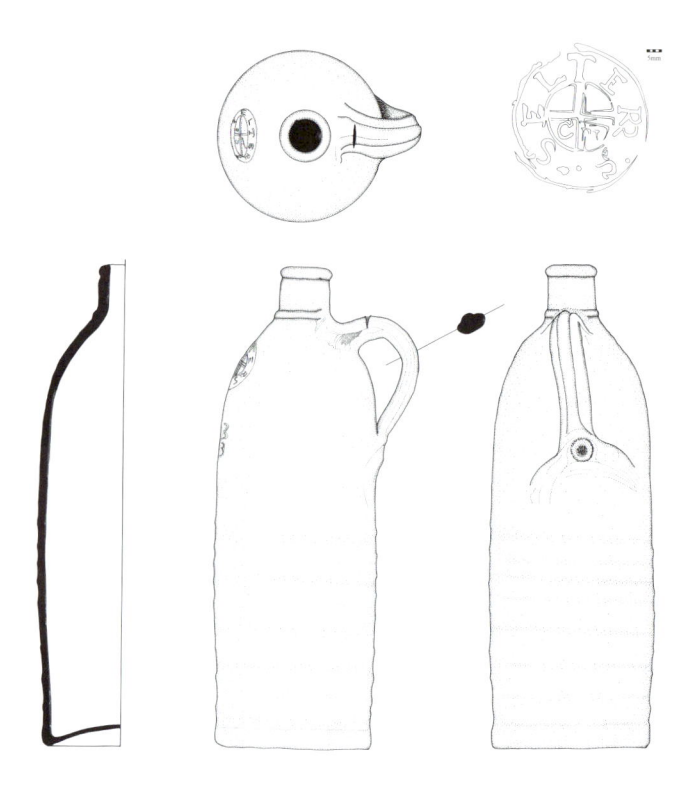

Documentation drawings and a picture of German Selters mineral water bottle.

Creamware

Creamware ceramics were first produced in the 1740s at a large number of centres throughout England, but the similar quality and shape from the different centres makes it difficult to attribute individual pieces to specific places. In England it was highly fashionable until the 1780s and despite a decline in popularity was still produced in certain areas in the 1820s. From the early 19th century this ware became established at centres throughout Europe.

Creamware is made from clay with calcined flint added and has a lead glaze which gives it a rich cream colour which became paler as firing and glazing techniques improved during the 18th century.

Fifteen pieces of creamware were recovered of which 6 were plates, 4 were serving dishes, and there was 1 gravy boat, 3 bowls and 1 lid. All of the plates had plain borders and all but one have the 'Bath' pattern with a slightly upturned edge, and the last a scalloped edge in the 'Royal' pattern. Three of the oval serving dishes have 'Bath' pattern borders and the fourth has a scalloped edge.

Five of the plates are marked. Three have the factory mark Sᵀ ANTHONYS, with two also having the workman's mark x, and one with the workman's mark ♦. The other two plates bear workman's mark *. St. Anthony's Pottery was founded in Newcastle-on-Tyne about 1780 and produced both creamware and earthenware. The mark on these pieces is thought to have been in use until 1804, although some scholars argue that it may have been in use up to 1820.

Pearlware

This term is used for a ware originally produced by Josiah Wedgwood from c.1779. To make his creamware less yellow and more like porcelain he added cobalt oxide to the glaze to provide a bluish tinge and this became the dominant ware in England from the 1790s to 1830s. The saucer has machine produced ribs and is decorated with a straw pattern in blue, while the lid is plain.

Chinese porcelain

Fourteen pieces of Chinese porcelain were recovered, including plates and a cup. Thirteen pieces are decorated in underglaze blue, and one in overglaze enamels. The underglazed blue wares consist of Nanking wares Canton ware and a group of miscellaneous ware.

Canton China transported by the ship.

Nanking ware

The decoration on Nanking ware is closely related to the Willow pattern which became common from the 1790s. These wares have higher quality than general export porcelain, and a specific square cell diaper border outlined with a spearhead border and more general landscapes. Only two vessels can be attributed to this group, an octagonal plate and an oval lid.

Canton wares

These wares were produced in the Province of Ching-Te-Chen and then sent by the East India Trading Company to the port of Canton where they were decorated by Chinese artists. Characteristic for this ware is the border which has a blue lattice network and inner border of wavy or scalloped lines known as clouds. They were subsequently shipped to Europe and America in the holds of cargo ships which resulted in them becoming known as ballast ware. These wares became common imports from the beginning of the 19th century.

Eight pieces of Canton ware were recovered including 3 hot-plates, 3 octagonal or sub-octagonal plates and 2 small circular plates. All of these have a landscape decoration in the willow pattern style.

Diverse underglaze blue wares

The remaining pieces, 2 plates and a dish, all have floral designs in underglaze blue. The motif in the dish includes a chrysanthemum which is a symbol for autumn.

Overglaze enamelled decoration

Only one vessel, a cup, is decorated in this way. The enamel has deteriorated and the decorative motif cannot easily be identified, but black dots around the rim and part of a floral design can be discerned. These elements are common on the poor quality export porcelain produced from the late 18th century.

European porcelain

The technology to produce hard-paste porcelain was rediscovered in Europe in the early 18th century and the first factory was opened at Meissen in 1710. Meissen guarded the secret closely for some 40 years, but during the second half of the 18th century porcelain was produced in this way by 23 factories in Germany. Factories were also established in France, Denmark and Sweden during the period.

Five pieces of European porcelain were recov-

Studying some of the recovered artefacts on deck.
Ayse D. Atauz, left, and Madli Hjermann.

European porcelain.

ered: a coffee pot, a teapot, a cup, and two lids. All the pieces are decorated with a type of straw-pattern in underglaze blue; the first three are decorated in a light blue, while the two lids are decorated in dark blue. The first three pieces are also marked; the coffee pot and the teapot both have a capital 'R' painted on the base while the cup has a hitherto unidentified painted mark.

The 'R' suggests the coffee pot and teapot were produced at the Gotha factory in Thuringia, Germany, which was in operation from 1757. The products retained the late rococo style with early decoration in underglaze blue, mainly blade, stalk or straw-pattern reminiscent of the Meissen straw-flower pattern. The 'R' mark was in use from 1795.

Iberian wares

Two vessels from the Iberian Peninsula were recovered, a *cantaro* and a bottle. The *cantaro*, a pitcher to hold liquid, is in a slightly micaceous redware and has a bib of green around the top and in two diagonal lines down the body. These vessels are still produced today in most areas of Spain in a variety of fabrics; redwares of this type are known to have been produced in Catalonia.

The bottle has a long neck and a flared mouth with a worn irregular rim. The fabric is a micaceous hard sandy dark red-brown. This type of ware is often known as Merida-type ware, but its production seems to have centred in the Alentejo, Portugal. Analysis of these wares has shown that there at least six distinct fabrics suggesting that they may have been produced over quite a large area of the Iberian Peninsula.

Martabani stoneware

This is an underfired cream stoneware with some red inclusions and with a glaze which is usually dark brown-black, but can vary and is often streaked as in the case of this vessel. The vessel forms are limited to storage jars varying from 30 to 120 centimetres in height and usually have a short neck and loops for tying on a lid or cover.

These storage jars were produced in south China, Indo-China, Burma and Siam, and were traded from Martaban which lies in Burma on the east coast of the Andaman Sea, east of the Irrawaddy delta and Rangoon. They were not traded to north-west Europe but went mainly to the Philippines and Indonesia. They were produced from the 13th/14th century up until the 19th century and the form is practically unchanged. The finding

Documentation drawing of a pottery bowl from the late 18th century.

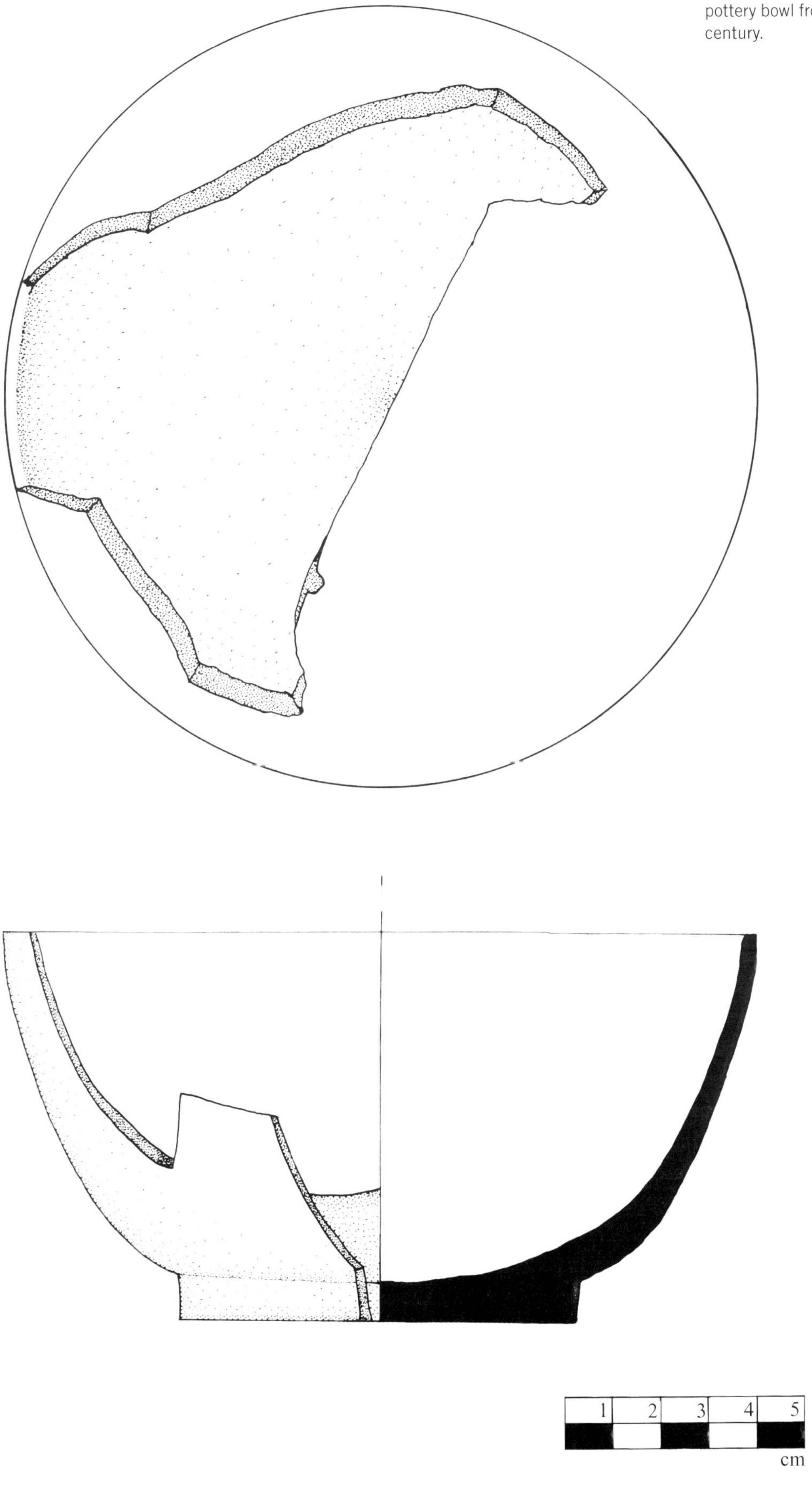

147

Cylindrical bottle from the late 18th century.

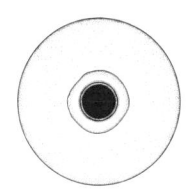

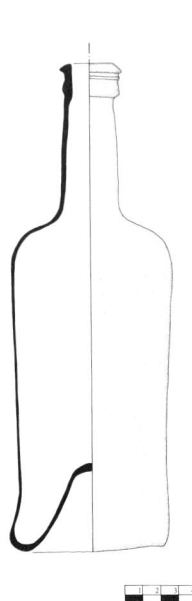

of single examples on sunken ships suggests that they were possibly used as water and oil containers rather than being products for trade.

Ian Reed's studies of ceramics provided quite a lot of detailed information about the ceramics and the chronology of the finds.

Until the excavation sediment box was lifted to the surface and its content examined on shore, it was not believed there were any clay pipes on board the ship. However, the investigation revealed several fragments of black and grey clay pipes, both stems and heads. Their colour and small size were probably the reason why none of these artefacts had been located during the exploration of the cultural layers of the site as they could easily be mistaken for marine biological forms.

Artefacts were also found in a number of other categories, including:

Rig components
Ten artefacts of rig components appeared to be elements of wooden blocks or pulleys produced from hardwood. The preservation of these artefacts varies from very good to poor.

GLASS
A total of 53 bottles and fragments of 23 others were recovered from the wreck site, some of them with quite distinct shapes. Bottles were generally used for shipping wine and spirits, but were also used to transport oils and other commodities. Although bottle shapes can give an indication of their country of origin it does not necessarily mean they were used to ship products from that particular country. It is well documented that large quantities of bottles were imported to Holland from various areas of Germany and also from France. It should also be remembered that bottles were typically reused and older types of bottles retained their usefulness over long periods.

Square case or cellar-bottles
The name derives from the fact that these bottles were generally transported in dozen lots in wooden cases or cellars for protection. A total of 13 such bottles were recovered and can be divided into two distinct groups: narrow-mouthed and wide-mouthed. Seven of the bottles were narrow-mouthed, while the remaining six were wide-mouthed.

All the bottles have a clear downward taper and

Emptying seabed sediments from one of the bottles.

a high kicked base so that the bottles appear to be standing on four short feet, a form typical of bottles produced after 1750. Bottles like this have frequently been called Dutch gin bottles, since they were used from the late 18th century for Hollands and Geneva. This does not, however, mean that all square sectioned bottles are Dutch in origin, as they were produced in almost every European country. The wide-mouthed variety was probably used to transport a variety of products including oils, olives, pepper and other spices.

French-style wine bottles

A total of 15 French-style bottles of the several hundred registered at the seabed were recovered. Thirteen are broader at the shoulder than the base, with tall necks. The remaining five are the weak-shouldered Champagne or Burgundy-type bottles which developed during the late 18th and early 19th centuries.

Cylindrical bottles

A total of 14 cylindrical bottles were collected. There are two observable types: those with a short body and a long neck and those with a long body and a shorter neck. This form of bottle developed to facilitate horizontal binning and save space. The types found here developed during the second half of the 18th century.

One particular bottle stands out. It has a long neck which widens towards the mouth. This bottle type has been found before in Holland where it is usually dated to the late 18th century or the early 19th century.

Other bottles

A number of other bottles were recovered as well, including storage bottles and bottles for pharmaceuticals.

One bottle has a long cylindrical form with a relatively wide mouth. It is 30.5 centimetres tall and made of a translucent green glass. Such bottles were mainly produced in France, but also occur in many other European countries. The narrower types of this type of bottle where used for such products as toilet water, brandy and other spirits, while the wider ones were used for preserving solids such as anchovies and gherkins. The collection also includes a relatively small flat-sided bottle. This type of bottle developed during the 18th century and was used for storage and shipping, with the later types having a very wide mouth.

A spyglass produced by Harris & Son in London.

Left: Part of a rigging block.
Right: A metal spoon.

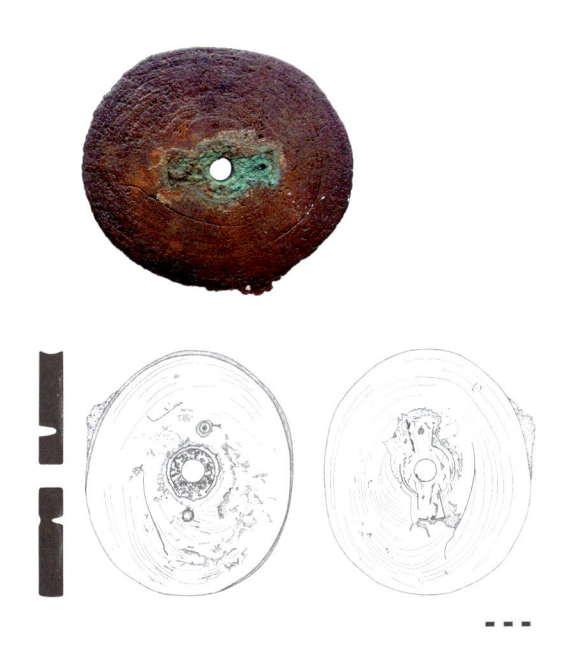

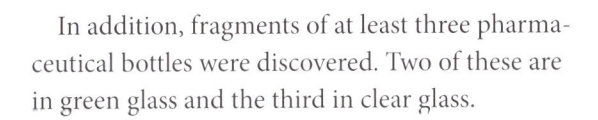

In addition, fragments of at least three pharmaceutical bottles were discovered. Two of these are in green glass and the third in clear glass.

METAL

The metal artefacts recovered vary in quality and material type. Many brass or copper artefacts were among the finds – mainly buttons, coins, ornaments and utensils. This category includes also items of gold (one coin), lead, iron, silver and pewter. The coin collection consists of 44 Russian copper Kopecks, from the period of Catherine the Great, i.e. late 18th century; one gold Dutch Ducat with the date 1802; one silver Danish 2 shilling dated 1785 or 1789; and one French copper coin dated to late 18th century.

There is some uncertainty as to whether four other items initially registered as coins are in fact coins.

Metal artefacts registered as *other* include quite a few artefacts that may belong to at least two compasses and probably a part of a bearing compass.

The 2005 excavations also uncovered many metal and wooden buttons. The metal buttons are mostly copper or brass, and are relatively small with a diameter less than 1.7 centimetres. Nearly all of them have a buttonhole loop more or less intact. One of the buttons has part of an inscription assumed to be "LONDON".

A group of five artefacts have been classified as weights, but may also be some kind of small handles. Another group consists of finds classified as hinges, securing screws for an octant and a nut with threads. Yet another group consists of copper coatings and different copper ornaments and handles.

The *Unknown* metal sub-category includes 25 artefacts such as pieces of corroded iron, pieces of copper plates and different indefinable metal fragments. One of the artefacts in this category is possibly a fragment of pocket sun-dial/compass.

The *utensils* sub-category includes five teaspoons and tablespoons in silver or pewter, as well as a candleholder in brass or copper and dated by typology to late 18th century.

Beside the glass bottles there are a few artefacts for storage and usage of fluids – faucets, consisting of both taps and tap handles, all produced in copper. Mortar, pestle and parts of kettles belong either to the ship's cooking utensils or were used for medical purposes.

❶ Two lead seabed sounders ❷ Part of a rigging block ❸ Octant

The excavation also uncovered a collection of three sea-bed sounders. These instruments were used to measure water depth under the keel, as well as to indicate seabed type beneath ships.

STONE

Stone is a very stable material and all uncovered artefacts are in a good state of preservation. The artefacts included two slates that may have been used as noteboards for navigation purposes. One artefact has been interpreted as a fragment of a stylus, a kind of pencil used for making navigation notes on slates/boards.

The collection also includes a whetstone and possibly a grinding stone. One large, heavy and almost quadratic (45.5 x 47 centimetre) stone plate has been interpreted as food preparation plate. There are clear traces of grinding that has formed a curve in the middle of the plate. Another artefact has been interpreted as a possible ballast stone.

WOOD

One wooden artefact in good state of preservation has been defined as an auger handle. This category also includes seven different handles and fragments of handles that could have belonged to different tools, all of which are produced from dark relatively hard wood, possibly ebony.

OTHER ORGANIC ARTEFACTS

There are not many artefacts in this category due to the poor conditions for preservation and the many disintegration processes on the site. Salt water in itself disintegrates wood, other organic material and even some non-organic artefacts. In addition, small wood-boring organisms such as shipworms (*Teredinidae*) and gribbles (*Limnoria lignorum*) disintegrate woodwork over time. Bacteria, microorganisms and fungus have also a destructive impact on organic material.

Marek E. Jasinski and Fredrik Søreide with some of the artefacts from the shipwreck.

The organic material includes two fragments of cordage, and two objects that were classified as possible fragments of textile or paper. However, these two particular finds may also be of modern origin, and need to be analysed to confirm their function and chronology.

The category also includes a fragment of leather with seam, which may have belonged to a shoe, and several olive kernels.

Nine domino pieces in bone or antler were uncovered in an excellent state of preservation, indicators of how leisure time may have been spent onboard during long sea crossings.

LABORATORY SAMPLES

The material examined by Thyra Solem at NTNU consisted of 17 samples, with most of the organic material being woodwork (lignoses) from deciduous trees heavily attacked by shipworm *Teredo* spp. Some of the samples include a very small amount of charred lignoses. Apart from capsules of buckwheat *Fagopyrum esculentum* from the northern hemisphere, a variety of plant seeds from the Mediterranean and Far East that occur as weeds in most crops were found in the gathered material.

A few insect fragments were observed, and it was hoped that two wings representing two different species of beetles could be identified. Two Norwegian entomologists specialising in beetles studied these sub-fossil fragments but could not identify the species, suggesting the beetles do not belong to the Nordic fauna. Considering food on board the ship was from places as afar as the Mediterranean and the Far East, it is possible the beetles also originate from these regions.

Fragments of obsidian were found in five samples. One of them also contained a small piece of pumice, which may possibly be traceable to a specific volcanic eruption. [2]

The collection of artefacts uncovered in the seabed sediments of the site has enormous informational potential and constitutes an excellent source of data to help put the historical puzzle together. The process continues and as is often the case in archaeological research it can easily become a "never-ending story". Paradoxically, the process often creates as many new questions as it answers. The interim conclusions reached by spring 2007 are discussed in the following chapter.

Documenting a fragment of stoneware.

The team recovered a collection of Russian 5 kopeck coins, indicating a Russian connection of some sort.

CHAPTER 17

THE HISTORICAL PUZZLE AND THE RUSSIAN LINK

The previous chapter provided detailed descriptions and some interpretations of the finds the ROV carried to the surface from the deepwater site. To put them in context, the information on hand after preliminary analysis of the archaeological material should be taken into account.

Firstly, the collection of artefacts perfectly reflects the international nature of the seafaring and maritime trade of the period. A brief background of Norwegian and international seafaring at the time adds some perspective here.

Generally speaking, the maritime field has always been one of the most globally-oriented in our civilisation. Since the very first watercraft was constructed, the act of journeying into the unknown and discovering new areas and peoples along or across bodies of water has been an important part of global cultural development. Our ancestors have long used the sea to transport much of their natural resources and local products, used seafaring to impose political and military power, and to spread intellectual impulses around the globe.

Interregional and even intercontinental seafaring started in the Mediterranean long before our time. In northern Europe, and especially in Scandinavia, long distance seafaring developed intensively before the first nation states, culminating in the Viking Age and early Middle Ages. Vikings and seafarers from Norway, Sweden and Denmark extended their political influence during this period through trade and warfare from Scandinavia to the coast of Greenland in the north, the coast of today's Canada in the west, to Constantinople and northern Africa to the south, and Russian states to the east.

Norwegian seafaring reached new heights when international trade started in the 13th century through the Hansa trading network in Northern Europe, in which Bergen was included around 1350. Norwegian dried fish, fish oil, timber, tar, furs, leather, whetstone, and even berries were for centuries important export articles transported by merchant boats to the continent from Norwegian ports.

In return, continental products from Germany, Holland, Britain, today's Poland (Danzig), and other areas were imported to Norway under Hansa's strict monopoly. Imports included corn, textiles and a number of luxury products.

The Black Death during the mid-14th century marks a significant decline in Norwegian seafaring and maritime trade. Soon after, in 1378, Norway

Remnants of an organic sack at the sea-bed. Buckwheat, a typical Russian staple, may have been the main cargo.

entered a union with Denmark that lasted until almost the end of the Napoleonic Wars in 1814.

In the first half of the 16th century, the Hanseatic domination of Norwegian international trade became gradually weaker and a new, more prosperous period started. Waterwheel-powered saw technology increased the export of Norwegian timber again, especially to Holland, and along the western coast of Norway as far as Bud and Molde other products were also exported to Scotland, Germany and England [1]. This period of prosperity continued with minor set-backs until the late 17th century, which was a period of economic expansion throughout western and northern Europe.

From 1700 to 1815, there were only 45 years of peace in Europe. More than half this period was marked by large-scale wars, which often included all the major maritime powers like England, Germany, France, the Netherlands, Spain and Russia. In the 18th century the kingdom of Denmark-Norway adopted a neutrality policy, and avoided these conflicts unless forced to react to a direct attack under the ever-changing alliances of particular wars.

Paradoxically, Norwegian shipping and trade flourished during the periods of war between leading nations of maritime commerce provided the kingdom of Denmark-Norway managed to maintain neutrality, enabling merchants to profit from the wartime economy by delivering goods and services to all warring parties. Danish and Norwegian trading companies were founded as royal monopolies and made substantial profit during the years of the War of Spanish Succession (1702–09), the Seven Years' War between France and Britain (1756–63) and the American War of Independence (1776–83), when the Kingdom managed to stay neutral.

When Denmark-Norway was forced to join particular conflicts, the war effect was detrimental to the Norwegian economy as trade was being transferred to the neutral ships of other nations. In periods of peace, the Scandinavian countries started to extend their economic spheres into the lucrative markets of the Indian Ocean, founding trading companies in that part of the world. Danish and Norwegian ships also sailed to Portuguese, Spanish and Mediterranean ports between 1745 and 1797.

The final years of the Napoleonic Wars, between 1807 and 1815 had catastrophic effects on Norwegian maritime commerce. Denmark-Norway was forced by a British attack on Copenhagen to join the war as a French ally, which subjected Danish and Norwegian merchant ships to attacks by British privateers. [2]

The collection of artefacts from the ship discovered on the Ormen Lange pipeline route can undoubtedly be placed in the the late 18th – early 19th century. The Dutch gold coin dated to 1802 shows that the ship wreck occurred after that date. One of the key questions is whether the ship wreck occurred before or after Denmark-Norway became engaged in the Napoleonic Wars on the French side in August 1807, thus becoming part of the continental embargo against Britain and its allies Germany and Russia.

What does the data collection include? As described above, the collection is essentially of international character in terms of where the artefacts come from. At least eight different countries or regions are represented: Great Britain, the Netherlands, France, Denmark-Norway, China, Russia, the Iberian Peninsula, and areas in the South China seas.

The line between cargo carried by the ship and utensils used by the crew onboard is not easily drawn. The wine and liquor bottles were undoubtedly cargo. The wine bottles are most likely of French origin although French wine, along with most other items in the collection, could have been taken onboard in any of European ports of the period by ships from any of the north-western European countries. The German Selters mineral water bottles are also most likely cargo, as the water from this particular well was believed in that period to be of great medicinal value.

It is probably also safe to include the Chinese and European porcelain as cargo, along with the stoneware products. This means the wine, liquor, and ceramics constitute the main cargo of the ship on its final journey. The few artefacts from the Iberian Peninsula and South China Seas were more likely equipment found in the ship's galley acquired by the crew during earlier voyages to these remote areas.

However, the total volume of the cargo detected by our archaeological team on the seabed was far from the total capacity of the ship, and there are two main possibilities. Either the ship was not fully loaded while sinking close to Bud, or the major part of the cargo consisted of organic products that have not been preserved such as flour, sugar, salt, etc.

Research into the Russian written documents. Gunnar O. Nilsen, left, filming and Dr. Oleg O. Ovsiannikov from the Russian Academy of Science in St. Petersburg working on board *Cehili*.

The port of departure for the final journey of the ship cannot be defined from the archaeological material, and the port of destination is also difficult to establish. However, some material traces have been uncovered that enable an educated guess. Firstly, the relatively large collections of Russian copper coins (kopecks) from the reign of Catherine the Great suggest a certain Russian link in the final history of the ship. These coins had a monetary value in Russia alone, and only there could the master of the ship easily use them for financial transactions. The Russian link is also supported to some extent by the results of botanical sample analysis.

Traces of buckwheat *Fagopyrum esculentum* also suggest contacts with the eastern part of the northern hemisphere. In addition, the excavation uncovered remnants of a bast-like container resembling a north Russian flour sack on the port side of the hull.

Commercial connections between northern Europe and northern Russia have a long history, and Norwegians in particular have always traded with their north-eastern neighbours [3]. Furs, corn, fish, and other commodities were frequently exchanged and traded between the two states. In the late Middle Ages, other northern European nations including the English, Dutch, Danish, and Germans joined the system.

In 1584, the Russian Tsar Ivan Vasiljevitsj ordered a new trading centre be established at the mouth of the Northern Dvina River close to the White Sea coast to help better control the international trade with his country. The town known since 1613 as Arkhangelsk soon after became a centre for European trade with Russia, and up until the 18th century was the only seaport of the Russian Empire in Europe. After Peter the Great founded the Baltic port of St. Petersburg in 1722 the two towns have remained closely connected by the seaway along the Norwegian coast that became somewhat of an internal Russian maritime route. Military equipment and internal Russian merchandise have been transported onboard Russian ships between the two ports.

International trade with Arkhangelsk at the end of the 18th and very early 19th century included alcohol, sugar and luxury ceramics among the standard merchandise carried to northern Russia from north-western Europe. Taking into consideration the geographical position of the wreckage site, the ship could presumably have either been on its way along the Norwegian coast to Arkhangelsk, or on its way back from there.

At first glance the first alternative sounds more likely as transporting wine from northern Russia seems very doubtful. It is however quite probable that a system of transporting empty bottles for reuse existed at that time due to the high price of bottles. It cannot either be excluded that the ship was sailing under the Russian flag and was in Russian possession during its last voyage.

During his reign, Tsar Peter the Great repeatedly commanded the building of new ships in a Western European manner as part of his attempts to modernize the Russian fleet. He had also by royal decree forbidden the construction of traditional Russian ships under the penalty of death. This policy was also continued to some extent after his death by Catherine the Great and other successors [4]. The purchase of Western European ships by Russian merchants and shipowners was thus not uncommon in this period.

Regardless of the origin and whether it was a Danish-Norwegian, West European or Russian ship that sailed to its demise in the vicinity of Bud the ship remains part of European seafaring history and an important monument of European maritime heritage.

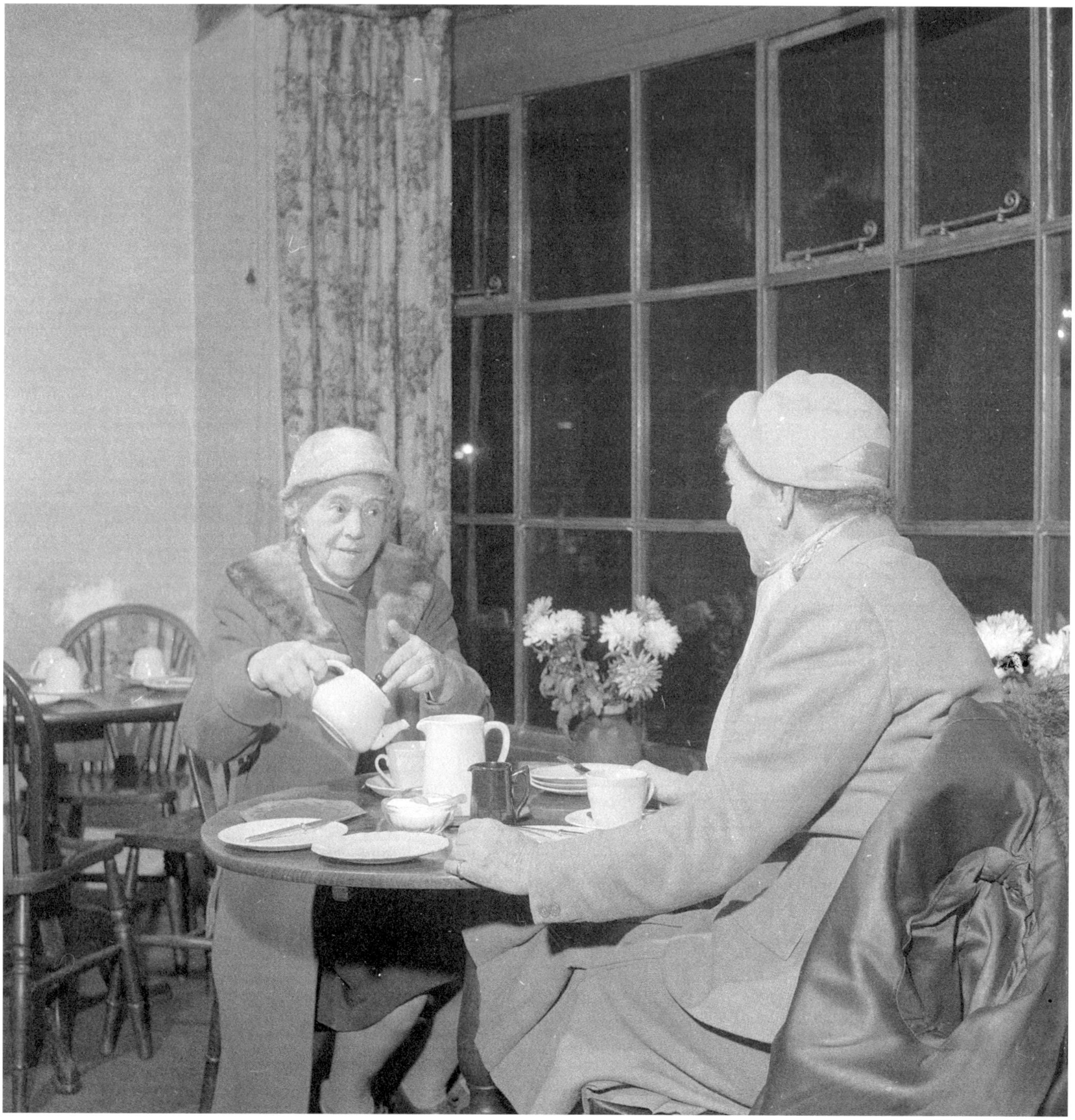

AFTERWORD

A CUP OF TEA AND A SHIPWRECK EXHIBIT

The Ormen Lange project has been a great success.

In conjunction with Statoil, responsible for the Langeled project and the Shell team drilling the production wells, Hydro has impressively managed the many challenges throughout the project. Without the experience of professional contractors from other demanding projects worldwide the development would not be possible, and certainly not within the planned budget and timeframe.

Ask anyone involved in the project and they would most likely say what a privilege it has been to be part of the Ormen Lange team. Discovery Channel produced a film about the Ormen Lange project and National Geographic Channel and German TV channels have also produced TV programmes. For Ormen Lange team members, this is a tribute to the outstanding result they have helped achieve.

Several film teams have also visited the marine archaeological project and included scenes from the operation as examples of the wide spectre of issues being dealt with in such an enormous project.

The marine archaeological team were able to cross one of the final frontiers of marine archaeology by matching the standards of conventional land-based archaeology: precision exploration, accuracy of positioning and measurements of structures and artefacts, and quality of documentation. Not only was this the deepest marine archaeological excavation ever carried out, in a number of aspects it was even of higher quality than is normal on land or in shallow water. The purpose-built technology and methods used on the site worked perfectly, from both a technical and an archaeological perspective.

The international interest in the Ormen Lange project is partly due to the importance of the energy supply to the European market, and to the UK in particular.

New pipelines and power cable infrastructure has gradually opened up the European energy market to increasingly flexible forms of trading and distribution. Energy will reach the customer wherever they are.

The gas from Ormen Lange is however intended for the British market. For the next 40 years or so gas from chilly Norwegian waters will keep British kettles boiling. Ormen Lange gas will be piped into millions of English kitchens, keep houses warm and British industry running. Hydro has designed the Ormen Lange development project in a robust way to ensure that gas will run through the pipes every day.

Connection to the Sleipner platform ensures that if production from Ormen Lange has to stop or is reduced for a shorter period, gas will still flow through the system. Our British neighbours can sleep well on a cold winters night knowing there will always be heat and a nice cup of tea in the morning.

Hydro will continue to develop the subsea system with one or two new templates in the Ormen Lange field at least until 2010. It will also continue the development of new technology to compress gas on the seafloor when the pressure in the reservoir starts to drop, something that will be required from around 2015 to maintain high production.

Shell will continue to drill new production wells and seek to operate the field to maintain high reliability, all the while with the intention of keeping things running smoothly for British consumers.

Awareness among the British of their dependency on Norwegian gas has increased during the development of Ormen Lange. When the gas terminal was built in Easington and inaugurated in the presence of Prime Minister Blair and Prime Minister Stoltenberg in October 2006, awareness increased. Britain and Norway have many traditional links and with the new Langeled pipeline two longstanding neighbours have gained a new interdependency.

Britain's increasing gas demand from abroad is partly due to declining production from UK gas fields and emphasises the fact that hydrocarbons are a limited resource with increasing market value. Ten years after the discovery of the Ormen Lange field it can be concluded that is a unique discovery. No other fields of a similar size have been discovered in Europe since 1997 and very few elsewhere around the world.

OPENING OF ORMEN LANGE

Trading gas with the UK is not merely a matter for oil companies. Before any gas pipeline could be planned, a treaty had to be established between Norway and UK, signed by Prime Minister Kjell Magne Bondevik and Prime Minister Tony Blair, through the Ministry of Oil and Energy in Norway and the Ministry of Transport in the UK.

Trading and co-operation between Norway and the UK has longstanding traditions. The shipwreck located outside Bud in the Ormen Lange pipeline

The 85 m long survey vessel *Geobay* becomes small when the sea becomes rough in the Ormen Lange area. Handling the harsh environment in a safe way has been an important part of the Ormen Lange Offshore development project.

route represents an earlier chapter in the history of trade between Norway and UK. British stoneware and other artefacts retrieved from the seafloor indicate trading between Norway, the UK, Russia and other countries in Europe and elsewhere. The ship's bell is dated to 1745 and the ship most likely sank in the first years of the 19th century, thus it may have traded longer than it takes to produce the gas from the huge Ormen Lange gas field.

It is hoped the story of the shipwreck will be shared with the public in Bud, close to the wreck site. Fræne Municipality is planning a Costal Culture Centre which would create a perfect frame to exhibit information about the gas project as well as artefacts and illustrations from the marine archaeological excavation at the coast of Fræna.

When looking from Bud out towards Ormen Lange on a stormy day as the waves break across the skerries, it is easy to imagine the challenges faced by a merchant ship sailing in rough weather and possibly even in the dark. Seeking shelter close to Bud was probably fatal for the trade ship. Even the modern fleet of offshore installation vessels working with Ormen Lange installations has been prevented from working and has also been forced to seek shelter in the fjord area close to Bud.

Fortunately however, the offshore work has been completed without any serious injuries or fatalities despite working offshore in harsh conditions year-round for many years. Providing a safe working environment for the people involved can be counted as a real part of the story's success.

In Norway, financing archaeological excavations is the responsibility of the developer, in this case the Ormen Lange owners or licence partners. The total costs for marine archaeological surveys and excavations together with archaeological investigations on land have totally NOK 120 million, which is a significant part of the budget for the Ormen Lange project. The Norwegian Directorate for Cultural Heritage has raised the status of communicating and education of the finds from archaeological excavations, and one of the arguments for retrieving artefacts from the wreck was to add to the knowledge of the shipwreck history for educational purposes.

The authors are hopeful that this book will contribute to spreading knowledge of the Ormen Lange project and excitement about the shipwreck and its discovery.

ORMEN LANGE-PROSJEKTET

Ormen Lange-feltet ble påvist ved boring i 1997. Feltet inneholder omkring 400 milliarder standard kubikkmeter gass og er det nest største gassfunnet på norsk sokkel. Mulighetene for et stort funn i dette området ble oppdaget av Hydros geofysikere flere år før området ble åpnet for utforskning.

I perioden fra 1997 til 2002 ble det boret flere brønner for å bestemme størrelsen på funnet og for å bekrefte kvaliteten av reservoaret. Samtidig ble det gjort et omfattende arbeid for å velge riktig utbyggingsløsning og avklare behovet for gass i det europeiske markedet. Hovedspørsmålet var om man skulle bygge en stor plattform på feltet med full prosessering av gassen for direkte transport gjennom en rørledning til det europeiske markedet eller om man kunne velge en undervannsutbygging på feltet. Undervannsløsning ville også inkludere gassledninger til land og et prosesseringsanlegg på land i Norge. Derfra skulle gassen transporteres i en stor gasseksportledning til det europeiske markedet.

For løsningen med landanlegg ble 14 lokasjoner vurdert, fra Sand kommune i sør til Tjeldbergodden i nord. Etter grundige vurderinger falt valget på Nyhamna på Aukra i 2002. Hovedkonseptet med en ren undervannsutbygging på feltet ble også endelig valgt i 2003. Valg av lokasjon for ilandføring av gassen ble vurdert i nært sammarbeid med Møre og Romsdal fylkeskommune, som hadde etablert prosjektet «Ormen til Møre» for å være med å sikre at denne delen av utredningen fikk høy prioritet og at Hydro fikk nødvendig hjelp til de detaljerte vurderingene som måtte gjøres før man kunne velge lokasjon for landanlegget. Det var derfor stor glede i Møre og Romsdal når ilandføring ble valgt som løsning og spesielt gledelig for Aukra kommune at valget falt på Nyhamna som lokasjon for gassprosesseringsanlegget.

Ormen Lange-feltet ligger på kontinentalskråningen ned mot dyphavet i vanndyp mellom ca. 700 meter og 1100 meter, og er det første dypvannsfeltet som er bygget ut på norsk sokkel. Reservoaret ligger sentralt i rasgropa etter Storeggaraset som ble utløst for 8200 år siden. Storeggaraset er verdens største kjente undersjøiske skred, med en bakkant som er 300 km lang og med en utløpsdistanse på ca 800 km. Raset skapte en stor tsunamibølge langs norskekysten og kysten av Skotland, Shetland og Færøyene. Lokalt var bølgen mer enn 25 meter høy, og steinalderbefolkningen langs kysten ble helt sikkert hardt rammet. Bakkanten av raset har en helningsvinkel på mellom 25 og 40 grader.

Før man kunne beslutte å bygge ut Ormen

Lange-feltet, med en investering på mer enn 50 milliarder kroner i første fase, var det helt nødvendig å undersøke om Storeggaområdet var stabilt, og om utbygging og produksjon av 400 milliarder kubikkmeter gass fra reservoaret kunne forandre stabiliteten. Hydro løste denne oppgaven i nært samarbeid med universiteter og forskningsinstitusjoner i Norge og ellers i Europa. Omfattende datainnsamling og forskningsarbeide ga grunnlag for å konkludere med at man trengte en ny istid for å kunne gjenskape den ustabile situasjonen man hadde før raset ble utløst for 8200 år siden. Alle de ustabile sedimentene i skråningen forsvant da raset ble utløst. Et kraftig jordskjelv er den mest sansynlige årsaken til at raset ble utløst.

Terrenget i raset der Ormen Lange-utbyggingen har foregått, består av store rasblokker av hard leire med mye stein, som er transportert ut på sokkelkanten gjennom flere istider. Rasterrenget har gitt utbyggerne store utfordringer. For å kunne legge rør har man måttet lage «rørgater» ved å grave vekk topper og fylle stein i lave områder mellom toppene for å gi støtte til rørledningene. Denne oppgaven krevde utvikling av ny graveteknologi og ny teknologi for kartlegging og nøyaktig undervannsnavigasjon.

Dypt vann, minusgrader på sjøbunnen og kraftig strøm skapte ekstra utfordringer for Hydro og kontraktørene som fikk oppgaver i forbindelse med utbyggingen. Også i nærlandområdet var undervannsterrenget med trange daler en utfordring. Hele 500 000 tonn med stein ble dumpet for å bygge understøttelse for rørene i dette området.

Ormen Lange-prosjektet har strukket grensene for hva man kan få til på mange områder. Det umulige er blitt mulig blant annet med ny teknologi utviklet gjennom flere år i et nøye planlagt utviklingsprogram. På mange måter er en slik utfordrende oppgave ingeniørens drøm.

På Ormen Lange-feltet installerte Hydro et undervanns produksjonssystem med to store brønnrammer i 2005, det største tungløftet i verden på så stort vanndyp. Forboring av brønner kunne starte når brønnrammene var på plass. I 2005 og 2006 ble de store gassproduksjonsrørene installert mellom Nyhamna og Ormen Lange-feltet. I selve rasområdet var dette en stor utfordring, men et grundig forarbeide med sjøbunnsbearbeiding og nyutviklet teknologi for undervannsnavigasjon gjorde dette mulig. I tillegg til gassproduksjonsrørene er det installert to styrekabler for å kunne styre feltet fra land og to ledninger for å tilføre frostvæske i gasstrømmen. Dette hindrer dannelse av gasshydrater. Totalt er det derfor 6 ledninger fra feltet og inn til landanlegget.

Statoil fikk oppgaven med å produsere og installere størstedelen av ledningen fra Nyhamna til Easington via Sleipnerplattformen. To fulle installasjonssesonger og to leggefartøy ble benyttet til å legge Langeledledningen. Langeled syd ble åpnet høsten 2006 for å levere gass fra Sleipnerområdet. Da var også gassterminalen i Easington klar.

Parallelt med installasjon av offshoreanlegg, sjøbunnsbearbeiding og installasjon av rørledninger, har Hydro bygget prosesseringsanlegget på Aukra. Med anleggsstart i april 2004 etter godkjenning av plan for utygging, har det tatt ca. tre år å bygge det gigantiske anlegget som dekker et område tilsvarende 120 fotballbaner. Et imponerende stykke arbeid på utolig kort tid.

Gassen fra Ormen Lange-feltet prosesseres på Nyhamna, og kondensat, som er en lett oljetype, skilles ut slik at gassen har den kvaliteten forbrukerne trenger. Frostvæsken som er tilsatt gassen, fjernes og renses og brukes på nytt. Så blir gassen sendt gjennom verdens lengste rørledning til havs, den 1200 km lange Langeled-rørledningen som går via Sleipnerplattformen til Easington i UK. I Easington er det bygget en gassterminal for å kunne ta imot gassen og sende den videre til forbrukerne gjennom rørledninger på land. Gassen vil dekke omkring 20 prosent av behovet i UK. Mange briter vil bli avhengige av gass fra Ormen Lange for å kunne ta sin tekopp en kald vinterdag. Hydro har sammen med mange flinke kontraktører klart å følge planen for utbygging og holde kostnadene omtrent på det nivået som var forutsatt for utbyggingen. Både for de som har vært med i prosjektet og for utenforstående er dette imponerende og flott. Illustrasjonene i denne boken gir et inntrykk av både størrelse og type utfordring Hydros ingeniører har måttet finne løsninger for.

I forbindelse med Ormen Lange-prosjektet måtte Hydro også forholde seg til et litt mer uvanlig problem. I henhold til den norske kulturminneloven måtte arkeologer fra Norges Teknisk Naturvitenskapelig Universitet (NTNU) kartlegge og undersøke rørledningstraseene for å sikre at Ormen Lange-utbyggingen ikke skulle ødelegge eventuelle skipsvrak og andre kulturminner på havbunnen. På forhånd hadde Hydros undersøkelser lokalisert en rekke moderne skipsvrak, men i august 2003 oppdaget arkeologene fra NTNU, Vitenskapsmuseet et historisk skipsvrak like ved rørtraseene på nesten 170 metres dybde i Bjørnsundet ved Bud i Fræna kommune. Skipets skrogrester samt hundrevis av vinflasker, porselen og en stor skipsklokke gjorde at arkeologene raskt kunne fastslå at skipet var et viktig kulturminne fra slutten av 1700-tallet og dermed beskyttet av den norske kulturminneloven. Siden det ikke var mulig å flytte traseen for rørene langt nok vekk fra funnet, krevde Riksantikvaren at Ormen Lange-prosjektet skulle bekoste en omfattende undersøkelse av lokaliteten og en utgraving av akterdelen av vraket.

Området rundt Bud, Nyhamna og Bjørnsundet utgjør et klassisk maritimt kulturlandskap med fjell, holmer, øyer og rikt kulturmiljø i skjæringspunktet mellom åpent hav og et sammensatt fjordsystem. På begge sider av Bjørnsundet befinner det seg et stort antall kulturminner fra forhistorisk og historisk tid, noe som viser at dette området har spilt en sentral rolle i den regionale kulturutviklingen gjennom tidene. Det skjermede og topografisk meget varierende sundet har vært et attraktivt fiske- og fangstområde til alle tider. Området er derfor sentralt både i forhold til terrestriske og maritime ressurser, og ligger i krysningspunktet for viktige terrestriske og maritime ferdselsårer. Allerede i steinalderen oppsto de første maritime kulturelementer gjennom bosetning rettet mot sjøfangst og fiske. I bronsealderen ble blant annet monumentale kystrøyser tilføyd landskapet, og fra jernalderen, vikingtiden, middelalderen og nyere tid har vi i tillegg til bosetninger flere sjøfartsrelaterte fysiske og ikke-materielle spor i form av havner, varder, nausttufter, seilingsmerker, skipsvrak, stedsnavn, sagn, etc.

Den aktuelle delen av skipsleden utgjør en del av hovedferdselsåren langs norskekysten med lange tradisjoner og av stor betydning for den maritime kulturutviklingen i regional, nasjonal og internasjonal skala. Det historiske skipet fant sitt siste hvilested på havbunnen ca 700 meter fra innseilingen til Bud nord for Molde. Denne havnen har i flere epoker spilt en viktig rolle i det maritime kulturlandskapet i området. Bud har gjennom tidene fungert som fiskevær og utskipningshavn for trelasthandel og tørrfiskhandel. I flere hundre år var stedet den viktigste handelsplass i regionen mellom Bergen og Nidaros, og i middelalderen spilte Bud en meget sentral sjøfartsrelatert og økonomisk rolle og var arena for politiske hendelser.

Molde fikk i 1742, trass sterk motstand fra Bergen og Trondheim, full handelsfrihet og ble kjøpstad. Utenlandske skuter ankret opp i Molde havn. I årene som fulgte hadde Molde opp til 40 registrerte besøk av utenlandske skip – danske, engelske, skotske, hollandske og spanske. Ved siden av fisk ble det solgt trelast, jern, husdyrskinn, røkt kjøtt, ost og bær. Det er ganske sannsynlig at vårt skipsvrak var et element av denne handelsprosessen.

For å kunne gjennomføre de pålagte marinarkeologiske undersøkelser av skipsvraket i Ormen Lange-traseen, måtte det marinarkeologiske teamet fra NTNU utvikle unik teknologi og nye marinarkeologiske utgravningsredskap. Prosjektet brukte avanserte posisjoneringssystemer og nyeste teknologi innenfor akustikk og digitale databaser. En spesialdesignet fjernstyrt undervannsfarkost ble utstyrt med en rekke sensorer og verktøy. I tillegg konstruerte teamet fra NTNU en stor utgravningsramme i stål som ble plassert over akterenden av vraket. Den fjernstyrte undervannsfarkosten kunne koble seg til rammen og ved hjelp av tannhjul bevege seg i alle retninger rett over vraket uten å ødelegge de delikate gjenstandene og trestrukturene mens den arbeidet med marinarkeologiske undersøkelser.

Ved hjelp av en skånsom slamsuger avdekket arkeologene deler av det mer enn 30 meter lange skipsvraket og dokumenterte det unike funnet på nesten 170 meters dyp. Nesten 500 nøye valgte gjenstander ble brakt til overflaten for å kunne lære mer om vraket og dets historie. Gjenstandene omfatter glass, porselen, skipsutstyr som taljer og gjenstander fra byssa. De marinarkeologiske undersøkelsene i forbindelse med Ormen Lange-prosjektet føyer seg inn i unike utfordringer som ble løst under prosjektarbeidet. Dette var første gang i verden at marinarkeologer gjennomførte en utgravning av et vrak på dypt vann utelukkende ved hjelp av fjernstyrt utstyr og med en presisjon helt på høyde med arkeologiske utgravinger på land og på grunt vann.

Forskerne ved NTNU, Vitenskapsmuseet holder fremdeles på med å undersøke og konservere gjenstandene. De har også lett i arkiver i hele Europa. Selv om de ennå ikke har funnet identiteten til vraket, er det mye som tyder på at det dreier seg om et skip som var på veg til eller fra Russland. Flere av gjenstandene og en samling mynter stammer fra nettopp Russland, men det er funnet gjenstander fra mer enn åtte land i vraket. Forhåpentligvis vil studier av gjenstandene eller nye arkivstudier hjelpe arkeologene med å avdekke identiteten til skipet. Gjenstandene fra skipet skal i fremtiden stilles ut i det planlagte informasjonssentret på toppen av Erganfortet i Bud.

FACTS ABOUT ORMEN LANGE

First Licence award	1996
Operator development phase (Also after 2007)	Norsk Hydro
Operator in production phase	Norske Shell
Operator for Langeled from 2006	Gassco
Ownership	Hydro: 18.0728% Shell: 17.0375% Petoro: 36.4750% Statoil: 10.8441% Dong: 10.3420% ExxonMobil: 7.2286%
Previous partner	BP (Replaced by Dong)
Estimated recoverable gas reseves	400 billion cubic meter
Estimated plateau production	70 million cubic metres pr. day
Estmated daily production of condensate	50 000 barrels pr. day
Length of reservoir	Approximately 40 km
Width of reservoir	Approximately 10 km
Water depth, production area	850 – 1100 metres
Temperature on seafloor	Approximately 1 degree C
Distance from shore	120 km
Type of development	Subsea production (No platform in the field)
Onshore gas processing plant	Nyhamna in Aukra municipality, West Norway
Production pipelines	Two 30" gas pipelines from field to Nyhamna
Export pipeline	Langeled, 1200 km. Approximately 800 km from Nyhamna to Sleipner and approximately 400 km from the Sleipner platform to Easington in UK
Gas terminal in Easington	Built by Statoil. Opened in October 2006
Onshore facilities in Nyhamna	Facilities for drying and compression of gas (65 000 Hp used for gas compression) Processing plant for separation and treatment of condensate (light oil) Anti freeze injection and recovery system (Mono Etylen Glykol – MEG) Caverns for storage of condensate Jetty for offloading of condensate to tankers Offices and control room
Drilling of production wells	Performed by Shell
Well capacity	Up to 24 wells
Plan for development	Approved in April 2004
Production start Langeled South	October 2006 (gas from Sleipner)
Production start Ormen Lange	October 2007
Ormen Lange development phase 2	2008 -
Further development of Ormen Lange	One or two additional production templates. Gas compression platform or alternatively a subsea gas compression unit from 2015 or 2016

BIBLIOGRAPHY

Chapter 1

1. Martinsen, O.J., Nøttvedt, A. 2006: Av hav stiger landet, section «Dyphavsavsetninger i Norskehavet» page 464 – 469. *Landet blir til, Norges geologi,* Norsk Geologisk forening.

Chapter 3

1. Bondevik, S., Løvholt, F., Harbitz, C., Mangerud, J., Dawson, A., Svendsen, J.I. 2005: «The Storegga Slide tsunami-comparing field observations with numerical simulations». *Marine & Petroleum Geology,* Vol. 22.
2. Haflidason, H., Lien, R., Seirup, H.P, Forsberg, C.F, Bryn, P. 2005: «Dating and morphology of the Storegga Slide». *Marine & Petroleum Geology,* Vol. 22.
3. Haflidason, H., Sejrup, H.P., Berstad, I.M., Nygård, A., Richter, T., Bryn, P., Lien, R., Berg, K. 2003: «Weak layer features on the northern Storegga Slide escarpment». In Mienert, J. and Weaver, P. (eds). *European Margin Sediment Dynamics: Side-scan sonar and seismic images.* Springer-Verlag Berlin 55–62.
4. Bryn, P., Solheim, A., Lien, R., Forsberg, C.F., Haflidason, H, Ottesen, D. Rise L. 2003: «The Storeegga Slide Complex: Repeated large scale sliding in response to climate cyclicity». In *Submarine Mass Movements and their consequences,* Kluwer academic publishers.
5. Bryn, P., Berg, K., Forsberg, C.F, Solheim, A., Kvalstad, T.J. 2005: «Explaining the Storegga Slide», *Marine & Petroleum Geology,* Vol. 22.
6. Bryn, P., Kvalstad, T.J., Guttormsen, T.R., Kjærnes, P.A., Lund, J.K., Nadim, F., Olsen, J. 2004: «Storegga slide risk assessment». OTC-paper 16560.
7. Lund, J. K., Olsen, J., Bryn, P., Brekke, G., Guttormsen, T.R., Kvalstad, T.J., Nadim, F. 2004: «Slide Risk Assessment in the Ormen Lange Field Development Area». The Seventh SPE International Conference on Health, Safety, and Environment in Oil and Gas Exploration and Production.

Chapter 5

1. Ottesen, D., Rise, L., Rokoengen, K., Sættem, J. 2001: «Glacial processes and large scale morphology on the mid-Norwegian continental shelf». In Martinsen, O.J. and Dreyer, T. *Sedimentary Environment Offshore Norway – Palaeozoic to Recent: Norwegian Petroleum Society Special Publication,* 10, 441–449. Elsevier Science B.V. Amsterdam.

Chapter 6

1. Ref. Jon Arne Sneli, Trondheim Biological Station.

Chapter 10.

1. Narmo, L.E. 1993: «Steinalder på Romsdalkysten». *Romsdalsmuseets Årbok* 1993 9–35. Molde.

2. Bostwick Bjerck, L. 1991: «Bolsøy – et påbegynt dikt». Spor 1991/1. Trondheim.
3. Døssland, A. 1990: «Med lengt mot havet». *Fylkeshistorie for Møre og Romsdal, I 1671–1835.* Det Norske Samlaget.
4. Larsen, P. (red) 1976: *Bygd og By i Norge. Møre og Romsdal.* Gylendal Norsk Forlag, Oslo.
5. Rødal, E. 1994: «Bønder og Fiskere. Økonomisk og sosial utvikling i Bud prestegjeld 1660–1800». Hovedoppgave i historie UNIT-AVH. Trondheim.
6. Jasinski, Marek E.; Søreide, F. 2007: «Die Sieben Weltmeere». Maritime Archäologie an der Norwegian University of Science and Technology. *Skyllis* 6(1–2), 94–108.

Chapter 11

1a. Jasinski, M. E. & Søreide, F. 2003a. Ormen Lange Archaeological Project. Marine Archaeological Survey. Survey Report – NH0374. August 2003. NTNU.
1b. Jasinski, M. E., Søreide, F. 2003b: «Ormen Lange Archaeological Project». Marine Archaeological Survey. Shipwreck Investigation and Survey Report – NH0380. October 2003. NTNU.
2. Delaporta, K., Jasinski, Marek E., Søreide, F. 2006: «The Greek – Norwegian Deep-Water Archaeological Survey. *International Journal of Nautical Archaeology* 35(1):79–87.
3. Jasinski, Marek E., Søreide, F., Ødegården, M. 2006: «Soli Deo Gloria – skipet på havets bunn. *SPOR* 21(1):12–15.

Chapter 12

1. Jasinski, Marek E. 1999: «Which way now?» Maritime archaeology and underwater heritage into the 21st century. World Archaeological Congress 4, Maritime Archaeology: Challenges For The New Millennium, Cape Town, South Africa, January 1999.
2. Søreide, F., Jasinski, Marek E. 2004: «Archaeological Oceanography – A new approach to marine archaeological heritage management». Oceanology International 16.03.2004–19.03.2004. *Oceanology.*
3. Hovland, M., Jasinski M.E., Søreide, F. 1998: «Underwater construction projects vs. marine archaeology: How solving conflict saved old shipwreck». *Norwegian Oil Review,* 24.7: 98–102.

Chapter 13

1. Jasinski, M. E., Søreide, F. 2003: «Ormen Lange Archaeological Project». Marine Archaeological Survey. Shipwreck Investigation and Survey Report – NH0380. October 2003. NTNU.
2. Jasinski, M.E., Soreide, F. 2004: «Ormen Lange Marine Archaeology Project». Archaeological Interpretation of Geobay Survey Data. Hydro cruise – NH0453. May 2004. NTNU

Chapter 14
1 Søreide, F., Jasinski, Marek E., Sperre, T.O. 2006: «Unique new technology enables archaeology in the deep sea». Sea Technology 47(10):10–13.
2 Søreide, F., Jasinski, Marek E. 2005: «Ormen Lange: Investigation and excavation of a shipwreck in 170m depth». Proceedings of the Oceans 2005 MTS/IEEE Conference & Exhibition.
3 Jasinski, Marek E., Søreide, F. 2006: «Ormen Lange Marine Archaeology Project». Report 2005. Trondheim. NTNU.
4 Ludvigsen, Martin & Søreide, Fredrik. 2006. Data fusion on the Ormen Lange shipwreck site. *Proceedings of the Oceans 2006 MTS/IEEE Conference & Exhibition.*

Chapter 15
1 Bakken, T. 2005: «Ormen Lange Marine Archaeology Project». Marine biology investigations. NTNU.
2 Jasinski, Marek E., Søreide, F. 2006: «Ormen Lange Marine Archaeology Project». Report 2005. Trondheim. NTNU.
3 Jasinski, Marek E., Søreide, F., Ødegården, M. 2006: «Vrakel ved Bud». I *Gammalt frå Fræna*. Elnesvågen. Fræna kommune 24–30.

Chapter 16
1 Ian R. 2005: «Analysis of pottery from the Ormen Lange Marine Project». Report. NTNU.
2 Solem, T. 2006: «Botanical investigation as a part of the project Ormen Lange Marine». Repport. NTNU.

Chapter 17
1 Sem og Slagen 2001: «– en bygdebok». 2. bind: *Kulturhistorie – første del*. Tønsberg: Høgskolen i Vestfold, 2001.
2 Berggreen, B., Christensen, A.E., Kolltveit, B. (red.) 1989: *Norsk Sjøfart*. Bind 1. Dreyers Forlag. Oslo.
3 Jasinski, Marek E., Ovsyannikov, Oleg V. 2006: «Routes to the Arctic Ocean. Aspects of medieval and post medieval portage systems in the Russian North». BAR *International Series,* Oxford 2006(1499):113–150.
4 Jasinski, M.E. 1994: «Tracing crossroads of shipbuilding traditions in the European Arctic». In Crossroads in Ancient shipbuilding. *Oxbow Monograph* 40:195–202;
5 Jasinski, Marek E., Ovsyannikov, Oleg V. 1998: *Vzgljad na evropeisku arktiku. Arkhangelskij sever: problemy i istotciki* (eng: *The European Arctic. Archangel region: research problems and sources*). Vol. II. St. Petersburg: Petersburskoje Vostokovedenje.

ILLUSTRATIONS

14 Chart Egil Ingebretsen Hydro **16** Illustration Ole Marthinsen Hydro **17** Seismic section Hydro **18–19** Illustaration Hydro **20** 3D image Egil Ingebretsen Hydro **21** 3D image Hydro **22** Illustration Hydro **24** Consept illustration Hydro **25** Petter Bryn **26** Chart Egil Ingebretsen Hydro **27** Chart Egil Ingebretsen Hydro **28** Illustration Egil Ingebretsen Hydro **29** 3D image Egil Ingebretsen Hydro **30** Illustration Hydro **31** Chart Norwegian Petroleum Directorate **32–33** 3D image Egil Ingebretsen Hydro **34** Chart Stein Bondevik UIT **34** Cart Hydro **35** Photo Stein Bondevik UIT **35** Photo Jan Mangerud UIB **36** Illustration Hydro **37** Photo Paal Rødahl **38** Chart Egil Ingebretsen Hydro **40** Sonar image Haflidi Haflidason UIB **42** Illustration Kongsberg Maritim **44** 3D image Egil Ingebretsen Hydro **45** Illustration Kongsberg Maritim **46** 3D image Hydro **46** Photo Hydro **46** Seafloor image Egil Ingebretsen Hydro **47** Illustration Kongsberg Maritim **48** Photo Endre Vestvik Hydro **50** 3D illustration Reinertsen Engineering **50** Seafloor Image Jan Erik Sikkeland Hydro **51** Photo Petter Bryn **51** 3D image Halvor Snellingen Nexans **51** Photo Petter Bryn **52** 3D image Reinertsen Engineering **52** 3D image Reinertsen Engineering **54** 3D image Egil Ingebretsen Hydro **54** Photo Hydro **55** Chart Dag Ottesen NGU **56** Photo Geoconsult **56** Photo Island Offshore **56** Illustration PSL **57** 3D image Egil Ingebretsen Hydro **58** Photo Van Oord **58** 3D image Egil Ingebretsen Hydro **59** Chart Egil Ingebretsen Hydro **60** Video grabGeoconsult /Veritas **62** 3Dimage Egil Ingebretsen **63** Photo Havforskningsinstituttet Bergen **64** (1) Video grab Geoconsult Veritas **64** (2) Video grab Geoconsult Veritas **64** (3) Video grab Geoconsult Hydro **64** (4) Video grab Geoconsult Veritas **64** (5) Video grab Geoconsult Veritas **64** (6) Video grab Geoconsult Veritas **64** (7) Video grab Geoconsult Veritas **65** (1) Video grab Geoconsult Veritas **65** (2) Video grab Geoconsult Veritas **65** (3) Video grab Geoconsult Veritas **65** (4) Video grab Geoconsult Veritas **65** (5) Video grab Geoconsult Veritas **65** (6) Video grab Geoconsult Hydro **66** Illustration FMC **68** 3D image Egil Ingebretsen Hydro **69** Photo FMC **69** Photo with the courtesy of Hereema Marine Contractors **70** Photo Seadrill **71** Photo Svein Roger Iversen Hydro **71** Photo Stig Arne Witsø Hydro **72** 3D image Egil Ingebretsen Hydro **72** Photo Lillian Aasheim Hydro **73** Photo Hydro **74** Video grab Geoconsult Hydro **75** Photo Hydro **76** Illustration Van Oord **77** Photo Hydro **78** Video grab DeepOcean Hydro **78** Video grab DeepOcean Hydro **79** Videograb DeepOcean Hydro **80** Photo Hydro **82–83** Photo Kim Laland Statoil **84** Chart Egil Ingebretsen Hydro **84** Photo Statoil **85** Photo Helge Hansen Hydro **86** Photo Øyvind Leren Hydro **88** Photo Øyvind Leren Hydro **88** Photo Øyvind Leren Hydro **89** Photo Vitenskapsmuseet **89** Photo Hydro **90** Photo Øyvind Leren Hydro **90** Photo Øyvind Leren Hydro **91** Photo Øyvind Leren Hydro **91** Photo Øyvind Leren Hydro **94** Photo Øyvind Leren **96–97** © Mappamundi – Knocke – Belgium **98** Archive of Romsdal Museum **100** Archive of Romsdal Museum **101** Archive of Romsdal Museum **102–103** Map Hydro. Photos: NTNU Vitenskapsmuseet **104** NTNU Vitenskapsmuseet **106** Hydro/Geoconsult/NTNU Vitenskapsmuseet **107** NTNU Vitenskapsmuseet **108** Museum of Cultural History, University of Oslo, Norway **110** Museum of Cultural History, University of Oslo, Norway **112** NTNU Vitenskapsmuseet (1+2) Marek E. Jasinski (3) **114** NTNU Vitenskapsmuseet **115** Fredrik Naumann **116–117** Hydro **118** NTNU Vitenskapsmuseet **119** Hydro **120** Fredrik Naumann **122** Fredrik Naumann **123** Drawings by Ayse D. Atauz **124–125** Fredrik Naumann/NTNU Vitenskapsmuseet **126** Hydro/NTNU Vitenskapsmuseet **128** Drawings by Brynjar Wiig, Photos Fredrik Søreide **129** NTNU Vitenskapsmuseet **130** Martin Ludvigsen, NTNU **133** Martin Ludvigsen, NTNU **134–135** NTNU Vitenskapsmuseet **136** Drawing by Ayse D. Atauz **139** Drawings by Ayse D. Atauz, Photo NTNU Vitenskapsmuseet **140** Drawings by Ayse D. Atauz, Photo NTNU Vitenskapsmuseet **141** Fredrik Naumann **142** Drawings by Ayse D. Atauz, Photo Fredrik Naumann **144** NTNU Vitenskapsmuseet **145** Fredrik Naumann **146** NTNU Vitenskapsmuseet **147** Drawing by Eirin Holm Rise **148** Drawing by Ayse D. Atauz, Photo NTNU Vitenskapsmuseet **149** Fredrik Naumann **150** Fredrik Naumann **151** Drawings by Ayse D. Atauz, Photo NTNU Vitenskapsmuseet **152** NTNU Vitenskapsmuseet **153** Fredrik Naumann **155** Fredrik Naumann **156** Fredrik Naumann **158** NTNU Vitenskapsmuseet **160** Marek E. Jasinski **162** Frank Martin/Stringer/Hulton Archive/Getty Images **164–165** Photo Hydro